Justice as Attunement

The meaning of an expression resides not in the expression itself but in the experience of a person's engagement with it. Meaning will be different not only to different people but also to the same person at different times. This book offers a way of attending to these different meanings. This way (or method) is a version of a trans-cultural activity that Richard Dawson calls attunement. The activity of attunement involves a movement of self-adjustment to a language, which a person transforms in her or his use of it. Consciously performing the activity can enable understanding of the processes by which we constitute ourselves and others when we use a language. This directly connects to the topic justice, which is concerned with constituting appropriate selves and relations.

Justice as Attunement engages with a wide range of texts – legal, literary, economic, philosophical, among others – and illuminates many useful and fascinating connections between them. There is a sense in which this book transcends disciplinary boundaries, for, in addition to students and scholars of law, literature, economics, and philosophy, it is written to a general reader who is interested in reflecting on and doing justice to their experiences in life.

Richard Dawson has held teaching positions in economics, law, and politics and published work on the economic role of government, on colonisation, and on literary dimensions of law.

Justice as Attunement

Transforming Constitutions in Law, Literature, Economics and the Rest of Life

Richard Dawson

Routledge
Taylor & Francis Group
a GlassHouse Book

First published 2014
by Routledge
2 Park Square, Milton Park, Abingdon, Oxon, OX14 4RN

Simultaneously published in the USA and Canada
by Routledge
711 Third Avenue, New York, NY 10017

Routledge is an imprint of the Taylor & Francis Group, an informa business

British Library Cataloguing in Publication
British Library Cataloguing in Publication Data

A catalogue record for this book is available from the British Library
Library of Congress Cataloging-in-Publication Data

A catalog record has been requested for this book

ISBN: 978-0-415-85751-2 (hbk)
ISBN: 978-0-203-79733-4 (ebk)

Typeset in Garamond
By Cenveo Publisher Services

FSC
www.fsc.org
MIX
Paper from responsible sources
FSC® C013604

Printed and bound by CPI Group (UK) Ltd, Croydon, CR0 4YY

Contents

Table of Cases

Foreword

My first acquaintance with Richard Dawson was an invitation to examine his doctoral thesis in law. This was conducted by video-link from one side of the planet to the other: me sitting in a room in England in the early morning and Richard sitting in a room in New Zealand in the early evening. As I recall, there were surprisingly few problems of attunement, despite the distance, and that has been my experience of engaging with Dr Dawson's work ever since. As I write, I have not had the pleasure of meeting Dr Dawson the old-fashioned way, but all being well this will be the year to put that right. Through technology we have the privilege to hold the entire span of the earth in our sights, but Richard Dawson understands, and I hope I do too, that for all the dazzling sights of the digital age it is deep attunement to the small sound of a personal voice that still matters most. How to bring that understanding into teaching and scholarship is something that must be learned and acquired slowly through practice, and Richard Dawson will agree with me that there is no better catalyst to that practice of learning than the works of Professor James Boyd White.

It is a happy coincidence that Richard Dawson's book was completed in 2013, for that year marked the 40th anniversary of the publication of Professor James Boyd White's pioneering work, *The Legal Imagination*. Dr Dawson has been deeply inspired and extensively influenced by the work of Professor White, and by *The Legal Imagination* in particular, but it is equally clear that the present volume is more than a work of tribute to James Boyd White. Professor White lays it down as a serious challenge that all of us should strive in our reading and listening to maintain critical independence of thought and to attain a compassionate personal response. Richard Dawson has met that challenge. He has attuned his ear to the voices of other writers and in the process he has developed the distinctiveness of his own voice. It is our turn to read and to listen and to become attuned.

It is a platitude to say that one has read a book with pleasure, so I will not put it that way. What I will say is that this has been in many respects an easy book to read. Not only is it written in short thematic chapters that are arranged in alphabetical order to give it the enticement of an encyclopaedia, but the writing style is always lucid and engaging. It is in these and other respects an easy read. But what pleased me most about this book are the respects in which it is difficult to read. Whereas it is not hard to read or to understand it at a surface level, what is very difficult is to read it deeply and to sound its depths and to become attuned to those deep sounds. The explanation for this challenge is straightforward: deep reading is always difficult. Deep appreciation *ought* to be difficult. The attunement of one person's mind to the mind of another should be perfectly challenging.

In *The Legal Imagination*, James Boyd White presents a panoramic portfolio of reading materials. He offers insightful perspectives on them and presents his readers with some of the puzzles that the materials produce. Richard Dawson offers his own responses to some of those puzzles (his chapter on Metaphor, for instance, is expressly a response to White), but equally impressive are the lengths to which he has gone to assemble a rich portfolio of his own. He has carefully expressed new contemplations, made new complaints and set new conundrums. I came to this book from a position of familiarity and empathy with the works of Professor James Boyd White, but Richard Dawson has deepened my appreciation of White's works and also broadened my appreciation to areas (notably economics) in which I had not previously thought to apply a Whitean approach. Richard Dawson's book does not offer a thesis so much as a *praxis*, or, to be more accurate, it seeks to prove the thesis that progress in human understanding and human judgment-making depends upon good practice. It seeks to prove this thesis through a demonstration of how to read well, listen well, hear well. He performs ways for us to attune justly.

Richard Dawson has taken risks in writing this book. Not least in his decision to present numerous short thematic chapters in alphabetical order to be read in any sequence that the reader might choose. At one point in the Prologue, he asks, 'What sort of literature is *The Legal Imagination*?' Later, in his Introduction, he answers his own question with the suggestion that *The Legal Imagination* might be placed in the genre of *Bildungsroman* (what he calls 'novels of character formation'). It might be better placed outside of any genre, and Dawson's own book might be placed with it. One of my all-time favourite books, Thomas Carlyle's *Sartor Resartus*, will keep them company in the select genus of genre-less works. Carlyle struggled for many years to find a publisher for his opus in large part because it did not fit within a known category. We should be grateful that Dr Dawson has not kept us waiting so long. In its purely formal or structural aspect Richard Dawson's alphabetized work is somewhat reminiscent of early modern digests such as John Selden's *Table Talk*. And perhaps that is the point – that we are invited to sit down together or 'lie down together' (as Milner Ball – another author featured in Dr Dawson's book – would have put it) in a mode of after-dinner conversation that is both controversial but companionable. Richard Dawson is a writer one can hear; a writer one can converse with. This is a refreshingly unpretentious book. For an author so well versed in the technicalities of both law and economics, he shows great sympathy for his readers in his effort to remove all barriers of vernacular and academic cant. He has cut up easy mouthfuls for us to chew over. The difficulty in his digest lies in the appreciation of every flavour and every nuance. Will we savour each section before we move on to the next? My own sense is that each section is sufficiently rich on its own to supply a Masters seminar with numerous talking points and much food for thought. Indeed, in each section there are the ingredients from which a discerning reader could work up a whole new book.

'Whole' is the word. This is a book that has to be appreciated holistically as one that integrates its many parts and as a work that has integrity of form and substance. Taken as a whole it is a fine work of deep research, sensitive reading, sustained critical engagement, intellectual integrity and sophisticated, clear expression. The highest praise I can give this book is that it lives up to the promise of its beautiful title: *Justice as Attunement: Transforming Constitutions in Law, Literature, Economics, and the Rest of Life*. Richard Dawson has challenged his readers to become better people through the process of attuning to what he and others have to say. I challenge anyone to read this book and not become a better person for it.

Gary Watt
The University of Warwick

Acknowledgements

This book draws heavily from my law doctoral thesis, written at the University of Canterbury. Financial assistance from a University of Canterbury Doctoral Scholarship enabled me to write the thesis. Thanks to those who had confidence in my work. Diane Proudfoot, in the Department of Philosophy, provided me with invaluable assistance during the early stages of my thesis. The two examiners of my thesis gave me much constructive and generous criticism, which has greatly assisted the rewriting process.

After submitting my thesis, which centres on the works of James Boyd White, I sent him a copy, hoping for some criticism. He provided an abundance (not only on the thesis but on an early draft of this book), for which I am immensely indebted to him. I am grateful to him for permission to use material from his work.

Jack Sammons offered helpful comments on two chapters. He also helped with the title of this book – providing me with insights on the central activity with which I am concerned.

I have benefited from comments on draft versions of the Introduction by Jeanne Gaakeer and Gary Watt.

Several fragments in this book draw from journal articles. I continue to benefit from comments by editors and referees from the following journals: *Canterbury Law Review*, *Otago Law Review*, *Waikato Law Review*, and the *Journal of Australian Political Economy*.

I have gained much from teaching several courses in Community Education at the University of Canterbury.

My debt to Martin O'Connor, my economics teacher, who first directed my attention to some disintegrative consequences of economic imperialism, is considerable.

In the early stages of writing my economics doctoral thesis, Warren Samuels invited me to contribute to a volume titled *The Founding of Institutional Economics* (1998). This helped to greatly expand my horizons in and out of economics.

In writing this book, I have found myself returning to and extending some ideas that reside in my book *The Treaty of Waitangi and the Control of Language* (2001). I remain indebted to the Institute of Policy Studies for providing a grant that enabled me to write it.

During 2002–04, several colleagues in the Waikato Management School, especially Maria Humphries, deepened my understanding of certain rhetorical dimensions of life.

In 2003 and 2004, students in POLS 311 – The Politics of Maori and Other Indigenous Peoples – at the University of Waikato taught me a great deal about communication.

In 2006, the Treaty of Waitangi Research Unit at Victoria University of Wellington published an Occasional Paper of mine, titled *Waitangi, Law, and Justice*, from which I have drawn. I continue to benefit from interchanges with the Unit's director, Richard Hill.

In a number of wide-ranging conversations, Kim Simmonds has given me much food for thought about the topic of justice.

A special thanks is due to Sarah Campbell, my wife, for her support – and for her patience when I have repeatedly got lost in a book.

A special thanks also to Gary Watt for his great Foreword.

I am grateful to the publishers mentioned below for permission to reproduce material.

No matter how accustomed we may be to reading, the better we know how to read, the more we shall feel the spectral sadness of the written word without a voice to fill it.

José Ortega y Gasset

After the *Maori Broadcasting* case, brought to try to get Maori language on New Zealand television, two of the plaintiffs said to me after the Court of Appeal hearing: 'Win or lose, we feel we have been heard at last'. We lost – but we should not underestimate the human desire to confront issues that matter in formal process before a disinterested tribunal.

Rt. Hon. Dame Sian Elias

The hearing is the heart of the law . . . ; but the hearing reaches its fullest significance only when it is coupled with the obligation to explain. Then the judicial opinion becomes a form with wonderful possibilities for meaning. It is a composition in which the speaker must choose a language for telling a story and justifying a result, and must do so against the reasonable claims of the losing side that he or she speak differently. . . . It is structurally multivocal, a system of translation that is open, in principle at least, in all directions. It is self-transforming. Since the opinion must make sense as a whole, the ultimate demand is one of integration. The instrument of integration is the voice – one's sense of self, of language, and of another. If one could strike a living balance among all these tensions and be attuned to all the conflicts one addressed, one would be making art of the highest kind, uniting in a single composition the concerns of truth, of beauty, and of justice.

James Boyd White

Prologue

What is this book you have in your hand, you may ask, and why is it called *Justice as Attunement*? 'Attunement' is for me a way of orienting oneself to meaning. It resembles the activity implied in the common phrase 'getting on the same page'. The word 'getting' is especially important, for there is a sense in which we can *never* be completely 'on the same page', since 'meaning' is in constant motion. On the flow of meaning, the lawyer Felix Cohen has said:

> Perhaps, if we look closely enough, a sentence never means exactly the same thing to any two different people. For no two minds bring the same . . . background to bear on . . . a sound or a series of marks. Indeed, I doubt whether any sentence means exactly the same to me the first time I hear it that it means the tenth time or the hundredth time. Of course, for many practical purposes, we are disposed to overlook such variations of meaning.
>
> (Cohen 1950: 240)

What I am calling 'attunement' is a way of paying close attention to what Cohen calls 'variations of meaning'. One practical purpose for paying attention to them is to do justice to our selves and to others.

Attunement to Attunement

As I say in the Introduction, my use of the word 'attunement' in this book draws from the linguist Alton Becker. Like Cohen, Becker attends to the role of background in the process of meaning. He does so, for example, in these autobiographical remarks:

> I once found myself, a small-town Midwesterner, at a rather prestigious East Coast institution. At lunch, I was repeatedly intimidated by the power and originality of the conversation, so much so that I stopped having lunch at all after a few weeks, for I felt my confidence as a teacher and a writer slipping away. . . . A friendly local native finally told me that the problem was only a deficiency of prior text, which could be

> overcome if every morning I read . . . the 'agenda,' the *New York Times*. I did, and it worked. I now shared with them a daily prior text . . . and I heard now the pervasiveness of prior text in all they said. They were not intimidating, and I could speak, now, with confidence and originality.
>
> (Becker 1992/1995: 285)

When we share a 'prior text' we will have a resource with which to participate in a 'conversation'. An aim of this Prologue is to provide some 'prior texts' for helping you, the reader, engage with the text that follows it. Becker might have put it this way: my aim is to assist the reader in the activity of attunement to the word 'attunement'.

I am reluctant to give a dictionary-style definition of 'attunement', for such a definition lacks the life of prior texts – in a dictionary there is no person using a word in a particular context, from which it acquires meaning worthy of the name.

To a General Reader

Part of this book's subtitle – *in Law, Literature, Economics* – is meant to suggest interdisciplinary activity. Given the tendency toward specialization in educational institutions, it is likely that some of the book will be unfamiliar to you. Unfamiliarity can be a source of many difficulties – including 'a deficiency of prior text'. In an essay on interdisciplinary work, the lawyer Jack Balkin notes that 'a sense of bewilderment' often emerges 'when people from different disciplines meet'. He continues:

> It is the sense not only of having to wade through a strange and abstruse vocabulary, but also the sense of puzzlement as to 'why does he or she find *that* interesting?' or 'why was so much effort wasted on showing *that* or discussing *that*?' To chance upon a discussion among persons of a different discipline can be like arriving at someone else's family reunion. Each discipline has its own ongoing controversies, its own distinctive debates to rehearse, its own characteristic points to score, and its own private demons to exorcise.
>
> (Balkin 1996: 956)

The 'why . . . ?', as Balkin appreciates, can have rewarding answers if time and energy are given to the question. We do not need to be economists to know that claims that 'effort' was 'wasted' will be based on assumptions that the reader might not share. One person's waste can be another's profit, which may be found in their 'strange and abstruse vocabulary', if treated justly.

While there is interdisciplinary activity in this book, it is perhaps more 'trans-disciplinary', for it is written to a general reader and it asks questions that are relevant to all people – ultimately questions of justice. Writing to a general reader has benefits and costs. One benefit is that it can help avoid the problem of a strange vocabulary. One cost is that it could well increase the likelihood of 'puzzlement' questions.

This Prologue is mainly for a reader who might be inclined to ask 'why does he find *that* interesting?' when reading the Introduction, especially the part about attunement to the work of James Boyd White. ('Why read his work?') One aim of this Prologue is to suggest what this activity involves and why it can be worth the effort.

When a Lawyer Writes a Complaint: Herbert A. Eastman

In 1995, the *Yale Law Journal* published an extraordinary essay, 'Speaking Truth to Power', by Eastman, director of clinical education at Saint Louis University School of Law. The essay is extraordinary for several reasons, one of which is that Eastman gives an extended criticism of his own work as a lawyer – two decades earlier. In 1976, then recently out of law school, Eastman joined a legal aid program for southern Illiniois and immediately found himself assigned to 'Hattie's case'. Hattie Kendrick has an important place in his essay, which opens as follows:

> I once had a client named Hattie Kendrick. She was a woman and an African-American, a school teacher and a civil rights warrior, spit upon, arrested, and tossed out of restaurants and clothing stores that did not 'cater to the colored trade.' She marched and spoke out for integration and against oppression. Her school fired her, but not before she had taught generations of black children in Cairo, Illinois, that participation in American democracy was their right and their duty. In the 1940's, she sued to win equal pay for black teachers, with Thurgood Marshall as her lawyer. And in the 1970's, she was a named plaintiff in a class action asserting the voting rights of black citizens in Cairo against a city electoral system rigged to reduce the value of their votes to nothingness. All she wanted was to cast a meaningful vote in a democratic election before she died – she was in her nineties, growing blind and weak. Such a woman. Such a story. And such a voice. Listen to how she discerns the problems of her town: 'Too long have the two races stood grinning in each other's faces, while they carry the fires of resentment and hate in their hearts, and with their hands hid behind their backs they carry the unsheathed sword.' Yet here is how the complaint filed in federal court identifies the named plaintiffs, including Hattie Kendrick: 'All plaintiffs are Blacks, citizens of the United States and of the State of Illinois, and residents of Cairo, Illinois registered to vote in Municipal Elections conducted in Cairo.'
>
> (765–6)

The complaint in *Kendrick*, for which a younger Eastman was responsible, gets much critical attention in the essay. The older Eastman has a complaint to make about the younger Eastman's complaint, which failed to do justice to his client.

We can read Eastman's essay as an attempt by him to work out a way of talking about the activity of being a lawyer, one who takes justice seriously. There is a sense in which he seeks to do justice to himself. This act begins by him attending to his own experience. Early on, he writes:

> This Article springs from the recurring disappointment and frustration I have felt after consultation with clients in cases presenting outrages that, in a phrase loved by my mother, cried out to heaven. . . . My frustration and disappointment began when I reviewed the pleadings I drafted for them. I could barely see over the chasm separating what those clients told me about their lives and what I wrote to the court as factual allegations in the complaint – sterile recitations of dates and events that lost so much in the translation. What is lost in a description that identifies a woman like Hattie only as a registered voter? . . . We lose the identity of the person harmed, the story of her life. But even more is lost. This was a class action aimed at remedying a systemic problem harming thousands, over generations. . . .
>
> The complaint omits the frustration of the democratic process and the powerful metaphors that claim an exception to the rules restricting the court's involvement. The complaint leaves intact the walls between the clients and the court, the clients and the lawyer. In a strange way, it even effaces the lawyer by denying her the dynamic and creative role of responding to the tragedy witnessed.
>
> I wondered how we, as lawyers, could plead the horror of wrong done on a mass scale. In reviewing the pleadings in other famous civil rights class actions, I found similar things. This Article explores why we fail and wonders whether we can do better.
>
> (766–77)

We might wonder if the editors of the *Yale Law Journal* expressed any concern about Eastman's use of the first person, the personal 'I'. Were there prejudices against the personal tone and the autobiographical elements in his article? We might also wonder if, then and now, any legal writing textbooks (a lawyer's 'prior texts') deal with 'cases presenting outrages that . . . cried out to heaven'. Do any such textbooks offer guidance on how to tell a 'story' and how to listen to one? Do any direct attention to 'powerful metaphors' that are not often recognized as such? Do any offer resources for dealing with that which might be 'lost . . . in the translation'? If the translator is a betrayer, as the old saying goes, we might do well to wonder if the image of lawyering as 'translation' opens up a productive line of inquiry for those who desire to be 'dynamic and creative'. Might the image help turn the legal hearing into a meaning-full hearing, in which there is some close listening?

What are the possibilities for doing 'better' when drafting a complaint? Eastman calls for 'thicker pleadings' (808). He explains what he means by that phrase in several ways, one of which is through a 'more literary revision' of the *Kendrick* complaint that he filed. About his new complaint, he writes:

> [T]he lawyer intertwines legal and nonlegal language. . . . By integrating the nonlegal language in a legal pleading, it calls upon the persuasive authority of both. . . . By pleading in the language of journalists and clients—and by quoting clients and others in the pleading—the complaint attempts to make the most powerful use of ambiguity. While the pleading begins and ends with language more recognizable and acceptable to a traditional audience—and retains the customary numbered paragraphs—the client stories dominate the pleading. In particular, Hattie's story is kept central, to draw upon the compelling attractiveness of her story. The story is allowed to develop, inviting and not coercing.
> (834)

> The pleading offers the language of voices rather than of concepts. . . . The lawyer's voice is included, as well. . . . In the hopes of practicing as a jazz civil rights lawyer and trying on a different paradigm for racial discrimination, the pleading tries to speak in terms of an entire community harmed by racism, rather than of a black people oppressed by a white people. In this sense, I emulate Hattie, who referred to white people as 'brother' even as she talked about subjugation. To further explore this paradigm, the complaint refers to European-Americans and African-Americans. This may help us to think in terms of a common immigrant history and also remind us of the diversity of persons with roots in those continents.
> (834–5)

We might wonder if any legal writing textbooks encourage their readers to think about what lawyers can learn from their clients. Contrary to what many legal writing textbooks say and suggest, 'ambiguity' has some important virtues, including the possibility of being 'inviting and not coercing'. And 'voice' matters. What value is a hearing without authentic 'voices'? We might wonder what could become of the law if 'the lawyer's voice' became normal in legal materials. Might a linguistic move away from 'concepts' to 'voices' be necessary for meaningful talk about justice? Might the legal hearing thus acquire new significance?

A Becker reader might be inclined to ask this question: what texts did Eastman read before critically engaging with his *Kendrick* complaint? (How did Eastman manage to distance himself from his younger self? What questions did he ask? What method did he adopt?) Throughout his essay, he refers to the work of James Boyd White, including his writing course book *The Legal Imagination*. A foundational question in White's book is this: 'What does it mean to learn to think and speak like a lawyer?' 'The readings and the writing assignments', White says, 'can be said to elaborate and complicate that question.' He continues:

> In the course of the book the student is asked to write as a lawyer, judge and legislator, and to reflect as a mind and a person on what he has done, to speak in his own voice about his experience of writing and thinking. He is asked to see what the lawyer does as a literary activity, as an enterprise of the imagination, with respect to which both success and failure – if he can define them – are possibilities for him. He must judge for himself what these possibilities are. The demand is upon his imagination, his ability to make sense out of what he does by looking beyond it.
> (White 1973: xix–xx)

White's imagined reader might find intimidating his invitation 'to see what the lawyer does as a literary activity'. We, however, have benefited from reading one of his actual readers. In having done so, to draw from Becker, we have avoided part of the 'problem' of 'a deficiency of prior text'.

White stresses that 'the law' is not an entity, as much talk about 'it' suggests, but a 'performance' culture. Listen to his 'thesis': 'that the activities which make up the professional life of the lawyer and judge constitute an enterprise of the imagination, an enterprise whose central performance is the claim of meaning against the odds: the translation of the imagination into reality by the power of language' (758). His reader might wonder how to justly respond to that thesis. How is she or he to 'hear' him?

White gives much life to his thesis in the 'writing assignments'. Consider this one:

> ***Drafting a Complaint***
>
> *Part One*
>
> Give an account of a death in some language other than legal language. Your account should not take the form of 'the statement of facts' in a legal brief or judicial opinion, but should be a living statement of its own.
>
> *Part Two*
>
> A. Draft a complaint, civil or criminal, based upon that event.
> B. Explain and evaluate what you have done as a writer of a complaint.
> C. Explain what sort of rhetorical resource the complaint affords. What interest or value has this sort of writing? What dangers?
>
> Here are some questions that may help you work this assignment out.
>
> 1. What sort of literature is the complaint? On what understanding is it to be read? Look at your complaint and ask what it has left out, what else might be said about these events. . . .

> 2. To the layman the complaint may seem a conclusory, dead instrument of no interest except as another example of the dishonest and nonsensical ways that lawyers speak. . . . Does it make sense, is it honest, to another audience, on some special understanding?
>   a. Examine your own complaint and ask how you have characterized the events you describe – with what specificity, what bias. . . .
>   b. . . .
>   c. By what process did you compose your complaint? What were the questions you faced? What inconsistent pressures did you try to accommodate . . . ?
> 3. . . .
> 4. In the portion of your paper in which you explain what it is you have done when you have drafted a complaint, you will necessarily characterize a part of a lawyer's life. In what terms do you do so? What inferences about the lawyer's life could be drawn from your account of what you did? Consider in particular the metaphors you use, and ask whether they do justice to your experience: 'start the machinery of the law,' . . . and so on. Try to find a way to express as fully as you can what drafting the complaint involved for you.
> 5. The temptation is to look at this in mechanical terms: the writer is a selector, like a cranberry-grader . . . perhaps. But your writing has a real audience and real purposes. To whom are you writing, and what are you trying to achieve with this document? Does it help to conceive of the complaint as a threat, say, or a challenge, or a bid, or a wish?
>
> (182–4)

We can be confident that Eastman had not read that assignment when he drafted the original *Kendrick* complaint. His *Yale Law Journal* essay, however, can be read as a response to most of it. In his essay, he says and suggests much about 'what' he had 'done' when he wrote the complaint in the *Kendrick* case. In explaining and evaluating his new complaint, he shows us that a complaint has important possibilities as a 'rhetorical resource' for doing 'justice', and that an important task for the lawyer is to pursue these possibilities as best as she or he can. In juxtaposing his two complaints, Eastman directs attention to the 'dangers' of a 'dead' complaint. An Eastman reader will know that a complaint does nothing less than frame the whole case, providing an image of who the parties are to one another, a way of thinking about the story they share, and what questions the lawyers and the judge need to address. What could be more important than that?

White's question about 'the questions you faced' might prompt us to attend to his questions and to ask some in response. Who is this James Boyd

White? What sort of literature is *The Legal Imagination*? On what understanding is it to be read? What experience lies behind it? To whom is he writing, and what is he trying to achieve with his questions? Does it help to conceive of his questions as a threat, say, or a challenge, or a bid, or a wish? Are they all of those at once, in the direction of doing justice?

In taking 'performance' seriously, we might do well to ask not what the present book is 'about' but what it *does*. It engages in the activity of close listening, to a writer who has said and suggested much about the possibilities of the hearing. I think that if we can attune ourselves to White, we will equip ourselves for doing justice both in and out of the law.

Introduction

Attunement to and from James Boyd White: Hearing the Hearing
'My Reader'
An Alphabetical Lexicon
A Guide for Confusion: Composition and Literary Criticism at Amherst College
Quotations: Political Listening
Pronouns

In Jane Austen's *Mansfield Park*, Henry Crawford reads aloud part of Shakespeare's play *King Henry VIII*. When he has finished, Edmund Bertram remarks to him: 'you read as if you knew it well.' This exchange follows:

> '. . . I do not think I have had a volume of Shakespeare in my hand since I was fifteen. I once saw Henry the Eighth acted, or I have heard of it from somebody who did, I am not certain which. But Shakespeare one gets acquainted with without knowing how. It is part of an Englishman's constitution. His thoughts and beauties are so spread abroad that one touches them everywhere; . . . .'
>
> 'No doubt one is familiar with Shakespeare in a degree,' said Edmund, 'from one's earliest years. His celebrated passages . . . are in half the books we open, and we all talk Shakespeare, use his similes, and describe with his descriptions.'
>
> (Austen 1814/2003: 312–13)

Like *Mansfield Park*, this book connects 'constitution' and language-'use'. I define an activity that all of us engage in all the time, often without being aware of it. In brief, the activity is: constituting ourselves and others when we use our language, which we transform in our use of it. I will define this activity largely by directing attention to examples and by my own performance in these pages, for I am myself engaged in it. Attending to this activity opens up an inquiry into the kinds of selves and relations that we do and could constitute. This inquiry lends itself to talking about justice as being concerned with constituting appropriate selves and relations.

Attunement to and from James Boyd White: Hearing the Hearing

The language that I use for talking about constitutions and justice draws heavily from the work of James Boyd White. In 2008, White retired from the University of Michigan, where for over two decades he had the titles of Hart Wright Professor of Law, Professor of English, and Adjunct Professor of Classical Studies. Not one to doff and don disciplinary hats, White offers an integrated way of imagining social life. To draw from the subtitle of his book *When Words Lose Their Meaning*, he is centrally interested in 'constitutions and reconstitutions of language' (White 1984). His interest touches various levels, including the person and society, as suggested here:

> Language is learned only by stages and only for use and by using it; and as one learns it, one naturally but imperceptibly undergoes changes: changes in attitude and perception and sentiment by which one becomes 'acculturated,' or 'cultured,' or perhaps 'cultivated.' But to learn a language is also to change it, for one constantly makes new gestures and sentences of one's own, new patterns or combinations of meaning. Language is part of a system of invention, an organized way of making new meaning in new circumstances. Some of these inventions are shared with others and become common property; others remain personal, part of the process by which the individual within a culture is differentiated from others who are similarly situated.
>
> The language marks the mind, and one will normally see that one's language is contingent, not necessary, only if one experiences a basic cultural dislocation: the sense that words have lost their meaning.
>
> (White 1984: 8 and 277)

In learning to speak, a child incorporates a language that structures her or his experience. From a young age, language can seem to be a part of nature, not a cultural artefact, until 'one experiences a basic cultural dislocation'. Such an experience may change one's sense of the nature of experience, for one may now sense it from a distance that was not previously available.

When words do 'lose their meaning', we can respond by telling a story about that very experience. The title of White's book draws from a passage in Thucydides' *History of the Peloponnesian War*, which tells a story about the destruction of the Hellenic world. After introducing details, he connects the *History* and his own book:

> An alteration in language of the kind I mean is . . . a change in the world and the self, in manners and conduct and sentiment. . . . One response to the world is to make a text about it, a reorganization of its resources of meaning tentatively achieved in a relation, newly constituted, between reader and writer. This is a way of acting in the world and on the world by using the language of the world. Thucydides' *History* is a response of this kind; so are the other texts we shall examine, and so, indeed, is this book itself. Other activities are also texts in this sense, including the conversations that take place among us, at home or at the office or on the street, whenever we talk about what matters to us. We struggle to make

> our words work as we wish, to redefine them to meet our needs, and in doing this we remake, in ways however small, our language and our world. The reconstitution of culture in a relation shared between speaker and audience is in fact a universal human activity, engaged in by every speaker in every culture, literate or illiterate, and the texts we shall read in this book can be taken as extraordinarily powerful . . . examples of this activity.
> (White 1984: 4)

White's own efforts at 'the reconstitution of culture' in *When Words Lose Their Meaning*, which defines a 'universal human activity' whilst reading a diverse collection of writers – Homer, Thucydides, Plato, Jonathan Swift, Samuel Johnson, Edmund Burke, Jane Austen, Chief Justice John Marshall – offers an experience of 'a basic cultural dislocation'. Whilst reading his text, writers who might at first seem to have little in common (say, Austen and Marshall) may come to be perceived as deeply similar, for they give 'extraordinarily powerful . . . examples' of the 'reconstitution of culture'.

When a person assumes that her language is adequate as a means of expression, she may readily fail to hear another person's language, and fail to do him justice, in and out of the culture that we call the law. White has much to say on the connection between language and justice. Here is one fragment:

> The law . . . provides a place that is at once part of the larger culture and apart from it, a place in which we can think about a problematic story by retelling it in various ways and can ask in a new and self-conscious way what it is to mean. Law works by a process of argument that places one version of events against another and creates a tension between them . . . ; in doing so it makes our choice of language conscious rather than habitual and creates a moment at which controlled change of language and culture becomes possible. The rhetorical structure of the law makes a place for each party and defines a relation between them by establishing the ways they may talk; in doing this it suggests a conception of justice as equality, for a person may find himself in any of these roles. The method of criticism most appropriate to the law as such is concerned less with the wisdom of a particular policy choice or the rightness of a particular rule or result than with the character that a court, legislature, or other legal speaker gives himself and his institution, the place it defines for others, and the relation it establishes between them. The law is less a branch of the social sciences than of the humanities in that it seeks not to be a closed system but an open one. It learns from the past and seeks new terms for the expression of motives, new forms for the establishment of relations; it is a method of learning and teaching; and its central concern is with the kind of relations that we establish with our inherited culture and with each other when we speak its language.

> To conceive of the law as a rhetorical and social system, a way in which we use an inherited language to talk to each other and to maintain a community, suggests in a new way that the heart of law is what we always knew it was: the open hearing in which one point of view, one construction of language and reality, is tested against another. The multiplicity of readings that the law permits is not its weakness but its strength, for it is this that makes room for different voices and gives a purchase by which the culture may be modified in response to the demands of circumstance. It is a method at once for recognizing others, for acknowledging ignorance, and for achieving cultural change.
>
> (White 1984: 273)

On many occasions, I have found myself returning to that passage. My rereading has involved connecting various words, including: character, community, conscious, criticism, culture, equality, justice, language, method, rhetorical, story, voices. Making these connections has been a challenging and rewarding experience. The challenging part has included trying to modify certain habitual modes of thought and expression, struggling with my choice of language. The rewarding part has included coming to a new appreciation for the hearing and for what acts of justice might involve – White's work offers to enrich the life of the ancient principle of justice, *audi alteram partem*, 'hear the other side'. I suggest that doing justice, in and out of the law, involves a struggle with one's choice of language. One goal of this book is to do justice to White's image of 'the heart of law'; it is part of my process of trying to 'hear' what he says about the hearing. This book will be a success for me if the reader returns to reread the above passage and has a similarly challenging and rewarding experience.

White's book on 'learning to read George Herbert' has served as a model for this book as it concerns the activity of reading White himself. The need for a 'learning to read' book for a long-dead poet might need no explanation. It seems obvious, for example, why we need a guide for reading Herbert (or Shakespeare), for his language is considerably unlike ours. White makes the point, however, that there is a sense in which each person's language is quite unlike any other person's language:

> My aim in this book has been to record the process by which I have begun to learn to read the poetry of Herbert, with the object both of helping others read their way into this difficult literature and, more generally, of suggesting a way of thinking about what it can mean to learn to read the work of another. For me . . . it is helpful to think of this kind of reading as learning the language of another, by which I mean not only that we come to appreciate more fully the special significance the writer gives to certain terms over the course of his work—'heart,' 'stone,' 'sunne'—but also that we become familiar with his voices, transitions,

> and gestures. . . . As we learn to read one gesture in light of another, one poem in light of another, we should acquire an increasing sense of attunement to the whole performance and feel our expectations engaged, surprised, and disappointed in increasingly coherent and familiar ways.
> (White 1994b: 231)

Learning to read Herbert is an extreme version of what we commonly do in our own social circles. If we can learn to 'learn to read' Herbert well, we can become better equipped to learn the language of another person well. A language 'attunement', I suggest, is at the heart of doing justice. No dictionary-style definition of 'attunement' will do, for the word acquires its vital meanings in the way it is used. This book's form, discussed below, is the product of an attempt to do better.

White's use of the word 'attunement' draws from the linguist Alton Becker, who used the word in the context of 'confronting a distant text' and 'the need for correcting . . . interpretation' (Becker 1988/1995: 387). 'Attunement' refers to the process of 'self-correction', which is 'the heart of any skill, from the very subtle adjustments of a violinist's fingers, attuning ear and muscle, to the fine coordination of the steering wheel, eye, and gas pedal that constrain the everyday contests of driving' (369). In reading a text, the 'correcting' can never be perfect. Whilst 'correcting', the strange may become familiar and the familiar strange. Through this process, we may hope to better understand the other, and ourselves.

Whilst a major part of this book can be read as an attunement *to* White, its heart is not about him but the 'universal human activity' of transforming constitutions of language. White is a model for a certain version of this activity, of doing justice with language. Attuning *to* him can serve as a resource *from* which to re-imagine the topic of justice, beginning with a basic sense of justice as a process of language attunement.

'My Reader'

White's work defies simplistic placement within conventional classifications. Whilst White has largely written to a general reader – who might be imagined as one of 'The People' – he has been read by specialists from a variety of disciplines, including anthropology, economics, law, literary criticism, philosophy, political science, and theology. I made the acquaintance of White's work when studying economics. Later, as an economist, I kept reading White mainly because he provided materials with which to challenge mechanistic thought at the core of a supposedly culture-free economics. After several years of doing such challenging, I went to law school. By my reading of his course book *The Legal Imagination*, I discovered that crossing could be a broadening and deepening of my work in economics, rather than an ending. Thinking critically about 'thinking like a lawyer' could serve as a resource for more thought about 'thinking like an economist'. White's work lends itself to enriching talk about disciplinary 'boundaries'. He suggests as much in *Acts of Hope* – a book that engages with, among other texts, Plato's *Crito*, William Shakespeare's *Richard II*, Emily Dickinson's poetry, Nelson Mandela's Speech from the Dock, and the US Supreme Court's judgment in *Planned Parenthood v. Casey*:

> While I hope this book can be read with interest by those who are expert in the various fields it touches, . . . it is not mainly addressed to a community of specialists. . . . In this book, as in much of my other work, I am trying to work out a set of questions that will connect texts, and their readers, across the lines of professionalism. . . . I mean to resist the view that texts such as these are the property of one group or another, or that it is necessary to speak the language of the specialist in order to speak well about them. In fact, I do not think of myself as writing out of a profession, but out of my own experience of these texts, to which I have turned for the life they offer. I would do this, if I could, no matter what my job was, for their importance to me as a person and mind. Likewise I write to my reader not as a Dickinson specialist, or a classicist, or a lawyer, but as the person who is these things and many other things as well, and I do this in part with the object of claiming these texts as an inheritance that is common to us all.
>
> (White 1994a: 270–1)

With the category 'profession' unfitting for placing White, we might consider rehabilitating 'amateur' (from the Latin *amator*, 'lover'). The literary critic Wayne Booth assessed White to be 'a kind of amateur, not in the sense of "amateurish" but in the traditional sense of genuine lover seeking no reward but the love itself' (Booth 1996: 380–1). We might wonder what 'set of questions' Booth asked when trying to place White. What questions could help a White reader do him justice? Asking questions of justice might lead his reader to claim his texts as 'an inheritance that is common to us all'. In doing so, she or he may well feel certain pressures to become an 'amateur', who writes to a fellow amateur.

An Alphabetical Lexicon

Authors create texts not out of a vacuum but out of prior texts. The meaning of a text to a reader is influenced by the texts that she or he brings to it. Writing and reading is at one level a process of moving between texts. In his book on Herbert, White has this to say about the process:

> We naturally read any poem, and any poet, in light of what we have already read, the other poems that have formed our expectations, trained our attention, and in this way shaped our responses and our tastes.

> To bring to Herbert a sense of poetry derived from Pope, say, would produce a very different experience of his texts from one based on Shelley or Browning. In my own case, the poet who most shaped my sense of what poetry was, and could do, was Robert Frost, and in reading Herbert I found illuminating parallels, especially in the fact that both seemed to build so much of their poetry out of voices. Frost's art and teaching are thus at work in my own reading. . . . In saying that Herbert's poetry of voices is in an important way like Frost's I of course reverse the proper sequence, for any influence went the other way. But to one educated at Amherst College, as I was, it did not quite feel like that, for at Amherst Frost was the model of what a poet could be, and much of his excellence was seen to lie in his capacity to manage his voices.
>
> (White 1994b: 15–16)

That passage offers what we might call cultural background: processes that 'formed our expectations' and 'trained our attention, and in this way shaped our responses and our tastes'. Writing conventions that put pressure on us to eliminate autobiography will pressure us to direct our 'attention' away from one's cultural background. These conventions can thus be an obstacle to our attunement to the reality of 'experience'-structuring cultures. White invites his reader to consider resisting these conventions. Let me take up White's invitation for the purpose of reading him, in light of others.

My experience of reading White has resembled my experience of reading the economist John R. Commons, who has a place in this book. (Commons revered the name 'political economy' for his discipline, a name worthy of rehabilitation, for reasons suggested in various pages below.) In the early 1900s, Commons helped draft a Wisconsin public utilities law and a law establishing an Industrial Commission. He came to appreciate that drafting is not a simple mechanical process but a complex art, one that involves anticipating various sorts of cases that may arise. After completing his task, he sought to develop an economics that centred on the legal hearing. In doing so, he brought the neglected topic of justice before the economist, a move that has large consequences for economics, for the ordinary meanings of various key words change. He connects each of these words and gives them new meanings. In doing so, he places great demands upon his reader. One Commons critic says this about the dynamics of reading him:

> To truly understand . . . any component of Commons' thought, one must first grasp . . . his 'whole' [framework]. . . . [T]hat challenge is in many ways similar to the undertaking of an anthropologist who is set down in the midst of a primitive social group and instructed to discover the meaning of activities and objects as understood by the members of this alien culture themselves. Only slowly, as the participant-observer gradually becomes familiar with the activities of the new culture and the contextual nuances of the language in which its members express their

> thoughts, do accurate meanings, and thereby genuine understanding emerge. In like fashion, one simply cannot grasp what Commons is driving at on an initial reading.
>
> (Ramstad 1986: 1095–6)

Commons returns repeatedly to some basic questions, but each time he comes at them from a different standpoint. This is the process by which he reinterprets familiar institutions – such as 'the market' and 'the law' – in such a way that they take on a new meaning. The familiar can productively become strange.

When writing about Commons' work in my economics doctoral thesis, I was at a loss as to how I should present it, for it was wide-ranging and I could not assume that my reader was familiar with it. I began by experimenting with an alphabetical lexicon. Each chapter was devoted to one of his key words, offering a mini-exploration, learning a little of Commons' world, before beginning again from another standpoint. I shelved the experiment with the lexicon for various reasons. I now regret this, for I have come to believe that it is the best way to read such an extensive work that centres on dynamics of cultural transformation. Any attempt to present these dynamics in a linear form would fail to do justice to the complexities of such transformation.

My change of mind happened when writing my law doctoral thesis on White's work. When I struggled to communicate with lawyers about it, the lexicon came to mind. Both Commons and White deal with an expansive whole, an evolving culture, and both require multiple rereadings if they are to be *really* read. Both have been profoundly misunderstood, no doubt partly due to the power of habits of thought in the culture that they criticize. The form of an alphabetical lexicon offers a collection of bases from which to engage with some of these habits.

In this book, I intend my use of the lexicon to understand the ways in which White has responded to the task of transforming constitutions. I do this partly because I think highly of his performances, but mainly to utilize him as an example of what we will have to do ourselves if we are to transform constitutions well. Thus, whilst 'attention' may be a key word for White, it may not be for my reader, who might choose different key words, and choose to work with them differently. One aim of this book is to stimulate awareness of such choices and to make them intelligible.

Many of the chapters in this book directly connect with others – a cross-reference is marked with an asterisk. There is no single road for reading them. Select a road that interests you. Change if the going is awkward.

Whilst this book makes a significant place for White's broad and deep explorations, I hope that its form can serve as a model for engaging with other similar explorations. It could be used, for example, with respect to anthropologists such as Mary Douglas and Clifford Geertz, cultural/literary critics such as Mikhail Bakhtin and Edward Said, educationalists such as John Dewey and Paulo Freire, linguists such as George Lakoff and Deborah Tannen, philosophers such as Hans-Georg Gadamer and Ludwig Wittgenstein, or theologians such as Walter Brueggemann and David Tracy.

A Guide for Confusion: Composition and Literary Criticism at Amherst College

The activity of attunement to White's way of imagining the world will involve connecting to his English education at Amherst College. We began doing so in the previous section and we will do a little more here before continuing to do so in several of the chapters below. Our interest here is the experience of confusion.

When White went to Amherst as a freshman, he encountered Theodore Baird, who directed English 1–2, a course in composition. At about the time White took the course, the *Harvard Educational Review* published a study of it. Here is a fragment:

> By midyear . . . an Amherst freshman finds it easy to believe the legend that one day Professor Baird pointed to a window in the classroom and asked the students to say exactly what they saw. When the whole class insisted that what they saw was a twelve-pane window, Baird went up to it, opened it, stepped through it onto the lawn outside, and told the class to follow. After leading the class around the building . . . and back into the classroom, Baird asked for a definition of the doorway they had just used. . . . The new definitions were more careful. Such legendary exercises . . . undoubtedly contribute to the success of the course. But primarily the Amherst undergraduate recognizes that English 1–2 forces him by a variety of novel means . . . to think for himself in a radical and honest way.
>
> (Broderick 1958: 46–7)

Baird sought to make the familiar unfamiliar. Partly by playing with 'definitions', he sought to help the student 'become conscious of words for their own sakes and of their importance' (Baird 1931: 9). Composing 'new definitions' can be a way of composing a new world.

Baird's students were given numerous assignments. These were 'sequential': 'they led from one place to another' (Gibson 1985: 139). The movement commonly involved returning to an earlier assignment and critically engaging with it. The student might get quite confused, as Baird suggested in this assignment:

> Reconsider the last five assignments dealing with the standards of correctness and the meaning of these standards in terms of people and society.

> The process of moving from one assignment to the next may be confusing, but this usually happens when you try to place yourself historically by describing the thought and feeling and behavior of other people in the past or in the present. You are not the first person to find conflicting standards existing . . . side by side. If you find survivals of the past around you this is to be expected. You are not the first to live with confusion. Express as well as you can your sense of conflicting standards in their largest sense. Do this not only in terms of English usage but also in terms of the life you see around you . . . . Finally, express what it means to 'live with confusion.'
>
> (quoted in Gibson 1985: 144)

A student will do well to 'express what it means to "live with confusion"' not with a tidy theory but by exemplifying it in her or his own writing. If a student imagines that talking in a confused way is a failing, she could be confused without being aware of it – a real failing.

Baird's assignment could serve as a resource in legal education. As lawyers know, the process of moving from one case to the next may be confusing. In Frost's phrase about poets, a lawyer perhaps could aspire to 'a momentary stay against confusion' (1939/1951: 18). This book is written out of this aspiration.

Quotations: Political Listening

There is extensive quotation in this book, for it is vital to attend to a whole way of thought and expression. One cannot, for example, say of White that X or Y is his position on an issue, for he often seeks to transform the language with which we talk about positions. This process needs to be fully represented in order to be understood. To avoid complexity, however, I have omitted footnotes in the original passages.

The use of lengthy quotations will sometimes help with the activity of attunement to different voices. In the process, we may hope to enhance our capacities for listening, an activity that has been given inadequate treatment in various disciplines. In the context of political thought, Susan Bickford has suggested that various forces have contributed to the depreciation of listening. One of them is the image of listening as a merely passive reception that does not require any real virtues. She resists that image:

> Listening . . . involves an active willingness to construct certain relations of attention . . . . [W]e cannot hear but *as* ourselves, against the background of who we are. But without moving ourselves to the background, we cannot hear another at all.
>
> [P]olitical listening cannot be grounded in passivity or an absence of self, for politics itself requires precisely the opposite. . . . It is the

> *interaction* of our efforts that results in a decision, a joint action; if I somehow absent myself when you speak, in order to 'hear' you, and you do the same for me, in what sense are we really together as peers? Politics requires self-involvement with others in action, where we do not 'draw back' but actively engage with one another with direction(s) and purpose(s).
>
> There must of course be an equality in terms of the role one plays. All must engage in shifting back and forth between perspectives, speaking and listening in turn.
>
> (Bickford 1996: 24, 146, and 147)

'Political listening' connects to the 'equality' principle of 'hear the other side'. How are we to listen to any side? Do we shift back and forth between perspectives?

This book is intended as a contribution to thought and expression on political listening. The contribution is at the level of performance rather than 'theory' (from the Greek *theatron*, 'a place for seeing'). The unusually lengthy quotations make a place for a certain rhetorical equality in the book and for the reader to judge acts of listening.

Pronouns

White's *The Legal Imagination* is 'a course in writing' (1973: xxi). At the outset, he seeks to 'create the sense that we are all colleagues here' (xxii). How are we to read his use of the pronoun 'we' in the context of his efforts to constitute a textual community? A helpful place to begin a response is this fragment from his book on Herbert:

> In talking about the experiences these poems offer their reader, I frequently use the first-person plural: 'we see,' 'we learn,' 'surprises us,' and so forth. This is an old-fashioned locution that some people dislike because they feel that it asserts a kind of cultural or attitudinal unity that they wish, often rightly, to deny. I know of no better way to talk, however, and hope it can be understood by my reader that I am not claiming that all of us somehow respond in exactly the same way—this book is in fact built on the opposite principle—but that this is my way of talking about how a poem works. I use the first-person plural to express a hope, not to dictate a result, and I want my own reader constantly to ask whether a particular use of 'we' or 'us' does speak for her or him. My aspiration is not that you will agree with everything I say, but that you will find this performance of what Herbert means to be useful in shaping your own understanding of his poetry.
>
> (White 1994b: xvii)

That passage has frequently come to mind whilst writing this book. When it did, I used it to guide my own writing, for it seems sound to me. Let *us* not get bogged down here with a discussion on various departures from the 'old-fashioned locution'. I have come to appreciate White's aspiration, to which I give new life in this book.

Like White, I have much to say and suggest about the relationship between the writer and the reader. There are no easy choices when it comes to using singular personal pronouns. Using 'her or him' can be cumbersome. When I am talking about White or another male writer, I will refer to his reader as 'she'. When talking about a female writer, I will refer to her reader as 'he'.

Activity

'Questions of a Certain Sort': Michael Oakeshott
'Now I Know How to Go On': Ludwig Wittgenstein

In the 1960s and 1970s, people from in and out of the law were wondering whether the apartheid regime was in a basic sense lawless. What lines of questioning* might have started a valuable line of inquiry for them? Here is one possible question: How might we imagine the law? In *The Morality of Law*, Lon Fuller suggests that that question is vitally important:

> It is truly astounding to what an extent there runs through modern thinking in legal philosophy the assumption that the law is like a piece of inert matter—it is there or not there. It is only such an assumption that could lead legal scholars to assume, for example, that the 'laws' enacted by the Nazis in their closing years, considered as laws and in abstraction from their evil aims, were just as much laws as those of England and Switzerland.
>
> (Fuller 1964/1969: 123)

For Fuller, the law is not an object (such as a set of rules) but rather is, as he puts it elsewhere, 'a purposive human activity' (1966/1999: 11). Attending to the law as an 'activity' can open up questions of justice*, questions that are beyond the pale for some people, occasionally speaking in the name of The Law.

A central aim of this book, to recall, is to define an 'activity' in which all of us engage: constituting ourselves and others when we use our language*, which we transform in our use of it. Like law, we will do well to imagine language not as an object but as an activity. What's in an activity?

'Questions of a Certain Sort': Michael Oakeshott

Like Fuller, the philosopher Oakeshott resisted imagining human phenomena as inert matter. He resisted, that is to say, dehumanizing acts of reification.[1] In *Rationalism in Politics*, Oakeshott offers a collection of essays that are 'concerned with doing, understanding and explaining; with different modes of these activities and with their relations to one another' (1962: Preface).

One essay, 'The Activity of Being an Historian', begins with these general remarks on the nature of activities:

> Activities emerge naïvely, like games that children invent for themselves. Each appears, first, not in response to a premeditated achievement, but as a direction of attention pursued without premonition of what it will lead to. How should our artless ancestor have known what (as it has turned out) it is to be an astronomer, an accountant, or an historian? And yet it is he who, in play, set our feet on the paths that have led to these narrowly specified activities. For, a direction of attention, as it is pursued, may hollow out a character for itself and become specified in a 'practice'; and a participant in the activity comes to be recognized not by the results he achieves but by his disposition to observe the manners of the 'practice'. Moreover, when an activity has acquired a certain firmness of character, it may present itself as a puzzle, and thus provoke reflection; for, there may come a point at which we not only wish to acquire and exercise the skill which constitutes the activity, but may wish also to discern the logic of the relation of this activity (as it has come to be specified) to others and to ascertain its place on the map of human activity.
>
> (137)

Oakeshott here pays 'attention'* to the significance of 'a direction of attention'. In reflecting on the nature of 'activities' and on the activity of 'reflection', Oakeshott is engaged in the activity that we call philosophizing. What 'place' does this activity have 'on the map of human activity'? What is the relation between being a philosopher and, say, a lawyer? Is there a place for the philosopher within the lawyer? Might making a place for the two people in one person help prevent us from delusively imagining 'a certain firmness of character' as a solid entity? We might wonder if that question emerged in South Africa during the Truth and Reconciliation Commission's Legal Community Hearings.

How might we put together a 'map of human activity'? Passing over in silence the activity of being a cartographer, Oakeshott suggests that we attend to our questions:

> Now, if we consider the concrete activity of an historian, a cook, a scientist, a politician or any man in the ordinary conduct of life, we may observe that each is engaged upon answering questions of a certain sort, and that his characteristic is that he knows (or thinks he knows) the way to go about finding the answer to that sort of question. But the questions which he knows to belong to his sort of activity are not known to be such in advance of the activity of trying to answer them: in pursuing these questions, and not others, he is not obeying a rule or following a principle which comes from outside the activity, he is pursuing an activity which,

> in general, he knows how to pursue. It is the activity itself which defines the questions as well as the manner in which they are answered.
>
> (97)

How are we to engage in the activity of reading* that passage? (Are there different kinds of reading that are associated with different lines of questioning*?) What questions do we want to ask? How might we categorize questions? How might we resolve our differences with people who live by different categories and who define differently what is 'outside' an activity? What activity will we be doing when we try to resolve our differences?

As I said in the Introduction to this book, White is not one to doff and don disciplinary hats. There is a sense in which he seeks to transcend conventional disciplinary boundaries. For anyone who imagines that such boundaries are fixed and 'natural' as opposed to fluid cultural artefacts, White's work offers the experience* of 'a basic cultural dislocation: the sense that words have lost their meaning' (1984: 277). The title of White's *When Words Lose Their Meaning* draws from Thucydides' *History of the Peloponnesian War*, in which there is an account of a social disintegration that is associated with a linguistic deterioration. For White, the account can help us attend to the ways in which 'language'*, 'character'*, and 'culture'* intertwine:

> I will both proceed from and seek to validate the premise implicit in the title of the book, that language is not stable but changing and that it is perpetually remade by its speakers, who are themselves remade, both as individuals and communities, in what they say. The basic question asked of each text is how it performs as a response to this situation. We shall thus be interested less in what differentiates the genres represented here—poetry and philosophy and history and moral essays and fiction and politics and law—than in what unites them, in the tree of which they are several branches. For they are all species of the more general activity that is our true subject: the double activity of claiming meaning for experience and of establishing relations with others in language. Each of the texts we shall read proceeds by working upon a world it defines and leading its reader to a position within it. To put it in a single word, I would say that our subject is rhetoric, if by that is meant the study of the ways in which character and community—and motive, value, reason, social structure, everything, in short, that makes a culture—are defined and made real in performances of language.
>
> (White 1984: xi)

If, like many people in our culture, White's reader would define 'rhetoric'* in part by opposing it to that which is 'real', she may well be deeply puzzled by his suggestion that it could be the name of a 'subject', or 'general activity', that can serve to 'unite' a 'world'. (A doubter within her might ask this question: Is White's rhetorical flourish about 'rhetoric', especially the metaphor* of the tree, deliberately deceptive?) If we can notice and appreciate the significance of a certain 'basic question', we may notice and appreciate the significance of a 'general activity'. (A possible source of misunderstanding on the part of a number of White's critics may reside in the fact that he is concerned with a question that seems to be beyond their horizons.) For White, 'rhetoric' is a word of integration*; it unites 'motive, value, reason, social structure, everything, in short, that makes a culture'. By resisting the common opposition between rhetoric and reality, White opens up lines of questioning that the opposition closes. After reading* White, we might be disposed to ask, for example: What kind of world does White seek to make real in his 'performances of language'? We might then ask: How might we judge our own performance* when responding to that question?

'Now I Know How to Go On': Ludwig Wittgenstein

In his *Philosophical Investigations*, Wittgenstein resists the common image of language* as a tool that serves to identify objects in the world. In doing so, he attends to different ways in which we can 'use' language:

> But how many kinds of sentence are there? Say assertion, question, and command? – There are *countless* different kinds of use of what we call 'symbols,' 'words,' 'sentences.' And this multiplicity is not something fixed, given once for all; but new types of language, new language-games, as we may say, come into existence, and others become obsolete and get forgotten. . . . Here the term 'language-*game*' is meant to bring into prominence the fact that the *speaking* of language is part of an activity, or of a form of life.
>
> (Wittgenstein 1953: §23)

When we learn a language, we learn to participate in an 'activity' – a somewhat elusive 'a form of life'. If we act as if language is merely a collection of labels, we will be insensitive to the 'life' left out. This insensitivity can be a source of in-justice*.

Speaking about the 'understanding'* of mathematical formulae, Wittgenstein advises that we 'try not to think of understanding as a "mental process" at all.' Instead, 'ask yourself: in what sort of case, in what kind of circumstances, do we say, "Now I know how to go on"' (§154). He is concerned not with our 'understanding' in the sense of repeating some 'idea' but with being able to 'go on' in an 'activity'.

Wittgenstein's image of understanding has a place in White's *The Legal Imagination* – in a section expressing dissatisfaction with certain acts of metaphor* in talk about the mind. After a passage from Plato's *Republic*, White offers these remarks and questions:

> One of the subjects of this passage is education, the process by which one goes from a state of darkness and ignorance to one of understanding and light, and of course Plato speaks of that metaphorically too: the critical event is a 'turning of the soul in the right direction,' or a 'conversion.' And our own language of education is also metaphorical: 'educate' comes from a Latin word meaning to 'lead out', for example. . . . Wittgenstein does propose a different version: sometimes, at least, it makes sense to explain understanding by saying that one who understands a proposition 'knows how to go on' from that point, that he knows what to say or do next. . . . Which of these ways of describing knowledge . . . would be more helpful to you if you tried to express what you have learned in law school?
>
> (White 1973: 694)

At various times, many law students seem to say, 'I don't know my way about', to use Wittgenstein's words for presenting the 'form' of a 'philosophical problem' (§123). They are lost in an unfamiliar city. Soon, however, they may find their way about like a native. This sense is readily applicable to 'what you have learned in law school': eventually one is able to competently handle the 'case arising'.

Wittgenstein's imagery also has a place in *When Words Lose Their Meaning*. Attending to 'attention'*, White talks about his approach to reading*:

> In this book I have sought to draw the reader's attention, and my own, to certain aspects of our common life and to hold it there. My object has been to make more fully accessible to thought the ways in which we constitute ourselves and our relations with other people when we use, and in using recreate, the language that makes us what we are. . . . The way of reading exemplified here is not an analytic technique that objectifies what it studies . . . ; rather, it is a way of responding to and thinking about the expressions of another mind. . . . It has been my purpose to record not merely a method or a set of terms but an activity of mind expressed in what I call a language. Such a language can be learned only by immersion in its processes. One understands it not when one can translate its terms into other equivalences but when one can do it oneself—when, in Wittgenstein's phrase, one knows how to go on—as I hope the reader has begun to do with the language at work in this text. The key words of analysis and criticism that I have been using accordingly acquire their meaning not from explicit definition but from the reader's experience of their use. While the book is not scientific in the usual sense, there is thus a sense in which it is nonetheless empirical, for

> its rests wholly on the reader's verification of its value in his or her own experience.
>
> (White 1984: 275–6)

How should we go about responding to and thinking about the expressions of White's mind? His reader will fail to do justice* to his 'way of reading' if she fails to pay 'attention' to her own 'experience'* of using his 'key words'. This experience will need to take the process of cultural 'immersion' seriously, not least because our 'experience' is a product of culture*. When White says 'merely a method', he is speaking of that which is supposed to get at certainty ('scientific in the usual sense'). There is a sense in which White offers a different kind of method. As mentioned below (*Method), his 'way of reading' resembles Lonergan's 'transcendental method'.

Alienation

The 'Alienation Effect': Bertolt Brecht
'The Art of Placing an Action at a Distance': Milner S. Ball

In 1990, scholars from various disciplines addressed the theme of alienation at the 12th World Congress of Sociology. Out of the meeting emerged 14 chapters in *Alienation, Society, and the Individual* (Geyer and Heinz 1992). In the spirit of Karl Marx, the chapters claim or imply that 'alienation' ('economic', 'psychological', among other forms) is an undesirable condition that we should strive to overcome. The organizers might have benefited from inviting White, who had then recently used the word 'alienation' in a markedly different sense. In talk about the activity* of reading*, White writes:

> The very process of engagement with a literary text is . . . transformative in kind: it teaches not only by offering 'insights' translatable into other terms – new propositions of fact or logic or value – but transforming the self, as we become our own version of what the reader has to be to understand and respond to it. Thus the reader of a Platonic dialogue, to read it well, must become a partner in the dialectic process that it not only recommends but performs; this will require her, like the Socratic interlocutor, to undergo an alienation from the commonplaces by which she has organized her life. So too, the reader of a Jane Austen novel, if he does his reading well, will find his own initial opinions, say of Emma's selfishness or Fanny's meekness, repeatedly disturbed and corrected, a process that should move him in the direction of greater generosity as well as greater accuracy of judgment.
>
> (White 1989: 2019–20)

In the 'process of engagement' with White, who makes connections between apparently unconnected works (such connections are acts of integration*), such as a Platonic dialogue and a Jane Austen novel, we may well 'undergo an alienation from the commonplaces by which we have organized our lives'. The 'transformative' experience* can be imagined as beneficial at the level of character* formation to the extent that it 'should move [us] in the direction of greater generosity as well as greater accuracy of judgment'*. This kind of movement* would suggest that there are some possible virtues of 'alienation'.

The 'Alienation Effect': Bertolt Brecht

The playwright and literary critic Brecht is a forerunner on such virtues. He used various techniques in staging and acting to dislocate an audience's identification with characters and story. These techniques led to an 'alienation effect', or 'A-effect' for short. Here is a fragment from his essay 'Alienation Effects in Chinese Acting':

> [T]he Chinese artist never acts as if there were a fourth wall besides the three surrounding him. He expresses his awareness of being watched. This . . . removes one of the European stage's characteristic illusions. The audience can no longer have the illusion of being an unseen spectator. . . . A further means is that the artist observes himself. Thus if he is representing a cloud, perhaps showing its unexpected appearance, . . . its rapid yet gradual transformation, he will occasionally look at the audience as if to say: isn't it just like that?
>
> (Brecht 1936/1978: 91–2)

For Brecht, when actors are seen as acting, the audience can readily involve themselves in (and learn from) the dramatist's engagement with the reality-'illusion' relationship.

The activity of questioning* has an important place in Brecht's work. In some notes on 'the A-effect as a procedure in everyday life', he says:

> The A-effect consists in turning the object of which one is to be made aware, to which one's attention is to be drawn, from something ordinary, familiar, . . . into something peculiar, striking and unexpected. . . . Before familiarity can turn into awareness the familiar must be stripped of its conspicuousness; we must give up assuming that the object in question needs no explanation. . . . A common use of the A-effect is when someone says: 'Have you ever really looked carefully at your watch?' The questioner knows that I've looked at it often enough, and now his question deprives me of the sight which I've grown used to and which accordingly has nothing more to say to me. I used to look at it to see the time, and now when he asks me in this importunate way I realize that I have given up seeing the watch itself with an astonished eye; and it is in many ways an astonishing piece of machinery. . . . If one sees one's teacher hounded by the bailiffs an A-effect occurs: one is jerked out of a relationship in which the teacher seems big into one where he seems small.
>
> (Brecht 1951/1978: 144–5)

Have you ever really paid attention to your questions? Have you ever really paid attention to 'attention'*? The A-effect may draw attention to the 'utterly ordinary' activity of paying attention*, which is influenced by one's questions, in order to make it 'peculiar' and elusive. Brecht concerned himself with our ways of managing our economies of attention, and thus with habitual modes of thought. An activity that we repeat may become a habit, and we may be able to perform it with little or no attention – we can become 'grown used to' it. Habits provide a habitation, a place and an orientation in the world. Brecht shared with others an image of art 'as a means of productive reorientation' (Brooker 1988: 68). There can be value in getting 'jerked out' of a particular orientation in the world, especially if it is a source of in-justice*.

White's work offers a plethora of A-effects. One that immediately comes to mind concerns stories. The activity of storytelling is one we humans do much of the time, often without awareness. In *The Legal Imagination*, White invites his reader to attend carefully to stories. Consider, for example, this passage:

> One might be tempted to say that telling stories is the mark of a primitive mind. It is a way of explaining experience, perhaps, but one that we have left far behind: it is magical, not rational; it is of the world of myth, not science. . . . But you know that the language of analysis has not replaced the narrative . . . and that one who believes that everything can be said in a language of theory and system is an impossible fool. We still read stories and tell them, finding a meaning there that we find nowhere else. The novel is read by millions, . . . Shakespeare is still admired, and so on. The story is still alive; nothing can compete with its hold on the attention. Can you explain why this is so? . . . What is it that narrative offers us, what possibilities for meaning, what resources for speech and thought? As you work out a response in general terms, shift your focus to the law and ask what the narrative offers the lawyer, what it offers the law.
>
> (White 1973: 863)

I am reminded here of Eastman's *Yale Law Journal* essay, with which we engaged above in the Prologue. Drawing from White's work, to recall, Eastman offers a rich story about the possibilities of taking stories seriously in law and legal education. The influential opposition in our culture* of truth versus story (or theory versus story) may readily lead us to treat stories as beyond the pale.

Continuously between the lines in *The Legal Imagination* is a Brechtian question such as this: Have you listened carefully to legal argument? 'What', his reader might ask, 'are we to listen out for?' Let White respond with a question: 'What is it about legal argument that makes it the occasion not for the inflamed stupidities of most public discourse or the endless contradictions of an ordinary quarrel, but for thinking and speaking well?' (807). Putting to work his key word 'conversation'*, White offers his reader this food-for-thought:

> Opposing parties are often so furious that between them no conversation is possible at all: each thinks he is right, and generous to boot, and as for

> the other –! Imagine what two angry litigants might say to one another if they met to discuss their differences, or even to submit them to decision by another. That is what you would call a quarrel, and at least potentially there is such a quarrel, such a complete social and intellectual breakdown, in the background of every legal case. You might draft a page or two of such dialogue. Now imagine the same dispute carried on by two lawyers, in negotiation or trial. There may be forcefulness of expression, there may be emotion, there may even be bad behavior; but there is form to it all, a sense of what one does and does not do, and this gives the argument shape and motion. Where does this sense of form, this energy for order, come from and how does it operate? Legal argument is a process by which hostility is at once expressed and controlled, at the same time and by the same means. Can you explain how this miracle occurs?
>
> (807–8)

With 'hostility' being 'at once expressed and controlled', we have a 'form' of talk with a real mystery. An economist attempting to explain it might be led (by an invisible hand) to speak of an 'invisible hand' – an influential metaphor* inherited from Adam Smith's *Wealth of Nations* (1776/1898: 345). After giving some thought and expression to that which White calls a 'miracle', we might consider adopting his word. Doing so might be a conversation-stopper: 'That's a word for religion, not law.' But why should it be a conversation-stopper? Might it be a conversation-starter if it prompts an orthodox lawyer to clear things up? The lawyer, after all, might come to sense as alien the language of sovereignty upon which she has built many of her legal arguments. With that experience*, she may feel a desire to contribute to the conversations that are clumsily called 'law as literature', with the hope of creating an integrated self (*Integration).

'The Art of Placing an Action at a Distance': Milner S. Ball

The Legal Imagination had a 'practical consequence' for Ball: 'The editor in chief of the *Stanford Law Review* convinced a reluctant board of editors to publish a piece of mine about courts as theater', and 'part of the case . . . made to his colleagues was the fact and precedent of White's book' (Ball 1989: 194, n. 6). Perhaps with an interest in explaining the 'miracle' of legal argument, Ball's essay introduces Brecht:

> Courts may not always or even frequently do justice, but their theatrical quality does contribute to their potential for doing justice by encouraging disinterestedness in the decisionmakers. As actors, judge and jury are asked to play parts in a government of laws and not of people. . . . Fulfillment of the roles enables judgments which rise above prejudice and which, therefore, will more likely be just. Not the least hoped for

> result of the theatrical trappings and conventions of judicial proceedings is to educe such performances.
>
> Judge and jury are audience as well as actors and in this capacity also may be encouraged to make unprejudiced judgments. Actors may be drawn beyond themselves by the roles they play, but they are not thereby totally absorbed in their parts for they maintain control of the characters they create on stage. An equivalent mix of involvement and detachment is also possible for the audience. A production which works absorbs the audience. The involvement is not total, however, for their remains a separation which arises from the consciousness that what is being witnessed is a theatrical action. The separation allows the audience to make impartial judgments about what it sees.
>
> Bertolt Brecht observed the phenomenon of audience involvement and separation and exploited it through the 'alienation effect.' Alienation, in this sense, is the art of placing an action at a distance so that it can be judged objectively and so that it can be seen in relation to the world—or rather, worlds—around it. Alienation stimulates conscious judgment by keeping the audience from simple identification with the characters of the play. . . . This . . . attitude of limited identification with attorneys or parties while observing them and forming judgments about them is the attitude appropriately developed in judge and jury as audience.
>
> (Ball 1975: 100–102)

The experience* of 'alienation' can help us to control the 'distance' between the self and a party being judged – it can help strike a 'mix of involvement and separation' and make a 'conscious judgment'*. Ball suggests that we will benefit from promoting conditions facilitating that experience in order to help a judge and jury 'do justice'. Justice*, we might say, begins in an attunement* to the linguistic constitutions of our selves and others. When members of a community are 'drawn beyond themselves by the roles they play', they have grounds for hoping that their constitutional transformations will be constructive 'performances' (*Performance; Play).

In *Living Speech*, White cites Ball's *Stanford Law Review* essay when comparing 'the cultural form of the Athenian tragedy' and 'the American judicial opinion' (White 2006: 169). White attends to a single judicial opinion, namely Justice Harlan's opinion in *Cohen v. California* (1971). Echoing some of the spirit (or, better, demon) of the era of the Vietnam War, Paul Cohen wore, in a courthouse, a jacket bearing the words 'Fuck the draft'. He was arrested and convicted for violating a California statute that made it an offence to 'maliciously and willfully disturb the peace or quiet of any neighborhood or person . . . by . . . offensive conduct'. The Supreme Court had to decide whether Cohen's speech was punishable because it fit one of the 'exceptions' to free speech protected by the First Amendment. White's interest in the case centres on the relationship Harlan establishes with the rude phrase. The place of the 'alien' is at stake: 'We can see . . . that the bringing on stage of that which is . . . alien . . . is at work through the entire opinion' (White 2006: 183). Harlan serves as a model for 'alienation' in Ball's sense – 'the art of placing an action at a distance so that it can be judged objectively and so that it can be seen in relation to the world—or rather, worlds—around it'.

Immediately before his engagement with Harlan's opinion for the Court, White examines particular aspects of Athenian tragedy. His interest is in how this genre 'has been seen to express the essential dignity and value of the human being' (168–9). In one passage concerning the theatre's treatment of women, he writes:

> In the world of Athens, women had a legal and social position mainly as possessions of men, whether fathers or husbands; even in procreation women were imagined to contribute nothing to the child except a kind of oven in which the male seed could grow; and they themselves had essentially no property and no civil rights. Yet by all three of the great dramatists of Athens they are represented on stage as psychological and moral actors who are in every sense (except power) the equal of men. . . . It is hard to know how to explain this phenomenon fully, but I think it is another expression of the general impulse to put on stage what is real but unseen—a part of life that is normally excluded from the vision of the male citizens who make up most of the audience. . . . This kind of drama is not merely a kind of entertainment, not an item of consumption, but a major public and political event, one of the purposes of which, at the hands of the three great geniuses whose work we have, is educative and transformative, bringing its audience to a new kind of life.
>
> (173)

This passage, which suggests a great deal about White's sense of the 'educative', brings to mind this claim by Adam Smith: 'The great secret of education is to direct vanity to proper objects' (1759/1974: 259). What is proper may be 'unseen', and it may take 'the hands' of 'all three of the great dramatists of Athens' to render the unseen visible. White attends not to the 'invisible hand' (Smith) but to the potential power of the literary hand to create a 'new kind of life'. In his passage, which offers a resource for defining the word 'equal' in terms of rhetorical capacity (*Equality; Rhetoric), White sets his 'stage' for his reading of Harlan's *Cohen* opinion. We can be sure that in bringing the two genres together White seeks to make a composition that is 'educative and transformative, bringing [his] audience to a new kind of life'.

After providing certain facts in *Cohen*, White begins his act of cultural cum judicial criticism. In doing so, he contributes to his image of law as a certain kind of 'conversation'*:

> The judicial process here brings into a zone of public awareness material that is normally unseen, most obviously and dramatically, and perhaps a

> bit embarrassingly, in the use of the word 'fuck'—a word that, although known to almost all English speakers, is even today, let alone in 1971, typically used only on certain kinds of occasions, with certain kinds of audiences, and is definitely excluded from most formal discourse, certainly the discourse of the Supreme Court of the United States. Justice Harlan marks the distance between this term and the language of the Supreme Court—and the decorous conversation he seeks to establish with his readers—by the way he recites the facts of the case, not in his own words but in those of the California court: 'On April 26, 1968, the defendant was observed in the Los Angeles County Courthouse in the corridor outside of division 20 of the municipal court wearing a jacket bearing the words "Fuck the Draft" which were plainly visible.' He thus uses the word, but distances himself from it, burying it between two sets of quotation marks, in this way at once confirming and violating the expectation that he would never use such a word in this context. This stimulates in the reader a kind of embarrassed uncertainty, which offers her a direct experience of the substantive question at the center of the case: What should we do about the complex set of feelings, both repressive and liberated, that are triggered by the use of this word in such a place?
>
> (175)

After reading Brecht on the A-effect, we might now be inclined to ask a question such as this: 'Have you ever really looked carefully at the F-word?' Harlan's dance with the word can remind us that language* is not a neutral tool as our talk about 'it' often suggests but, rather, a medium for creating characters and communities of one kind or another. It seems readily imaginable that when he displayed the slogan 'Fuck the Draft', Cohen would have been surprised to learn that it could be placed in a 'decorous conversation'. To the extent that the meanings of words are influenced by their 'use', the meaning of the phrase could dramatically change for him.

White goes on to draw attention to some aspects of *Cohen* that concern the politics and ethics of 'attention'*, which is at the heart of his approach to justice:

> What is happening in the *Cohen* case, from one perspective, is just another event in the long struggle over the meaning of the Vietnam War. But the law cannot think in such terms; it must fashion itself to meet the particularities of the case as these emerge in thought and argument that are themselves shaped by the particularities of prior cases, prior arguments. When the bright light of attention is focused on what we have not seen, or seen clearly, it almost always reveals a complexity and richness of significance that we had missed, thus putting in question, among other things, our own prior habits of mind and imagination. It frustrates

> and educates our expectations. In the *Cohen* case, the larger issue—that of the draft, and the war itself—is, of course, on everybody's mind and the source of deep, sometimes violent, internal national conflict. What the law does here is take a tiny fragment of that larger story, this simple act of protest, and examine it not in the terms of the national political debate—prowar or antiwar—but as a constitutional problem, to be analyzed, argued, and decided in the terms established by this branch of the law.
>
> (177–8)

To the extent that the opinion leads us to 'question . . . our own habits of mind and imagination', we are on the way to achieving a certain healthy disinterestedness in relation to the case. White's reading of the case has the potential to disturb certain slogans that we carry with us. 'Law is politics', for example. Well, yes and no. Of course 'law is politics', but a certain kind of politics that can be distinguished from another. We can be sure that the slogan 'law is politics' need not and should not be a conversation*-stopper for White. The confident user of the slogan is likely to have a sense of alienation from the world that White does not share.

White's reading of *Cohen* can be read as a part of his image of the law as a 'culture of argument' (*Culture), which is much richer that the dominant static image of 'law . . . as a set of rules' (White 1984: 267). For White, to recall, 'Law works by a process of argument that places one version of events against another and creates a tension between them . . . ; in doing so it makes our choice of language conscious rather than habitual and creates a moment at which controlled change of language and culture becomes possible' (White 1984: 273). With his reading of *Cohen* in the background, we might fittingly add to that image: White's cultural criticism works by a process of argument that places one subculture against another and compares them; in doing so it makes our images of them conscious and offers a resource for re-imaging these images, with the hope of maintaining or enriching one's culture. In reconnecting the *Cohen* case with ancient Greek theatre, White writes:

> Like the drama, then, the opinion brings before us what is remote in time and space and in doing so creates a world of imagination, simultaneously drawn from the world we otherwise know and an alternative to it. The idea in both cases is not to offer the audience an escape into fantasy, but to create an imagined reality that can run against that other imagined reality we call the 'real world,' both to test it and to be tested by it. . . .
>
> . . . [Like] the earliest forms of Greek drama . . . the law works . . . by the opposition of character against character, plaintiff against defendant, each representing a different vision of the world—and of the law—and seeking to establish his or her own as the dominant one. The central legal institution we call the hearing works by a disciplined opposition that is intended to lead—and sometimes does so—to deeper understanding,

> indeed, to the revelation of central questions theretofore obscured by our ignorance, or by our habits of thought and imagination.
>
> (White 2006: 178–9)

In putting together a fragment of 'the law' with 'the drama', White offers with his own version of the activity* to which he directs his reader's attention, namely 'a disciplined opposition that is intended to lead . . . to deeper understanding'. His composition offers to extend talk about reasoning by analogy in the law by explicitly using analogical reasoning for re-imagining the law. In doing so, we can read White as seeking to 'create an imagined reality', one that can help his reader make sense of what he means by 'to create an imagined reality'. Reiterating his efforts in *The Legal Imagination* (1973: 878), White challenges those who would set 'imagination'* and 'reality' in opposition to each other.

Attention

The Love Rule: Simone Weil
'A Certain Negro Woman': *Prigg v. Pennsylvania*
Economizing on Attention: Arjo Klamer

The word 'attention' is commonly used in ordinary life. 'Everyone knows what attention is', said William James (1890/1981: 381). Well, yes and no. That which seems ordinary can often be transformed into the extraordinary when given attention.

The Love Rule: Simone Weil

During her short life, Weil suffered from severe headaches. In *Waiting for God*, she develops a language of pain, which includes a distinction between affliction and suffering. In '[a]n hour or two of violent pain caused by a decayed tooth' we can experience 'suffering' without experiencing 'affliction' (1951/1973: 117–18). Weil uses the latter word to name a process that consists of 'an uprooting of life, a more or less attenuated equivalent of death, made irresistibly present to the soul by the attack or immediate apprehension of physical pain' (118). It is in a state of affliction, Weil claimed, that we can learn to 'decreate' parts of the self that obstruct the will of God (see Little 1993: 25). She hoped that by means of decreation, her own unnecessary wants would cease to get in the way of God's love for the world: 'If only I knew how to disappear there would be a perfect union between God and the earth I tread, the sea I hear' (quoted in Plant 1996: 37). This 'I' can be thought of as an 'imperialistic' (Little 1993: 25), which an ideal self would do well to reconstitute. We can be sure that Weil would have little respect for the dictum 'I think, therefore I am' as a foundational utterance. A better start might be 'Here I am', to echo an attentive Abraham (*Genesis* 22: 1).[1]

In her talk about attention, Weil suggests much about the inadequacy of the commonly used opposition of active versus passive. There is a sense in which we need to actively get passive: 'Attention is an effort, the greatest of all efforts perhaps, but it is a negative effort' (1951/1973: 111). She refers to a famous story:

> Christ taught us that the supernatural love of our neighbor is the exchange of compassion and gratitude which happens in a flash between two beings, one possessing and the other deprived of human personality.

> One of the two is only a little piece of flesh, naked, inert, and bleeding beside a ditch; he is nameless; no one knows anything about him. Those who pass by this thing scarcely notice it, and a few minutes afterward do not even know they saw it. Only one stops and turns his attention toward it. The actions that follow are just the automatic effect of this movement of attention. The attention is creative. But the moment when it is engaged it is a renunciation. This is true, at least, if it is pure. The man accepts to be diminished by concentrating on an expenditure of energy, which will not extend his own power but will only give existence to a being other than himself, who will exist independently of him.
>
> (146–7)

This passage in not one to 'pass by': it connects with the lawyer's question (*Luke* 10: 29), 'And who is my neighbour?' We might wonder what might become of the economist's fiction *Homo economicus* if she or he had the capacity to ask that question in a way that differs radically from the conventional utility-seeking question, 'What can I get?'

In her essay 'Human Personality', Weil defined 'justice'* as 'a certain kind of attention' (1943/1977: 313). This attention involves a capacity 'to listen to someone' (332).[2] She considered it important to 'learn to distinguish between two cries' (334): 'Why am I being hurt?' and 'Why has somebody got more than I have?' The first cry should have privileged status, for when it 'arises from the depth of a human heart . . . there is certainly injustice' (315). Weil goes on to talk about the place that this cry should have in public life:

> Apart from the intelligence, the only human faculty which has an interest in public freedom of expression is that point in the heart which cries out against evil. But as it cannot express itself, freedom is of little use to it. What is first needed is a system of public education capable of providing it, so far as possible, with means of expression; and next, a régime in which the public freedom of expression is characterized not so much by freedom as by attentive silence in which this faint and inept cry can make itself heard; and finally, institutions are needed of a sort which will, so far as possible, put power into the hands of men who are able and anxious to hear and understand it.
>
> (316)

Weil, to be sure, would have a distinctive emphasis placed on the activity that is commonly called 'thinking like a lawyer'. This emphasis, called 'attentive silence', could perhaps be called 'hearing like a just lawyer'. Justice begins in 'silence'* and in listening*.

Weil greatly admired Homer's *Iliad*, writing an essay in literary criticism on the epic, titled 'The *Iliad* or the Poem of Force' (1941/2003).

White's engagement with the epic in *When Words Lose Their Meaning* draws from Weil's essay:

> The primary way in which Homer moves his reader from a position within his imagined world, and accepting of it, to an external position from which he can be seen and judged is by organizing the traditional epic materials into patterns of meaning that have significance different from anything that is or could be said directly in the epic language itself. He works by an art of juxtaposition that at once distances the reader from the heroic culture and defines a central value by which it can be judged.
>
> Simone Weil speaks to this point in a famous essay celebrating what she calls the 'extraordinary sense of equity' in the *Iliad*. Homer describes Achaean and Trojan deaths . . . in identical terms, expressive of identical feelings; and in doing this he enacts for us a central value of the poem—a value distinct from those expressed by any character in it: the recognition of the equal humanity of the people who must suffer on both sides. 'One is barely aware that the poet is a Greek and not a Trojan.'
>
> . . . This is an 'equity' that goes far beyond impartiality between Achaean and Trojan. It is an acceptance of the conditions of existence so strong as to become a marvelous hospitality to life in all its forms and aspects, a love of the world itself.
>
> (White 1984: 39–40)

With that passage, White's reader may readily catch a sense in which his chapter on the *Iliad* 'is really about law' (xi), especially its possibilities for a meaningful kind of equality*. What more could anyone want from a judge than an 'extraordinary sense of equity', with 'the recognition of the equal humanity of the people . . . on both sides'? As we read the chapters that follow his chapter on the *Iliad*, we will do well to notice White's Homeric 'art of juxtaposition', including 'a remarkable equality of treatment' of materials from the law (including the Chief Justice Marshall's opinion in *McCulloch v. Maryland*) and from that which we commonly call 'literature', a treatment that offers to transform our sense of both and that is worthy of the word 'love'.

'A Certain Negro Woman': *Prigg v. Pennsylvania*

In 1837, Edward Prigg kidnapped Margaret Morgan and forcibly took her and her children over the Pennsylvania state line into Maryland, where she became a slave. A trial court convicted Prigg of kidnapping under a Pennsylvania statute passed in 1826 ('An Act to give effect to the provisions of the constitution of the United States relative to fugitives from labor, for the protection of free people of color, and to prevent Kidnapping.') Prigg's attorney argued that Prigg had legally seized Morgan, exercising his right under the Constitution and the Fugitive Slave Act,[3] and that the Pennsylvania statute was in conflict with the federal law and should be struck down. The relevant part of the Constitution (Article IV § 2, cl. 3) is: 'No person held to Service or Labour in one State, under the Laws thereof, escaping into another, shall, in Consequence of any Law or Regulation therein, be discharged from such Service or Labour, but shall be delivered up on Claim of the Party to whom such Service or Labour may be due.' This is the so-called Fugitive Slave Clause – 'so-called' because the composers of the Constitution avoided the word 'slave'.[4] The Constitutional Convention delegates did not discuss what this clause was supposed to accomplish or how it was to be implemented (Finkelman 1993: 613–14). Why the silence*? Were they avoiding a constitutional breakdown?

Margaret Morgan was the child of a couple who had been born into slavery. They had been the slaves of a Maryland master named Ashmore. Although he never formally emancipated them, sometime before 1812 Ashmore allowed Margaret's parents to live as free blacks. Thereafter Ashmore 'constantly declared he had set them free' (Finkelman 1993: 610). Margaret was born after her parents had been informally set free. She married Jerry Morgan, a free black, and in 1832 they moved across the Maryland border to Pennsylvania, where they had several children. These children were free under Pennsylvania law and they did not fit the constitutional definition of fugitive slaves (persons 'escaping into another state'). Margaret's marriage to Jerry Morgan and her move to Pennsylvania occurred with the apparent acquiescence of Ashmore. Under either Pennsylvania or Maryland law, Margaret may have been legitimately free. She may well have considered herself to be free (Finkelman 1993: 610–11).

Justice Story, for the Supreme Court, refers to Margaret Morgan, 'a certain negro woman' (*Prigg* 1842: 608), only once. We might say that he failed to reach for the Homer within him. For White, the Court's opinion was a poor judicial performance, being one-sided:

> After a brief statement of the facts—itself of interest because it is so clotted with legalisms as to distance both judge and reader from the human reality of which it speaks—Story moves directly to the fugitive slave clause of the Constitution. . . . [His] method of interpreting the . . . clause . . . is to look through its language for the intention that lies behind it, an intention he sees on the one side as insistence that maximum protection be given to southern slaveowning interests, and on the other as acquiescence in this claim. . . . Story's method eliminates the aspirational or idealizing element that is essential to what we think of as law: it reduces talk about what 'ought to be' to talk about what 'is,' or what 'was,' thus reducing aspiration to mere will. The ultimate question for him is not what result makes best sense of the instrument as that document was originally composed, but what the South wanted. This is to destroy the ground of authority upon which law rests: the authority

> that derives not from the power of the person who makes the law but from the character of the law that is made, from the kind of conversation by which it is to become real in the world. Instead of participating in an argumentative or discoursing community that struggles with the questions, what kind of world we ought to have, what the authoritative language ought to mean, we are offered a world in which the only question is what someone wanted. The vice of this opinion is worse than authoritarianism: it is to destroy authority.
>
> (White 1990: 117 and 120–21)

For White, Story's defective 'method'* of reading* is an act of dis-integration*, in that 'it reduces talk about what "ought to be" to talk about what "is" . . .' White's character*-related distinction between 'authoritative' and 'authoritarianism' can help us talk about the opinion. For him, Story seems to imagine himself not as participating in a collaborative enterprise with his readers – as, for example, Marshall does in *McCulloch* (*Constitution) – but as telling them in perfectly plain terms that such-and-such *is* The Law. Story, to put it differently, has created an authoritarian character and, in doing so, has destroyed, for the moment at least, law worthy of the name.

White's reading of *Prigg* brings to mind remarks of his about the basic question that one asks. 'The way a court works', he says, 'is deeply affected by the kind of question it addresses' (White 1984: 264). To that we could add: The way a cultural and legal critic works is deeply affected by the kind of question he or she addresses. We can be sure that White asks an integrative question, which, for example, intricately combines 'is' and 'ought', and also the general and the particular (*Integration; Questioning). White writes his judicial criticism out of his 'ultimate question', namely, Is it just?[5] 'Just' here concerns a certain kind of attention (*Justice). We can be confident that a judicial opinion 'clotted with legalisms as to distance both judge and reader from the human reality of which it speaks' will have difficulty in providing this attention. For White, the problem with Story's opinion is that it is written out of a different question. The *Prigg* case, particularly Story's act of 'reducing aspiration to mere will' offers White and his reader food-for-thought on the separation of law and justice.

Giving attention to Margaret Morgan in his reading of *Prigg*, White goes on to offer a resource for thinking about the integration of 'ought' and 'is':

> . . . I think the proper result in *Prigg* would have been to uphold the Pennsylvania kidnapping statute, in *Dredd Scott* to find the plaintiff a citizen of the United States. In addition I think that the reading of the Constitution in a more lawyerly way would have led to substantial difficulties, emotional and intellectual, with the results reached in these cases—difficulties which the formulations actually employed by the Justices enabled them, and their readers, to avoid. To focus, for example, upon the circumstances of Mrs. Morgan's freeborn child in a way that

> recognized that he was a person, entitled to freedom but needing his family, would have been to realize that Mrs. Morgan and indeed her unfree children were people too; a realization, which, if articulated with sufficient clarity, would have tended to erode, not the discourse of law, which it would have exemplified, but that part of it which maintained slavery.
>
> Today we have no slavery, but we do have people suffering greatly, victimized greatly, who in the law and elsewhere are talked about in highly distancing and objectifying ways. Real attention to the fundamental character and commitments of legal discourse, by lawyers and judges and others, might help us bring to our collective attention, however reluctantly, the circumstances of the successors of Margaret Morgan and her children—of all races—and prepare us to address them with more responsiveness and responsibility alike.
>
> (139–40)

The *Prigg* case centred on a person who was 'suffering greatly'. For White, 'legalisms' got in the way, silencing her, and this meant that in a sense the law had lost itself, that lawyers had lost themselves – they were doing an activity* other than law. He would direct our 'collective attention' to the process of working out a fitting direction of attention for law on the map of human activity. If we attend to fashioning an integrated language*, especially with regard to 'ought' and 'is', we can be confident that at the same time we will be fashioning an integrated society.

Economizing on Attention: Arjo Klamer

The first writing assignment in White's *The Legal Imagination* is titled 'What Do Different Speakers Want to Know?' (1973: 36). The scene is this: 'there has been a stabbing in a barroom brawl.' White asks: 'What does each of the following speakers want to know about this event? . . . (a) the doctor called to the scene; (b) the assailant's priest; (c) the brother of the stabbed man; (d) the lawyer for the defendant.' White prods attention toward their lines of questioning*: 'Draft passages in which you show each of these people framing the questions he would ask about this event.' White's reader might well wonder about the questions that White frames. If so, the final part of the assignment may be helpful. It is concerned with 'drawing inferences from speech' – an activity* that we 'all' do 'all the time'. White invites his reader to twist her attention:

> In this course you will be asked to draw inferences from your writing in a double way: first, you will be asked to look at the portion of a paper in which you show a lawyer – yourself? another? – functioning and talking as a lawyer, and to draw what inferences you can about the possibilities of legal life there defined. Then you will be asked to turn to the part of

> the paper written in your own voice, as an independent mind, and ask how you define yourself there. The ultimate question, of course, is what connection you can establish between these two sorts of performance, these two kinds of writing, these two selves that you define.
>
> In a sense the whole rest of the course is devoted to working out these problems. At this stage, perhaps you will find the following questions helpful in figuring out what inferences might be drawn from your writing. . . . [A]sk of each of the paragraphs you have written, 'Would anyone, given any choice in the matter, want to read this paragraph? Why?' The skeptical question every reader asks of everything (except for a teacher reading term papers) is, 'Why should I pay any attention at all to what this person writes?' How do you as a writer attempt to provide your reader with an answer to that question?
>
> (40–41)

A first reading of White's questions had a disabling effect on my capacity to write. (Perhaps there was an unproductive competition among my 'selves' to speak, and that meant that my limited 'attention' was being channelled in too many directions, leading to a paralysis.) An internal conversation* began about how I should speak. This question emerged: 'Which "I" should speak?' Another question came forth: 'Who was that last self speaking?' Then another: 'Do I have some centre of my multiple selves?' That last question connects to this utterance in Shakespeare's *King Richard II*: 'play I in one person many people' (*Imagination). It seems to me, to my many selves, that White's questions prod us to attend to the reality of a 'we' within each of us, a reality that opens the door to the justice*-related task of trying to create a harmony within. Doing so might help prevent an internal brawl. What might an economist at such a brawl want to know about the event?

'Where are the people in economic models?' So says an imagined 'literary critic' in Klamer's essay on the topic of 'rationality' in economics (Klamer 1987: 163). Unlike many economists, he takes the question seriously, and he has sought to fashion a humanistic economics. Such an economics, as suggested in *Speaking of Economics*, has a place for attention:

> Students are more than pleased to get the attention of their supervisor and finish their dissertation with his or her assistance. . . . Doing a dissertation is one thing, getting published is another, but getting *noticed* is an entirely different ball game. It had not occurred to me that others in the conversation might ignore the book. But how could this not be? I should have realized this before as a reader. A profusion of bookstore shelves, university library stacks, and catalogues of publishers abound with the work of others seeking attention. How is anyone going to notice a particular book or article when there are so many others?
>
> (Klamer 2007: 52)

Why did it not occur to Klamer that his book might be ignored? Where was he directing his attention? What questions were channelling his attention? What cultural forces were at work in his questions? With his 'how'-questions, the reflective Klamer offers a point of departure for re-using a key word in economics, namely *scarcity*. Economists commonly concern themselves with scarcity at the level of 'trade-offs' resulting from 'limited resources'. Klamer goes on to set up an uncommon line of inquiry concerning the study of how scarce resources of attention are allocated to the desires of people to be heard.

What are the costs and benefits of channelling our attention on attention? Klamer alerts us to some possible scarcity-related costs:

> Intense attention is what characterizes the scientific life. . . . This intense attention . . . accounts for the autism of so many scientists. They are self-absorbed – and have to be – in order to fix their attention on their problem, to focus on what is really important in their research, thus earning the well-deserved reputation of being absent-minded. They are too preoccupied to pay attention to the other conversations that are going on around them, rendering them bad company in non-academic settings. . . . It is a matter of different focus, or being in another attention space.
>
> (54–5)

Here is a resource for thinking about why people disagree and how they might come to agree. Without being aware of it, parties disagreeing may be in a different 'attention space'. Becoming aware of the possibility of being in different attention spaces could prod the parties to engage in the activity of attunement* to each other's space.

Klamer's attention to 'attention space' is part of his effort to re-imagine the familiar activity that we call 'conversation'*:

> The conversation is the manifestation of attention. Instead of thinking of attention as something going on in people's heads, as psychologists like us to do, I suggest we think of attention as a characteristic of the conversation. Ideas have attention only if they are in the conversation. Conversations are thus attention spaces.
>
> (55)

Where might the metaphor of conversations as 'attention spaces' be placed in the marketplace of ideas? If it catches the attention of many economists, might the metaphor of the 'marketplace of ideas' crash in the marketplace of ideas?

Klamer pays much attention to metaphor*, which can enable us to economize on attention-consuming extended explanations. His vocabulary of metaphor includes 'constitutive metaphors', which help frame the way we imagine the world. These metaphors 'lie so deep that we are usually unaware of them' (114). The constitutive metaphors of mainstream economists 'come in the form of systems of equations and conjure up images of machines, of humans as calculating robots, and a mathematical system'. A collection of heterodox economists, on the other hand, are 'inspired by an organic vision of the world; their constitutive metaphor is cast in anthropomorphic terms and makes us think of people who are equipped with emotions, subject to uncertainties, and knowledgeable only in a limited sense' (129). When mainstream economists meet heterodox economists, patterns of attention can productively shift: 'Only in confrontation with others who think in different (constitutive) metaphors might we become aware of them' (114). The patterns, however, might not shift:

> [C]onstitutive metaphors and stories define a conversation. Once inside a conversation we cannot think without them. And we can be inside the conversation only if we understand how to work the constitutive metaphors and stories. That's what graduate school instills: how to think the constitutive metaphor and enact the constitutive story without being aware of it. It's like riding a bicycle; people do it without thinking how they do it. We may be so steeped in our conversations that we cannot imagine that others think and talk differently, that there are other serious conversations out there.
>
> (128)

Imagine being unable to 'imagine that others think and talk differently, that there are other serious conversations out there'. A defining feature of an economic imperialist would seem to be a one-track imagination, or a direction of 'attention' that is fixed solid and that has no interest in self-'aware'-ness. Klamer's attention-centred book can be read as being devoted to the promotion of self-awareness by economists. This could cultivate an interest in the politico-economic activity of transforming constitutions of language, in the direction of justice*.

We have noticed Klamer's book. How might we talk about the economics of our attention if we not only read it but engage in re-reading*? The following passage from White's *The Legal Imagination* may help:

> You have probably noticed that neither the good opinion nor the good poem can be read through once only, that both require reading again and again in light of where they come out. Both must be addressed with the whole mind, both demand all the attention one can give; and one consequence of reading of this sort is not only an increased understanding of what lies outside of oneself, but a change in the reader himself, an expansion of sympathy or an opening of a new capacity to perceive. Good writing in the poem or opinion works directly on its reader and changes him.
>
> (803)

We might say that 'good writing' engages its reader in a kind of conversation, part of which is conversation about the conversation. As the reader changes, she can reread with the intention of making sense of the changes that have taken place, of the person the text has helped her become. Any 'conclusions' will be tentative, for we can expect to revise them, as with earlier conclusions. There will be a to-and-fro movement* 'outside of oneself' and inside. Making sense of the movement, the material of transcendental method*, will 'demand all the attention one can give'.

Attunement

'When One Learns a Distant Language': A. L. Becker
'Learning as Attunement': Frances Trix

About ten years ago, I picked up Kierkegaard's *Fear and Trembling* for the first time. I soon put it down, failing to understand much at all. He seemed to be rambling. Several years later, I read a book on Kierkegaard, by Edward Mooney, that talks about the structure of *Fear and Trembling*, a structure that I had failed to appreciate. Here is a passage from Mooney's book:

> Its unfolding structure seems symphonic or operatic: there is an opening program note (or preface), a tuning section which sets the stage, a lengthy overture, three dialectical acts or movements, and a closing coda. The section immediately following the program note has a title best translated 'Attunement.' This . . . rings of 'tuning up'—readying audience and performer alike for an ensuing performance. . . . Kierkegaard . . . sounds variations on the Genesis story of God's terrible command to Abraham. These abbreviated, disturbing, and distorting 'attunements' are rehearsals, false starts. . . . By their dazzling obscurity, these exercises tease our dialectical and musical ears, preparing us for longer renditions yet to come. . . . [S]urely here Kierkegaard anticipates—and fulfills—Nietzsche's call for a music-playing Socrates.
>
> (Mooney 1996: 89–90)

That passage can serve as a resource for talking about 'the negotiation of meaning' (Lakoff and Johnson 1980 – *Metaphor), which often involves the use of the metaphorical imagination* with the aim of productively making the unfamiliar familiar, and thereby enabling understanding*. The suggestive musical metaphors in the passage can help a Kierkegaard reader tune in to him. Without the help, a reader may hear him as a cacophony, to speak from my own initial experience.

Just as Mooney seeks to help his reader to hear Kierkegaard, I am seeking to help my reader to hear White, along with my more general claims about 'justice as attunement'. This chapter is perhaps best read as a 'tuning section', 'readying' for a 'performance'*, 'preparing us for longer renditions to come'.

'When One Learns a Distant Language': A. L. Becker

In 1958, Becker took up a position teaching English in Burma. Whilst learning Burmese, he had the experience of a major cultural disorientation (*Culture), with words losing their meaning. In *Beyond Translation*, he provides a collection of stories about it. Here are three fragments:

> When I tried to tell a story in Burmese, I put in past time markers in imitation of English tense—and totally confused people. Time took on new distinctions, lost old ones.
>
> People over and over said they were '*ah nah deh*,' which might translate as '(my) strength hurts (me)'. It was a reluctance to put themselves forward—their own power made them uneasy—a signal that more persistent inviting was needed, a positive emotion of 'shame' that I learned very slowly to value. And I began to understand a new set of metaphors involving new pains and with them a new set of emotions.
>
> Like a rain of fresh new poetic metaphors, Burmese defamiliarized the image of the world that I took for granted.
>
> (Becker 1995: 11, 11, and 12)

The metaphors that we live by are the product and producer of an 'image of the world'. They are often not recognized as metaphors until we encounter 'a rain of fresh new poetic metaphors'. Metaphor* can serve to transform the strange into the familiar and the familiar into the strange – a potentially productive movement* of alienation*. The process, especially if it involves 'an experience of the collapse of language under strain' (White 1973: 760 – *Experience; Language), may give rise to 'new pains'.

When Becker was in Burma, a missionary gave him a book from which he learned about the Burmese language. The book impressed him, and he wanted to learn more about its author, the linguist Kenneth Pike. Becker ended up doing a PhD in linguistics. As dissenter in the tribe, he suggested that linguists might benefit from attending to the way they talk about language:

> The dominant metaphor in most current linguistics sees language as a timeless code, encoding timeless, universal 'thought' or 'concepts' in different ways. An alternative to this is to think of languaging as an endless social process of orientating and reorientating ourselves and each other to a constantly changing environment. The Javanese call this process *jarwa dhosok*, pressing old texts into the present situation. Here we will do well to replace the word *language*, as an accomplished system or structure, with the word *languaging* as the performance of a repertoire of games or *orientations*, à la Wittgenstein . . . . [L]anguaging is one means by which we continually

> attune ourselves to context. In a distant language, we have to relearn to attune ourselves, which means primarily building new memories.
> (288)

The word 'languaging' may sound strange at first, perhaps from 'a distant language'. (It is the present participle of the neglected verb 'to language'.) Language is a process of languaging. It may be worth appropriating 'languaging' into our languaging – making it our own – for it can remind us that language is not a system of names but an activity* that we do. 'Languaging . . . is a kind of attunement between a person and a context' (9), a process of 'self-correction' and 'very subtle adjustments' (369). 'Performance'* matters here.

Let us keep languaging in the direction of an attunement to Becker's way of imagining language. He stresses the importance of time and memory:

> Burmese seems exotic because I lack the stock of remembered prior texts, the lingual memory, to make it seem familiar. I seldom know if what someone says is new and original or old and familiar. I do not 'get' jokes.
> (12)

> Languaging is inherited not as grammatical rules . . . but particularity, in particular memories of particular instances of languaging, what I have called *prior texts*. Knowing a way of languaging means having a repertoire of prior texts—all the particular instances of languaging any one of us remembers, always imperfectly. When we speak or write, we take those imperfectly remembered prior texts and reshape them into new contexts.
> (15)

Beckerese may or may not seem exotic, depending upon one's stock of remembered prior texts. Learning Becker's languaging is learning particular instances of 'it'. We may hope that our engagement with Becker provides us with some valuable prior texts with which to reshape into new contexts, including attuning ourselves to the contexts against which others create texts.

Becker's concern with 'particularity' may be irritating or frustrating for those with a will to speak in a universal voice* in the service of clarity and neutrality. There is a sense, however, in which Becker's work could speak to a universal audience:

> Our goal, following Wittgenstein, is description, as careful and self-conscious as we can make it. And why describe languages—that is, languaging in different societies? I think the answer . . . is to learn to converse with those we have difficulty conversing with. Whether they are our own neighbors and family or people halfway around the world, the same kinds of differences are involved, I think, and learning about one teaches about the other. Recognizing the dramatic differences I confront in speaking to a Balinese prepares me to recognize the more subtle differences

> I confront in speaking to my wife or my children, and it teaches me to respect them, not out of some abstract moral principle but as the practical first step in having my own differences respected.
>
> (422–3)

To take the particularities of a society seriously, including its way of languaging, can be an educative step in the direction of taking the particularities of a person seriously, including her or his way of languaging. If we can learn to converse with the Other, then we may be able to get into a position to really converse with the Self (*Conversation). Who is this person Becker? Can we 'recognize' that he is different from you and me? Doing so could be a first step in being able to respect – and to do justice* to – differences. While Becker might be reluctant to talk about 'some abstract moral principle', he certainly provides a resource with which to give content to the ancient principle, 'hear the other side'.

For a number of years, Becker taught in the Department of Linguistics at the University of Michigan, Ann Arbor, where he retired in 1985. White began teaching at the University of Michigan a year before Becker retired. The two of them became good friends. As I mentioned in the Introduction, White's use of the word 'attunement' draws from Becker's usage of it. This passage from White's book on 'learning to read George Herbert' will have a familiar ring to a Becker reader:

> My aim in this book has been to record the process by which I have begun to learn to read the poetry of Herbert, with the object both of helping others read their way into this difficult literature and, more generally, of suggesting a way of thinking about what it can mean to learn to read the work of another. For me . . . it is helpful to think of this kind of reading as learning the language of another, by which I mean not only that we come to appreciate more fully the special significance the writer gives to certain terms over the course of his work—'heart,' 'stone,' 'sunne'—but also that we become familiar with his voices, transitions, and gestures . . . . As we learn to read one gesture in light of another, one poem in light of another, we should acquire an increasing sense of attunement to the whole performance and feel our expectations engaged, surprised, and disappointed in increasingly coherent and familiar ways.
>
> (White 1994b: 231)

That passage could serve as a valuable resource for thought and expression about the activity of learning White's language. We need to attend not only to the meaning he gives to his key words – 'activity', 'attention', 'attunement', . . . 'voice'– but also to his 'voices, transitions, and gestures'. Reading the passage in light of our reading* of Becker, who lives by an image of language* that resembles White's, should help us acquire an increasing sense of attunement to White's whole 'performance'*.

'Learning as Attunement': Frances Trix

In the Introduction to this book, I mentioned that White's book on learning to read Herbert has served as a partial model for my efforts in this book to read White. Trix's book *Spiritual Discourses* (1993), on 'learning with an Islamic master', resembles White's book in various respects, one of which is the use of the word 'attunement'. There is a connection to Becker here: he is her former teacher.

Trix's book provides an account of the relationship between a *talib* ('seeker') and her or his *murshid* ('spiritual master'). She gives a detailed account of her own relationship with Baba Rexheb, a leader of the Bektashi order at a *tekke* (monastery) in Michigan. 'In linguistic terms', the aim of her book 'is to describe dialogue in a specific situation of learning' (18). Trix notes in the Introduction that he and she 'speak different dialects of Turkish: he a West Rumelian dialect, I a generally more standard Istanbul dialect'. Through their interchanges, however, their differences have diminished: 'Baba's and my dialects are becoming more and more like varieties of the same dialect' (20). This shift, as she says, is the material of what sociolinguists call 'linguistic convergence' (20). Trix connects that suggestive term and other related terms to 'attunement'.

The 'attunement' that Trix describes is 'a gradual lingual enrichment of Baba and myself toward a new coherence' (19). Her description of the movement* indicates it was non-linear. The movement connects with her use of the word 'attunement':

> The notion of attunement evolved from the challenge to describe the interaction of Baba and myself in our lessons . . . . The most intriguing aspect of those exchanges was the way Baba appeared to sit back. Despite his unquestioned authority in spiritual matters, Baba never initiated lessons, never issued directives, never appeared even to correct me. There was no outside syllabus that I could recognize. Instead I was left to initiate discussion. . . . [D]espite the appearance that the wrong person was taking the initiatives, and despite the wide range of reference and variety of verbal play that Baba and I engaged in, there still appeared to be a direction in our lessons—to better questions on my part, to greater resonance of narratives, . . . and throughout to the continual affirmation of Baba's and my relationship. This drift was not a development in a logical sense, but nonetheless there was a development, and it is this quality that I labeled 'attunement.'
>
> (149–50)

We may take it that Trix's teacher believed that that which we call education is done not *for* students but 'with' them. The student needs to learn to ask questions and to distinguish which ones are 'better' (*Questioning). How is she meant to do that? Does she simply follow her curiosity?

Trix defines 'language attunement' as 'increasing coordination through play-full recollecting of dialogue with another' (19–20). This definition, as she says later on, 'implies that Baba and I get better at playing verbal games with each other, the more shared experiences we had to build on' (150). After reading Becker, we might suspect that she began to 'get' jokes.

A key word in Trix's definition is 'play'*, a word that she appropriates from Paul Ricoeur. On her appropriation, she writes:

> Ricoeur's understanding of the power of a text is particularly stimulating. He sees this power as the potential to disclose a world. Therefore, 'To understand is not to project oneself into the text; it is to receive an enlarged self from the apprehension of proposed worlds which are the genuine object of interpretation.' . . . Instead of speaking of 'enlarged self,' . . . Bektashis and other Sufis speak of 'loss of self,' of 'death before dying.' These expressions reflect partly the precariousness of trusting into the Unknown, as well as the reframing that can ensue. But these contradictory metaphors should not blind us to the agreement between Ricoeur and the Bektashis that the event of interpretation or spiritual growth is fundamentally one in which one receives but does not control or direct. Ricoeur calls this event of interpretation 'appropriation,' or 'the making one's own what was initially alien.' However, the term 'appropriation' has the grave disadvantage of implying that the interpreter is in control. Ricoeur acknowledges the problem, and tries to overcome it by describing the actual process of interpretation as a sort of 'play' toward the world proposed by the text.
>
> (21–2)

How are we to play with that passage in order to 'understand' it and its author (*Understanding)? How are we to struggle against distance and alienation*? In struggling, might we each hope to receive an enlarged self? Might this first require 'trusting into the Unknown'? Who is in 'control' here? What is 'control'? Is that last question a 'controlling' question? Might the word 'guiding' be a better word than 'controlling'? Is the distinction between 'controlling' and 'guiding' mere word play? After hearing from Trix about her teacher's invitational approach to 'lessons', it would seem that the distinction is an important one, in the service of 'lingual enrichment'.

Trix gives numerous examples of 'lingual enrichment'. One concerns the word *hu*:

> For many years, although I knew 'hu' came from the third-person singular Arabic pronoun for 'he,' I assumed its use and therefore meaning to be similar to 'amen.' Then one day when reading to Baba I suddenly recognized 'hu' in places I had never noticed it before, leading to my new understanding that 'hu' was both a name of God, in the Muslim sense that God is referred to by 'hu' ('He') in the Qur'an, and that it can refer

> indirectly as well to one's murshid. . . . [M]y re-understanding of 'hu' had been a sort of swift illumination. Despite the dramatic quality . . . , [it was] based on much previous contact with the terms and with the illuminator.
>
> (151)

What's in a name? In this case, a name can lead to a dramatic 're-understanding' of the murshid–talib relationship, for it may be compared to the God–human relationship. Trix, we can be sure, asked a question of character* like this one: Who is this Baba, and how shall I address 'him/Him' in a way that recognizes that 'he/He' may be different from me? Its companion question is: Who am I becoming in this process of attunement?

Now that we have done some attuning to 'attunement', we are more fully equipped to hear more about its nature and about the 'particular aim' of Trix's book:

> [T]he engendering quality of attunement is . . . observed in interactants' ability and proclivity to use experiences of past attunement as a grounds for present attunement. With recurrent interaction, attunement becomes a recursive process, ever expanding in reference and subtlety, leading to the creation of a shared language.
>
> Shared language of this sort is celebrated in a Bektashi context in sessions of *muhabbet* in which participants sing nefes [spiritual poems] back and forth to each other. In a more mundane way, attunement also can be reached periodically in talk between people who have interacted over a long period of time. My particular aim is to describe strategies that facilitate both the periodic attunement and the more far-reaching attunement, for my understanding of the murshid is that he teaches through such strategies.
>
> (19)

This passage brings to mind Becker's remarks about learning Burmese: the activity of remembering is crucial. It is only from re-membering that 'experiences of past attunement' can be a source of learning. We can get a virtuous circle, with the activation of 'past attunement' leading to further attunements, which can lead to further attunements, and so on.

Trix's talk about the dynamics of attunement resembles parts of White's engagement, in *When Words Lose Their Meaning*, with Austen's *Emma*. This is 'a novel of education' (White 1984: 163), in which the heroine moves from a 'disturbed language' in which she 'constitutes her self and her social world' (she treats people unjustly) to 'a condition of health and knowledge' (164) – we might now call this from–to development a 'lingual enrichment'. As the novel proceeds, Emma comes to develop a more complex way of thinking and talking about herself and others. Her education is formed in part through a series of painful encounters and through her developing relationship with Mr Knightley. Emma and he are involved in 'conversations', 'rational' and 'playful', to use the narrator's terms for describing what Emma's father cannot meet her in (terms included in the title of White's chapter). In these conversations, we can sense that she has a 'set of capacities for thought and speech and life', a side of her that 'can be called on to correct' the disturbed side (167). It is through the conversations that her 'contrasting modes of being' become 'in conscious opposition'. For White, 'much of the life of the novel lies in the development of what these conversations mean.' In particular, *Emma* will 'be only in part a novel of correction, in which Emma's distorted ways of speaking and being are broken down by experience; it is also a novel of change through affirmative experience' (167). Austen offers her reader a similar 'experience'*. Let White speak about the 'textual friendship':

> Jane Austen's ideal of friendship is given meaning and definition not only in the relationship between Emma and Mr. Knightley but in the relationship that she as a writer establishes with her reader in this text. The textual community of *Emma* in fact directly parallels the imagined community between Emma and Mr. Knightley: it is educative in its concerns, it works by pleasure and conversation . . . . The analogy between Emma and the reader begins with the very act of reading, as we both try to observe things accurately and to understand what they mean. For as Emma must learn to 'read' her world if she is to judge and act and speak well within it, we must learn to read the text well if we are to understand what happens to us as readers. Like her, we are constantly trying to locate ourselves with respect to what we are told, to figure out what to respect and how to respond; like her, we are always asking what things mean, and we ask that question of the same things she does. . . .
>
> Although we share her questions, we do not directly share Emma's experiences of error and correction. . . . We do not share Emma's point of view, nor do we enjoy a position of secure omniscience; instead, we experience the events of the text with a partial and incomplete intelligence, different from that of any of its characters; it is almost as if we were ourselves actors within it. Our task, like Emma's, is to read our way into understanding.
>
> A part of this reading, as of all reading, is re-reading. Emma does this through her memory, going back over what she has observed and the way she interpreted it, trying to understand her mistakes, and this is what we do in our ordinary lives. But as readers of this text we can repeat the actual process of reading the text and so learn to see more and more clearly what at first we saw awkwardly and dimly or missed entirely. This is a text that must indeed be reread to be read at all, for an essential part of the experience it offers the reader is the correction of his earlier misreadings, by which it teaches him or her to become the audience, the partner, that the text defines and requires.

> In this sense the text engages its reader in a kind of conversation, like those between Emma and Mr. Knightley, in which at every clarification one feels recognized and rewarded with pleasure and knowledge. The reason the text offers its reader such continual freshness, such a sense of surprise and learning, is that one's sense of it, and of oneself, is always changing. At each discovery one finds oneself invited, as one who has *now* seen such-and-such a point, to ask how this clarification affects the rest of one's reading; this in turn leads to another set of questions and puzzles and clarifications; and so on. The experience is a little like taking a progressive series of tests, each of which is intelligible only when you have passed its predecessor. It is in some sense the same paragraph one reads, but each time one both sees it differently and feels differently addressed. One hears Jane Austen's voice in new ways, asking new questions, . . . and in the process one moves into an increasingly confident and intimate understanding of the text and its author. It is the movement of mind into harmony with mind that is responsible for the sense, shared by so many readers of Jane Austen, that one has a secretly privileged and personal relationship with her, a special kind of friendship; this sense is, for one who has read her well, literally true.
>
> (185–6)

That passage has provided me with much in the way of 'surprise and learning'. When I first read it, I was yet to imagine that literary criticism – a somewhat strange activity of writing about writing – had much value. 'What is the point?' I came back to the passage after my early skim-readings of *The Legal Imagination*, wondering what White was up to with all his questioning*. In the process of re-reading, I could sense that I had had some initial prejudices against literature and literary criticism and that the prejudices were problematic. (This was an 'experience'* of a productive alienation* from one image of the world and attuning to another.) In repeating the process of 'reading'* the text I could hear White's voice in new ways, and in the process of asking new questions, I felt I was moving into an increasingly confident 'understanding'* of the text and its author, a 'movement'* that we could call an 'attunement'. (We could readily use the language of Lonergan's transcendental method* – especially the interdependent components of 'experience', 'understanding,' and 'judgment', all of which are driven by 'questioning' – to talk about 'what happens to us as readers'.) It became clear to me that the textual community of White's *When Words Lose Their Meaning* (and of *The Legal Imagination*) directly parallels the textual community of *Emma*: it is educative in its concerns, it works by pleasure and conversation*.

Character

'Prejudices': Edmund Burke's *Reflections on the French Revolution*
'Integrity': Jane Austen's *Persuasion*
'Rational Fools' and *Homo Economicus*: Amartya Sen

A key word in economics is 'specialization'. Economists have written a great deal about various benefits of specialization, and they commonly cite Adam Smith's *The Wealth of Nations* in doing so. While Smith does talk about such benefits at the start of his book, he also talks about costs later on. Economists have had much less to say about this later part. Let Smith speak:

> The man whose whole life is spent in performing a few simple operations . . . has no occasion to exert his understanding, or to exercise his invention in finding out expedients for removing difficulties . . . . He naturally loses . . . the habit of such exertion, and generally becomes as stupid and ignorant as it is possible for a human creature to become. The torpor of his mind renders him, not only incapable of relishing or bearing a part in any rational conversation, but of conceiving any generous, noble, or tender sentiment, and, consequently, of forming any just judgment concerning many, even, of the ordinary duties of private life.
>
> (Smith 1776/1898: 613)

We might wonder what might 'become' of a tribe of economists who spend the whole of their lives working with a narrow definition of the word 'rational', one that has no place for 'conversation'*, 'judgment'*, and 'just[ice]'*. If the tribe becomes a dominant force in a society, what might become of the famous Smithian 'invisible hand', which harmonizes the pursuit of one's 'own interest' with the 'public interest' (345)? Might the hand turn into a visible foot that destroys the society?

'Prejudices': Edmund Burke's *Reflections on the French Revolution*

Burke begins the *Reflections* as a letter to a 'very young gentleman at Paris' who has asked him about his position on the French Revolution (1790/1898: 3). The gentleman believed that, as a supporter of 'liberty', Burke would support it. He was wrong:

> I should . . . suspend my congratulations on the new liberty of France until I was informed how it had been combined with government; with

> public force; with . . . morality and religion; with the solidarity of property; with peace and order; with civil and social manners. All these (in their way) are good things, too, and without them liberty is not a benefit whilst it lasts, and is not likely to continue long. The effect of liberty to individuals is that they may do what they please; we ought to see what it will please them to do, before we risk congratulations which may be soon turned into complaints.
>
> (9–10)

Burke resists thinking of the word 'liberty' in isolation – its meaning, contrary to what a black-letter lawyer might say, is not independent of how it is 'combined'. There is, to be sure, more at stake for Burke than just the meaning of a word: he is concerned with the way words mean. He is resisting the image of words as entities that can contain fixed meanings, which can be passed around from one person to another like a rock. For Burke, words are evolving cultural artefacts that shape us and are shaped by us as we use them.

In the spirit of the great common lawyers, Burke was critical of forms of reasoning that ignored the significance of 'circumstances':

> Circumstances (with which some gentlemen pass for nothing) give in reality to every political principle its distinguishing colour and discriminating effect. . . . Abstractly speaking, government, as well as liberty, is good; yet could I, in common sense, ten years ago, have felicitated France on her enjoyment of a government (for she then had a government) without enquiry what the nature of that government was, or how it was administered?
>
> (8–9)

For Burke, the French revolutionaries were engaged in a power grab that would result not in 'liberty' worthy of the name but in a destructive disruption of collective identity.

Burke's *Reflections* is at one level a critique of the Age of Reason, an age in which 'reason' (or its companion 'rational') was set in opposition to 'prejudice'. He challenged the common presumption that prejudices are a vice that a person of 'reason' would want to eliminate. He imaged a living 'British Constitution' based on virtuous 'prejudices' (*Constitution):

> [I]nstead of casting away all our old prejudices, we cherish them to a very considerable degree . . . . Many of our men of speculation, instead of exploding general prejudices, employ their sagacity to discover the latent wisdom which prevails in them. If they find what they seek, and they seldom fail, they think it more wise to continue the prejudice, with the reason involved, than to cast away the coat of prejudice, and to leave nothing but the naked reason . . . . Prejudice is of ready application in the emergency; it previously engages the mind in a steady course of wisdom and virtue, and does not leave the man hesitating in the moment

> of decision, sceptical, puzzled, and unresolved. Prejudice renders a man's virtue his habit; and not a series of unconnected acts. Through just prejudice, his duty becomes part of his nature.
>
> (102–3)

Burke here invites his reader to think about the value of the existing institutions and the 'prejudices' in them that revolutionaries would demolish. This is an invitation to resist the denigration of what some Rationalists called 'ancestor-wisdom'[1] – or that which gets called 'customs', 'superstitions', and 'traditions' – the material of 'prejudice' handed down from an irrelevant past and that which is an obstacle to 'reason'.

Burke goes on to talk about 'the composition of the National Assembly'. By 'composition' he does 'not mean its formal constitution . . . but the materials of which in a great measure it is composed, which is of ten thousand times greater consequence than all the formalities in the world' (47). Burke would have us attend not to a written constitution but to the unwritten constitution that may give it life or death:

> Judge . . . of my surprise, when I found that a very great proportion of the Assembly . . . was composed of practitioners in the law. It was composed not of magistrates, who had given pledges to their country of their science, prudence, and integrity; not of leading advocates, the glory of the bar; . . . —but for the far greater part . . . of the . . . merely instrumental members of the profession. . . . They must *join* (if their capacity did not permit them to *lead*) in any project which could procure them a *litigious constitution*; which could lay open to them those innumerable lucrative jobs which follow in the train of all great convulsions and revolutions in the state.
>
> (49–50)

Burke here distinguishes the lawyer-statesman from the narrowly self-interested lawyer.[2] Unlike the latter, who lacks 'integrity' and attends to his private ends, the former not only takes the public good seriously but also has the capacity with which to work out the content of a rational public good. The lawyer-statesman is distinguished by the practical wisdom or 'prudence' that he shows.

That which Burke calls 'a litigious constitution' turns out to be the vortex of society, leading to a destructive and disturbing confusion:

> Humanity and compassion are ridiculed as the fruits of superstition and ignorance. Tenderness to individuals is considered as treason to the public. Liberty is always to be estimated perfect, as property is rendered insecure. Amidst assassination, massacre, and confiscation, . . . they are forming plans for the good order of future society.
>
> (150)

Burke points to a 'Babel'-like linguistic collapse that is associated with the social and political one.[3] Now no one could talk with much meaning about 'liberty' and 'property' when there was not the cultural stability required for them to have a meaningful place.

White's reading of Burke in *When Words Lose Their Meaning*, part of which we engage with below (*Constitution), outlines Burke's presentation of intimate relations between 'language'*, 'character', and 'culture'*:

> Burke offers his reader a language that . . . defeats cliché by complication, distinction, and composition. This is meant to be a language of generality to which the reader may turn from any of the activities of life in order to claim a meaning for what he does and to connect it with the rest of life; it is truly a constitutional language. . . . Burke imagines . . . a reciprocal relationship between self and culture, which can work to good ends or bad. When it works well, as it does under his 'British Constitution,' we find good men in positions of authority, capable of conserving what is best in what they have inherited and of reforming whatever is defective; such men maintain and improve a constitution that tends to produce, and place in authority, other men of similar ability and virtue, and so on. When it works badly, as it does in 'France', deterioration of culture leads to deterioration of character, and vise versa, in a continuing accelerating movement of dissolution.
>
> (White 1984: 208–11)

The 'reciprocal relationship' brings to mind Gunnar Myrdal's principle of cumulative causation. Myrdal described a process in which parts of a whole social system respond to or affect other parts, and changes in the system can accumulate, causing changes in one or another direction through the whole system. There can be a 'vicious circle', with the dynamic process moving in a harmful direction, and a 'virtuous circle', with forces moving in a positive direction (Myrdal 1944/1996: 75–6). Burke's *Reflections* can be read as a guide – with 'parts' including language, character, and institutions – for the British for staying out of the vicious cycle in France and for continuing with their virtuous cycle.

'Integrity': Jane Austen's *Persuasion*

Various passages of Burke's *Reflections* that distinguish 'the British constitution' from 'the French constitution' echo his earlier re-configuration of the relationship between the sublime and the beautiful. He associated the sublime with the 'male' and the beautiful with the 'female'. He also associated the sublime with 'constancy', 'fortitude', and 'firmness', and the beautiful with 'tenderness', 'timidity', and 'weakness'.[4] Mary Wollstonecraft challenged his language in *A Vindication of the Rights of Men* and in *A Vindication of the Rights* *of Women*. She claimed that it enslaves women to flawed views of masculinity and femininity.[5] Her response to Burke was awkward, for at places she adopts his language in her treatment of him, transforming him into a 'weak' woman.[6] Austen, in *Persuasion*, suggests that the binary oppositions are too simple for adequately describing characters. The user of the oppositions, as Austen's hero learns, can readily make a mis-judgment* about a character. The experience* of doing so can be a valuable alienation* from a defective language – a resource for making a constructive and self-conscious constitutional transformation.

The action of *Persuasion* takes place between the summer of 1814 and February 1815. Just after the Napoleonic Wars, many naval officers were returning home. Sir Walter Elliot, 'a foolish, spendthrift baronet' (1817/1998: 234), rents his ancestral home to an Admiral Croft. (Shakespeare seems to be missing from Sir Walter's perhaps un-English constitution.[7]) Croft's wife is the sister of Captain Frederick Wentworth, who, eight years earlier, had been engaged to Sir Walter's daughter, Anne. She has 'an elegance of mind and sweetness of character, which must have placed her high with any people of real understanding' (11–12). The narrator tells us of their falling in love:

> He was . . . a captain Frederick Wentworth . . . , who being made commander in consequence of the action off St. Domingo, and not immediately employed, had come into Somersetshire, in the summer of 1806; and having no parent living, found a home for half a year, at Monkford. He was, at the time, a remarkably fine young man, with a great deal of intelligence, spirit and brilliancy; and Anne an extremely pretty girl, with gentleness, modesty, taste, and feeling.—Half the sum of attraction, on either side, might have been enough, for he had nothing to do, and she had hardly any body to love; but the encounter of such lavish recommendations could not fail. They were gradually acquainted, and when acquainted, rapidly and deeply in love. It would be difficult to say which had seen the highest perfection in the other, or which had been the happiest; she, in receiving his declarations and proposals, or he in having them accepted.
>
> (29–30)

Anne, however, faced resistance. Sir Walter 'gave it all the negative of great astonishment, great coldness, great silence, and a professed resolution of doing nothing for his daughter' (30). Anne's godmother Lady Russell also resisted. (Anne was 19 years old.) She, the narrator mentions earlier, 'was, generally speaking, rational and consistent—but she had prejudices on the side of ancestry' and 'had a value for rank and consequence, which blinded her a little to the faults of those who possessed them' (17). Whilst it is uncertain what impact her 'prejudices' had in this situation, it seems that her opposition to the engagement was based upon a variety of reasons, including her sense of 'propriety'[8] (relating to, among other things, engagements that are likely to last for a long time due to financial constraints) and of Frederick's 'dangerous character' – 'headstrong' (31). The narrator goes on to say:

> Such opposition . . . was more than Anne could combat. . . . Lady Russell, whom she had always loved and relied on, could not, with such steadiness of opinion, and such tenderness of manner, be continually advising her in vain. She was persuaded to believe the engagement a wrong thing—indiscreet, improper, hardly capable of success, and not deserving it. But it was not merely selfish caution, under which she acted, in putting an end to it. Had she not imagined herself consulting his good, even more than her own, she could hardly have given him up.—The belief of being prudent, and self-denying principally for *his* advantage, was her chief consolation, under the misery of a parting—a final parting.
>
> (31)

> Anne . . . had to encounter all the additional pains of opinions, on his side, totally unconvinced and unbending, and of his feeling himself ill-used by so forced a relinquishment.—He had left the country in consequence.
>
> (31)

The path that the novel takes from this point may impel Austen's reader to return to the above excerpts for a closer reading*, with lines of questioning* that he failed to ask on a first reading. What weight did Anne give to the various parts of Lady Russell's opinion? By what mode of reasoning did Anne do her weighing? Are the words 'indiscreet', 'improper', 'success', 'deserving', 'selfish', 'prudent', etc., ones that Anne used? If so, what did she mean by them? About what exactly was Frederick 'unconvinced'? These questions are all concerned with the life of the interchange between Anne and Lady Russell and Frederick. (We might ask: What kind of rhetoric* did each person display? Was it, for example, coercive or invitational?[9]) We need to know *what happened* in order to judge who these characters are in relation to one another and the sort of community they brought into being.

The withholding of such important details is far from innocent. Why do we not hear Anne's 'elegance of mind' at work? From the start of the novel through to the above excerpts (in the fourth chapter), the narrator has given Anne's 'word' little 'weight' (12), treating it in much the same way as her family does. The claim that Austen has deliberately composed her text this way is persuasive: She is luring her reader into accepting Frederick's forthcoming judgment* of 'weakness and timidity' on Anne.[10] Her reader, if Austen has 'success', will be offered an experience similar to the one Frederick will have, namely a space for making sense of a mis-judgment. The principle of 'hearing the other side' may come to have renewed force. Doing justice* includes attuning to the language and reality of the other (*Attunement).

Soon after the break-up, Frederick became a man of 'rank and consequence'. When he now visits the Crofts at Kellynch, Anne is staying with her sister

Mary Musgrove at nearby Uppercross Cottage. At the time of his visit, he is looking to marry. 'He was rich, and being turned on shore, fully intended to settle as soon as he could be properly tempted' (62). Anne has no place within his horizons:

> Frederick Wentworth . . . had not forgiven Anne Elliot. She had used him ill; deserted and disappointed him; and worse, she has shewn a feebleness of character in doing so, which his own decided, confident temper could not endure. She had given him up to oblige others. It had been the effect of over-persuasion. It had been weakness and timidity. (62)

We learn later that Frederick had not forgiven Anne partly because he understood neither her nor himself. He had been wounded by Anne's rejection of his marriage proposal, but he was, and still is, oblivious to the wound. We shall see that distinctions crucial to his self-understanding are blurred. He learns that being 'totally unconvinced and unbending' may be a virtue in some circumstances, but it may be a vice, especially if there is on his side a failure to hold himself open in a conversation* and to attempt to reach a common understanding* – if, that is, he is 'headstrong'.

Frederick failed to imagine the possibility that Anne felt the pull of her love for him as well as an opposing pull to break the engagement in deference to the judgment of her godmother. Contrary to what he assumed, Anne continued to love him even though she broke the engagement. Anne, who continuously tries to read herself and to tell a coherent story about her life, can be considered to be a person of 'integrity' (17), to use a word that the narrator problematically applies to Lady Russell. For Anne sought to identify and to bring into harmony, through deliberation, different pulls within her. As Frederick will come to learn, sound self-knowledge is a requirement for integrity, for a self must be attuned to the different pulls.

Frederick soon comes to have 'a heart for either of the Miss Musgroves, if they could catch it; a heart, in short, for any pleasing young woman who came in his way, excepting Anne Elliot' (62). During a walk, Anne's sister Mary dissuades Henrietta Musgrove from visiting Winthrop, the home of Henrietta's suitor, Charles Hayter. Elitist Mary considers him an inappropriate suitor – 'It is very unpleasant, having such connexions!' (84). Louisa, however, successfully insists on the visit. When alone with Frederick, Louisa, unaware that Anne can hear her, remarks: 'I have no idea of being so easily persuaded. When I have made up my mind, I have made it' (85). Louisa's words here sound like words composed for Frederick, who on hearing them would remember an imagined Anne resisting Lady Russell. Praise from Frederick, who might be seeking to justify to himself his judgment on Anne, is forthcoming:

> 'Happy for her, to have such a mind as yours at hand! . . . [W]oe betide him, and her too, when it comes to things of consequence, when they are placed in circumstances, requiring fortitude and strength of mind,

> if she have not resolution enough to resist idle interference in such a trifle as this. Your sister is an amiable creature; but *yours* is the character of decision and firmness, I see. If you value her conduct or happiness, infuse as much of your own spirit into her, as you can. . . . It is the worst evil of too yielding and indecisive a character, that no influence over it can be depended on.—You are never sure of a good impression being durable. Every body may sway it; let those who would be happy be firm.'
>
> (85–6)

Frederick here uses 'weak' and 'firm' as opposite and unqualified terms of reproach or praise. (A Burke reader, who has the word 'liberty' echoing, will appreciate the dangers of such simplicity.) However, the meanings of 'weak' and of 'firm' are not independent of 'circumstances' – of particular people, relations, places, and times.

Frederick, continuing his discourse with Louisa, and interacting with his immediate physical environment, exercises his analogical imagination*:

> 'Here is a nut,' said he, catching one down from an upper bough. 'To exemplify,—a beautiful glossy nut, which, blessed with original strength, has outlived all the storms of autumn. Not a puncture, not a weak spot any where.—This nut,' he continued, with playful solemnity,—'while so many of its brethren have fallen and been trodden under foot, is still in possession of all the happiness that a hazel-nut can be supposed to be capable of.' Then, returning to his former earnest tone: 'My first wish for all, whom I am interested in, is that they should be firm. If Louisa Musgrove would be beautiful and happy in her November of life, she will cherish all her present powers of mind.'
>
> (86)

How, with all due 'play'*, can a hazelnut make vulnerable its identity and its self-'possession' so as to 'fall' into conversation and to fall in love? Analogies can serve to make coherent what we have or do not have in common with other people and to make coherent our own memories and expectations. There are, however, apt and inapt analogies and a variety of degrees in between. To live by the hazelnut analogy (that is, to live by the single rule 'be firm'), as Frederick will soon learn, is too simple to be coherent and workable. When Frederick comes to experience* this incoherence, his understanding of others and of himself will be significantly transformed.

Frederick's principal disorientation takes place at Lyme Regis, where his friend Captain Harville resides. The visiting party includes the Miss Musgroves, Charles and Mary Musgrove, and Anne. At Lyme they meet Harville and his wife and a Captain James Benwick, who is staying with them (a wounded-in-action James had been engaged to Harville's sister Fanny, who recently died). On Lyme's famous Cobb, Louisa *insists* to Frederick that she be 'jumped down' a 'steep flight' of steps – 'the sensation was delightful to her'. Whatever the sensation might have been to him, Frederick was 'less willing' because of the 'hardness of pavement': 'He advised her against it, thought the jar was too great; but no, he reasoned and talked in vain; she smiled and said, "I am determined I will:" he put out his hands; she was too precipitate by half a second, she fell on the pavement on the Lower Cobb' (106). Next:

> 'Is there no one to help me?' were the first words which burst from Captain Wentworth, in a tone of despair, and as if all his own strength were gone.
>
> 'Go to him, go to him,' cried Anne, 'for heaven's sake go to him. I can support her [Henrietta] myself. Leave me and go to him. Rub her hands, rub her temples; here are salts, —take them, take them.'
>
> Captain Benwick obeyed . . . . Captain Wentworth, staggering against the wall for his support, exclaimed in the bitterest agony,
>
> 'Oh God! her father and mother!'
>
> 'A surgeon!' said Anne.
>
> He caught the word; it seemed to rouse him at once, and saying only 'True, true, a surgeon this instant,' was darting away, when Anne eagerly suggested,
>
> 'Captain Benwick, would not it be better for Captain Benwick? He knows where a surgeon is to be found.'
>
> Everyone capable of thinking felt the advantage of the idea. . . .
>
> 'Anne, Anne,' cried Charles, 'what is to be done next? What in heaven's name, is to be done next?'
>
> Captain Wentworth's eyes were also turned towards her.
>
> 'Had not she better be carried to the inn? Yes, I am sure, carry her gently to the inn.'
>
> 'Yes, yes, to the inn,' repeated Captain Wentworth, comparatively collected, and eager to do be doing something.
>
> (107–8)

In this emergency, when the kind of prejudice admired by Burke does not leave the woman hesitating in the moment of decision, Frederick's 'first words' ('Is there no one to help me?') are in a 'tone' that will be new to Austen's reader's ears, and perhaps to his own. His words make an opening for Anne's 'word'. He finds himself playing catch with her – 'He caught the word'. (This fragment connects well to Gadamer's work on 'play'*.[11]) In catching her 'word', an act which 'seemed to rouse him at once', he evidently interiorizes an expression which has come from her interior, an interior which has spontaneously assumed and expressed itself in the role of captain. Both Captains spontaneously 'obeyed' her. Whilst Frederick is 'eager to be doing something', we might wonder if he appreciates what has been done to him.

Anne ends up joining Frederick and Henrietta in returning to Uppercross. When Henrietta expressed regret about the walk to the Cobb, Frederick 'burst forth, as if wholly overcome' with these words: 'Oh God! that I had not given way to her at the fatal moment! . . . But so eager and so resolute! Dear, sweet Louisa!' To these exclamations, Anne's mind turned to the topic of justice*:

> Anne wondered whether it ever occurred to him now to question the justness of his own previous opinion as to the universal felicity and advantage of firmness of character; and whether it might not strike him, that, like all other qualities of the mind, it should have its proportions and limits. She thought it could scarcely escape him to feel that a very persuadable temper might sometimes be as much a favour of happiness as a very resolute character.
>
> (113)

'Question'-ing* in the direction of justice, we can be sure, is important to Austen. Talk about the importance of 'proportions and limits' will sound familiar to an Aristotle reader.[12] A re-reader of the novel will know that Frederick admits to Anne that at Lyme he had 'begun to understand' himself by 'receiving lessons of more than one sort' (228). Notably, with respect to Lousisa, he had 'learnt to distinguish between the steadiness of principle and the obstinacy of self-will, between the darings of heedlessness and the resolution of a collected mind' (228). He has learned that his language of judgment was too simple. The fall knocked him from his habitual modes of thought, providing him with a spur to re-imagine both himself and Anne.

By the end of his first reading of the novel, Austen's reader may be persuaded to reread the narrator's summary of the 'persuasion' that went on between Anne and Lady Russell when Anne was 19 years old. While rereading, he may now be equipped with some new questions. A modern reader of *Persuasion* may benefit from reading White's *Heracles' Bow*. Consider the following passage, in which he gives some content to his claim that '[t]alk about justice is at its heart talk about character and relations':

> An example from domestic life may help clarify what I mean when I say that justice is at heart a matter or relations and attitudes rather than results. Suppose the parents of a teenaged child ask, as they often understandably do, what rules they should adopt governing such things as curfews, dating, housework, allowances, school work, conduct towards siblings, music lessons, and so on. What answer could you—or Dear Abby or anyone else—possibly give them? Obviously there is no one set of correct or just or wise rules. Many fine parents have resolved these matters with their children very differently; many bad parents have no doubt used rules that looked very much like those used by parents of whom one would approve. Within very wide bounds what is critical is not the content of the rules but the relationship out of which the rules grow and which they in turn help to reconstitute. *What* the parent

> decides matters less than *how*; with what attention to the child's needs and circumstances, with what respect for his or her feelings and claims, with what voice, with what kind of listening (or 'hearing'), and so forth. If this analogy is thought to be inappropriately paternalistic, the same point could be made in connection with relations more explicitly equal—in a marriage, a professional partnership, certain business relations, and so on. The point is that the heart of what we mean by justice resides in questions of character and relationship and community—in who we are to each other—for this determines the meaning of what is done. If these things are got right, the material manifestations—the rules, the results—will take care of themselves; if they are not got right; the rules and results will be wrong, and this is true in the family, in the custody hearing, in the sentencing proceeding, in the ordinary trial, in national political arrangement, and in international relations.
>
> (White 1985a: 134)

To connect the passage to *Persuasion*: *How* did Lady Russell advise Anne about the merits of her engagement? With what 'attention'* to her circumstances, with what respect for her feelings and claims . . . ? What attention did Anne give to her own circumstances? Did she get her 'listening'* and 'voice'* right? As I suggested above, the narrator failed to address the ethical and literary 'who' questions. It is often easy to miss what is absent. When Austen's reader comes to later interchanges that do address these questions, he may well notice what was absent earlier.

'Rational Fools' and *Homo Economicus*: Amartya Sen

Imagine that you are a certain Nelson Mandela, who has a deep friendship with Walter Sisulu. Both you and Sisulu are freedom fighters in South Africa, committed to resisting racist laws, first through wholly legal means, then through non-legal means. You both ultimately engage in acts of sabotage, exposing yourselves to imprisonment if you get caught. The state manages to get only enough evidence to convict you both of a relatively minor offence, for which the penalty is five years in jail. You and Sisulu are in separate cells; both are told that if one confesses while the other one remains silent, the confessor will only get one year in jail, while the other spends life in jail. If both confess, both will get an intermediate sentence of ten years. Will you confess or remain silent?

Some years ago, I gave that question to a third-year economics class. For them, the question had a familiar ring: 'this is the "Prisoner's Dilemma" game' – one that can be applied to just about any topic studied as 'the economics of . . .'. A large majority of the students responded with 'confess'. The standard explanation was confidently expressed: each prisoner is 'rational', considering costs and benefits that accrue directly to themselves – they are 'self-interested'. Irrespective of what the other prisoner does, each prisoner gets a shorter sentence by confessing. The 'game' is one in which the pursuit of 'self-interest' is self-defeating: the 'dominant strategy' is to confess, and both prisoners would have been 'better off' remaining silent.

Some students remarked that we were dealing not with 'Prisoner X and Prisoner Y' but Mandela and Sisulu and that words such as 'friendship' and 'committed' made a difference. In this spirit, I directed the class to Sen's 'Rational Fools' article, in which he criticizes economists for 'avoidance' and 'evasion' in relation to the meaning of 'rational'. He offers to enrich rationality talk by connecting 'rationality' to 'commitment' (1977: 323). In doing so, he distinguishes 'sympathy' from 'commitment':

> If the knowledge of torture of others makes you sick, it is a case of sympathy; if it does not make you feel personally worse off, but you think it is wrong and you are ready to do something to stop it, it is a case of commitment. I do not wish to claim that the words chosen have any great merit, but the distinction is, I think, important. It can be argued that behavior based on sympathy is in an important sense egoistic, for one is oneself pleased at others' pleasure and pained at others' pain, and the pursuit of one's own utility may thus be helped by sympathetic action. It is action based on commitment rather than sympathy which could be non-egoistic in this sense. . . . In the terminology of modern economic theory, sympathy is a case of 'externality.' Many models rule out externalities . . . . [T]he existence of sympathy . . . would not require a serious revision of the basic structure of these models. On the other hand, commitment does involve, in a very real sense, counterpreferential choice, destroying the crucial assumption that a chosen alternative must be better than (or at least as good as) the others for the person choosing it, and this would certainly require that models be formulated in an essentially different way.
>
> (326–8)

Sen stops short of giving a guide as to how models might be 'formulated in an essentially different way'. He simply offers the 'thesis' of 'the need to accommodate commitment as part of behavior' (344), not the least to explain why, for example, 'people playing the Prisoners' Dilemma frequently do the unselfish thing' (341). If *Homo economicus* could do this too, we might say that she would be capable of conceiving a certain generous sentiment, and, consequently, taking the topic of justice* seriously.

In *Heracles' Bow*, White reads Sophocles' *Philoctetes*, in which there is an example of Sen-like 'commitment'.[13] He connects the play to the limits of 'ends-means rationality':

> [T]he play is at heart about the conditions under which ethical and practical thought take place, about their ontology and epistemology if you will.

> Here its major point is that the only circumstances under which ends-means rationality might be rational never exist, for our thought must always take place on conditions of uncertainty that render that kind of 'rationality' worse than useless. These conditions require us to think in other, more difficult, ways and to attend first and last to questions of character and community. The only rational 'ends'—the only ends we can confidently use as guides to conduct—are conceptions of ourselves and of our relations with others, not materially describable states of affairs.
>
> (White 1985a: 23)

For those inclined toward judging actions according to the value of their consequences ('consequentialism'), we will do well to extend the word 'consequences' to include the kinds of 'character and community' that we make in our actions. This inclusion will not facilitate determinate solutions, but it could help create meaningful social realities. White's reality is one that fuses the concerns of the 'practical' and of the ontological (ontology deals with the question of 'what there is'). To tune one's mind to this reality is to equip oneself for attending to the activity of transforming constitutions.

For the economist who values models that begin with the isolated individual (Defoe's Robinson Crusoe is the conventional model), Sophocles' play can be read as calling for another beginning. Generalizing from the play, White says:

> Our practical and moral lives are radically communal—unless perhaps we live alone on an island—and this means that our thought about what we want and who we are must reflect the freedom and power of others, without whose free cooperation we can have nothing of value, be nothing of value. This in turn means that hardheaded practical thought and sound ethical thought alike require us to recognize the existence of others and our dependence upon them.
>
> (25)

We do not need to refute claims by economists and others that an important matter is the individual. We simply need to attend to *what* the individual *is* (we are back to 'hardheaded practical' ontology), to 'recognize' that the individual emerges in, and is constrained by, a collectivity. We cannot escape the need to work out the terms by which we manage pervasive interdependencies between individuals. A key question that each faces is this: How can we enhance our relationships with each other? This brings the question of justice* to the fore, a question that can prod us into constructively re-imagining the shallow, calculating *Homo economicus*.

Constitution

'An Entailed Inheritance': Edmund Burke's *Reflections on the French Revolution*
'WE THE PEOPLE' and *McCulloch v. Maryland*
Reimagining South Africa's 'Transformative Constitution'

In 2000, I attended a conference titled 'Building the Constitution', held in Wellington. Its aim was 'to bring together representatives of all points of view in the developing debate on the constitution and to point to a way forward on the debate' (James 2000: xi) It may have been helpful for participants at the outset if the organizers had circulated the definitions of 'constitution' in the *Oxford English Dictionary*. Here are six:

1. The action of constituting, making, establishing, etc.: see the verb.
2. A decree, ordinance, law, regulation; usually, one made by a superior authority . . .
3. The way in which anything is constituted or made up; the arrangement or combination of its parts or elements, as determining its nature and character; make, frame, composition.
4. Physical nature or character of the body in regard to healthiness, strength, vitality, etc.
5. The mode in which a state is constituted or organized; especially, as to the location of the sovereign power, as a *monarchical*, *oligarchical*, or *democratic* constitution.
6. The system or body of fundamental principles according to which a nation, state, or body politic is constituted and governed.

At least one version of each of these was used during the conference. The diversity perhaps contributed to misunderstandings, which could have led those involved to talk about 'constituting' a workable harmony. In this regard, a helpful conference paper was by Alex Frame, 'Beware the Architectural Metaphor', calling for caution in using the 'building' metaphor* in the conference. One reason 'is the danger that the "architects" envisioned by the metaphor, however skilled and well-intentioned, neglect or lose contact with the life and energies of the peoples and cultures the edifice is intended to serve' (Frame 2000: 427). Frame went on: 'law tends to grow organically, and will resist the attempts of technicians to force it into shapes designed to serve the interests of "social engineering" . . .' (428). His metaphor could promote talk about how we might *constitute* talk about 'the constitution', knowing that the talk shapes the 'thing'.

'An Entailed Inheritance': Edmund Burke's *Reflections on the French Revolution*

With the signing of the Constitution of the United States, the word 'constitution' became increasingly used for referring to a written document that organizes governance. When Burke, in the *Reflections*, expressed admiration for 'the British constitution', some readers resisted the phrase. 'A constitution', said Thomas Paine, 'has not an ideal, but a real existence; and whenever it cannot be produced in a visible form, there is none' (Paine 1791/1998: 122). Paine's assertion that the word 'constitution' must be a written document was nothing short of 'a revolutionary attempt to redefine . . . what constitutes a legitimate government' (Blakemore 1988: 11). In seeking to exclude former meanings of 'constitution', Paine was engaged in that which we are calling 'transforming constitutions' – the (re)constitution of language*, self, and other.

Perhaps with Shakespeare's *Richard II* as part of his constitution (*Imagination), especially the 'image of inheritance' (White 1994a: 60), Burke claimed:

> [F]rom Magna Charta to the Declaration of Right it has been the uniform policy of our constitution to claim and assert our liberties as an *entailed inheritance* derived to us from our forefathers, and to be transmitted to our posterity – an estate specially belonging to the people of this kingdom . . . . By this means our constitution preserves a unity in so great a diversity of its parts.
>
> (Burke 1790/1898: 38)

Burke here resists a line of mechanistic thought – one that runs through Thomas Hobbes, who sought to extend methods of geometry to politics – that would set 'diversity' in opposition to 'unity'. In doing so, he provides a base for modern constitutional talk (in the sense suggested by James Tully –*Integration).

Burke was a dissenter in the Age of Reason, which, having little or no respect for the past, opposed the traditional. His dissent centred on the inheritance metaphor*:

> [O]ne of the first and most leading principles on which the commonwealth and the laws are consecrated, is lest the temporary possessors and life-renters in it, unmindful of what they have received from their ancestors, or of what is due to their posterity, should act as if they were the entire masters; that they should not think it amongst their rights to cut off the entail, or commit waste on the inheritance, by destroying at their pleasure the whole original fabric of their society; hazarding to leave to those who come after them, a ruin instead of an habitation, and teaching these successors as little to respect their contrivances, as they had themselves

> respected the institutions of their forefathers. By this unprincipled facility of changing the state as often, and as much, and in as many ways, as there are floating fancies or fashions, the whole chain and continuity of the commonwealth would be broken. No one generation could link with the other. Men would become little better than the flies of a summer.
>
> (111–12)

For Burke, a distinctive capacity of humans is to create institutions, including languages, which create an order on a potentially chaotic world, an order that can produce a meaningful and coherent 'we'. Another human capacity is to be 'unmindful' of these institutions – to take them for granted, and to experience them as 'natural' rather than 'cultural'. A cultural earthquake, such as the French Revolution, can make us mindful about our capacity to be unmindful. Burke directs our minds to the dangers of being unmindful: we may 'become little better than the flies of a summer'.

As I remarked above (*Character), the *Reflections* can be read as a guide – with 'parts' including language, character, and institutions – for the British for staying out of the vicious cycle in 'France'. The guide metaphor, however, is inapt. In *When Words Lose Their Meaning*, White suggests that Burke's essay is not so much a guide as an actual contribution to the reconstitution of a 'part', namely language, which can constructively contribute to the reconstitution of other parts, and so on – in a process of cumulative causation. In a passage that defines through contrast Burke's act of 'composition', White writes:

> Burke's purpose in the *Reflections* is not to communicate ideas that are already perfectly statable in existing languages but to make a language in which new ideas and new sentiments can be expressed, a new constitution established, in the text and in the world: a language he wishes his reader first to learn and then to own and use. It is essential to his purpose that this language be literary in character, not 'theoretical.' In reading this text, one cannot extract a word from its context, give it a stipulative meaning, and then place it in a statement of abstract theory without doing violence to Burke's text and mind and to our experience of both. Each word is attached by a dozen strings to other words (as we quickly see when we try to isolate one for analysis), and each of these in turn, is similarly connected with other words. Thus . . . 'property' and 'religion' are as inextricably linked in Burke's language as they are (in his view) in the world, and that world is itself, in part, the creation of the text.
>
> (White 1984: 217)

There is an intimate relationship between 'experience'* and 'language'*. '[T]o make a language' is to make not so much an object (or a collection of objects – letters, words, sentences) but an experience. For White, Burke's organic constitutionalism invites, or perhaps demands, us to resist dividing a language into parts and treating them independently of the whole and of the relations among the parts. The 'meaning' of a word is not an object that can be captured in a dictionary but rather an experiential process of becoming whilst the word is used with other words in a particular context.

For White, Burke's great 'achievement' in writing the *Reflections* is the expression of 'a new idea of what a constitution is' (228). At the same time, this is also the expression of 'what an individual is, and what kind of relation can exist between the individual and his world' (228–9). In this regard, White writes:

> The center of Burke's achievement is to see that culture and the self exist in a reciprocal relation, subject to perpetual reconstitution, that the processes by which such reconstitution occurs are both personal and social, taking place within the self and in conversation with another; that to be rational in any sense they must proceed on the basis of what we actually are, not on the theoretical preferences based on abstract considerations; that the language in which they occur must be what I have called literary—merging fact, value, and reason, fusing the particular and the general, uniting thought and emotion, logic and image—rather than theoretical or conceptual; and that to understand these processes, and to subject them to conscious and intelligent regulation, we must find or make a place that is at once within the culture and outside it, a place from which we can observe and criticize what we do. To make such a place is the aim of his text; in a different way, it is the aim of my own.
> (229)

That passage can help us make sense of White's invitation in *The Legal Imagination* to 'make a place . . . from which the world, and our contributions to it, can be seen and judged in a new way' (1985b: xi). The passage for me helps bring home what is so deeply wrong with much economics. We might now be inclined to ask an economist to ask herself: Who is the 'self' in her customary talk about self-interest? Better still, we might ask her who she is becoming as she talks about self-interest. Also: How 'rational' is it to treat the self and culture as separate from one another? How should we talk about rationality? Can we do so from 'a place that is at once within the culture and outside it'? What is this 'it' that we call 'culture'? Might 'it' be not an entity but an inseparable process of selving and culturing?

'WE THE PEOPLE' and *McCulloch v. Maryland*

McCulloch v. Maryland (1819) is concerned with the meaning of 'the people' in the Preamble to the Constitution.[1] The question about the meaning arose during a dispute about Congress's power to establish a national bank and about the right of a state to tax it. The issue of Congress's power had been around for almost 30 years. Seeking cabinet advice, President Washington had put the question to Jefferson and Hamilton in the early 1790s, when Congress chartered the Bank of the United States. For Jefferson, the creation of such a bank was not within the powers of Congress enumerated in Article I nor within the General Welfare Clause (Article I, Section 8: 'To lay . . . Taxes . . . , to provide for . . . the general Welfare of the United States') nor the Necessary and Proper Clause (later in Section 8: 'To make all Laws which shall be necessary and proper for carrying into Execution the foregoing powers, and all other Powers vested by this Constitution in the Government of the United States . . .'). For Hamilton, Congress had certain implied powers, and the creation of a national bank could be reasonably claimed to be among them. The differences between them were connected with different ways of imagining the identity of the parties to the Constitution. For Jefferson, the Constitution was a compact among 13 sovereign Peoples, and Article I should be interpreted narrowly in accordance with the rule that treaties generally be interpreted narrowly. For Hamilton, the Constitution was a grant of power by one People to a special set of national agents: 'This restrictive interpretation of [Article I] is also contrary to this sound maxim of construction; namely, that the powers contained in a constitution of government, especially those which concern the general administration of the affairs of a country, its finances, trade, defense, etc., ought to be construed liberally in advancement of the public good' (quoted in Amar 1987: 1453).

The bank did get established with a planned life of 20 years. After it expired, Congress established the Second Bank of the United States, partly for the purpose of ending the economic disorder. Southern and western states expressed their belief that the Bank inhibited the growth of capital in their regions and that it engaged in some problematic fiscal practices. In response, some states taxed it significantly. The state of Maryland claimed that the Bank owed it $15,000 in state taxes. James McCulloch, the cashier of the Baltimore branch, refused to pay the tax. A legal case began.

Concerning the identity of 'the people', counsel for the state of Maryland considered the Constitution 'as the act of sovereign and independent states'. By this claim, 'The powers of the general government . . . are delegated by the states, who alone are truly sovereign; and must be exercised in subordination to the states, who alone possess supreme dominion' (*McCulloch* 402). Chief Justice Marshall offered a lengthy response, part of which is as follows:

> It would be difficult to sustain this proposition. The convention which framed the constitution was indeed elected by the state legislatures. But the instrument, when it came from their hands, was a mere proposal, without obligations, or pretensions to it. It was reported to the then existing Congress of the United States, with a request that it might 'be submitted to a convention of delegates, chosen in each state by the people thereof, under the recommendation of its legislature, for their assent and ratification.' This mode of proceeding was adopted . . . . The government proceeds directly from the people; is 'ordained and established' in the name

> of the people . . . . The constitution . . . bound the state sovereignties. The government of the Union, then (whatever may be the influence of this fact on the case), is, emphatically, and truly, a government of the people. In form and in substance it emanates from them. Its powers are granted by them, and are to be exercised directly on them, and for their benefit.
> (402–5)

Marshall's qualification ('whatever may be the influence of this fact on the case') seems to suggest that it may not make any difference to the result of the case whether he starts out from the position that the Constitution was a compact between sovereign Peoples or a grant by one People. Some readers may well have wanted Marshall to elaborate on it, perhaps without the metaphor* 'emanates'. We might wonder from whom that metaphor emanates.

Marshall stressed that the Constitution had to be drafted broadly and that it was not to be regarded as a 'legal code':

> A constitution, to contain an accurate detail of all the subdivisions of which its great powers will admit, and of all the means by which they may be carried into execution, would partake of the prolixity of a legal code, and could scarcely be embraced by the human mind. It would probably never be understood by the public. Its nature, therefore, requires that only its great outlines should be marked, its important objects designated, and the minor ingredients which compose those objects be deduced from the nature of the objects themselves. That this idea was entertained by the framers of the American constitution, is not only inferred from the nature of the instrument, but from the language. Why else were some of the limitations, found in the ninth section of the 1st article, introduced? It is also, in some degree, warranted by their having omitted to use any restrictive term which might prevent its receiving a fair and just interpretation. In considering this question, then, we must never forget that it is *a constitution* we are expounding.
> (406–7)

How are we to read that oft-quoted passage? What does the phrase 'it is *a constitution* we are expounding' mean? In considering that question, we must never forget that words do not speak for themselves.[2]

I say in that last sentence 'we'. What, or who, is in that pronoun? We might do well to ask the same question of Marshall's 'expounding' sentence.

White reads *McCulloch* in *When Words Lose Their Meaning*. Immediately after quoting the 'expounding' passage, White offers this comment on the direction in which Marshall has taken his reader:

> We can now see that everything that Marshall has said so far has been intended to reduce the embarrassment presented by the following

> obvious argument: 'The United States is a government of enumerated powers; the power to create a bank is not among them; therefore, it is in excess of them and invalid.' Marshall's effort has been to establish the conditions on which he could claim that such a reading, which would perhaps be appropriate to a 'legal code' or to an interstate agreement, is inappropriate to a 'constitution,' which by its nature requires not mere explication but what he calls 'expounding.'
>
> (White 1984: 255)

White here claims that the activity that Marshall calls 'expounding' is more complex and demanding and creative than that which goes by the name 'explication'. To that claim, we might add this: that which we commonly call 'interpretation' cannot simply replace 'expounding' – a distinction needs to be made, for we are concerned with an uncommon kind of reading*.

After his paragraph on Marshall's 'expounding' paragraph, White's reading takes something of a spiral, coming at the character of 'expounding' from a different angle:

> What is there about the Constitution that leads to these consequences? Part of the answer . . . is the fact that any attempt to reduce all the powers to explicit statement would be impossibly complicated. But there is another line of argument, never made explicit by Marshall, and it is even more fundamental. It rests on . . . the question whether the Constitution is the act of the people or of the states. For who are these 'people,' and where are they now? In Marshall's rhetorical universe, the 'people' are defined by their one great collective act of self-constitution. They existed once in time only, when the Constitution was made, and have since resolved themselves into their constituent units and groupings—as states, officials, individuals, and factions. The 'people' thus no longer exist among us, and never can again. They have left behind them this instrument, the Constitution, which is technically amendable but was meant in its essentials to endure forever. Unlike the legislatures, unlike the states (had the Constitution been regarded as a compact among them), the 'people' are not here to correct what we do, and the instrument was composed with the knowledge that they would not be. This is why it contains no technical rules telling us how it should be construed, or, as lawyers say, what 'construction' it should be given. And this is also why it would be impossible for it to address every contingency in detail. The 'people' of whom Marshall speaks existed only in their act of constitution, in a kind of momentary incarnation; everything achieved by the Constitution had to be achieved at one time; it could not be developed in stages or by gradual adjustment to experience. The people thus left behind them a testamentary trust that has something of the character of a sacred text. It is an instrument that requires a special kind of reading Marshall will give it.

> This view of the Constitution establishes not only Marshall's point about the way in which the grant of powers should be read but his own position as the authoritative reader of it. As the expositor of the text that expresses the will of 'the People,' . . . Marshall claims to be the only instrument through which their will can be done. Far from holding a lifetime appointment against the rules of democracy, . . . Marshall implicitly says that his position is, of all positions, the most perfectly justified by the central principle of our democracy, for he alone expounds the instrument that is the single act of 'all the people.' He is indeed the voice of the people. His role is like that of a priest as well as that of a trustee, and he is entitled to this position by his excellence at the activity he calls 'expounding.'
>
> (255–6)

White here can be read as expounding on what Marshall means by 'expounding', as giving a special kind of reading to 'a special kind of reading'. Marshall's opinion, for White, vibrates a certain authenticity: a process of law-making is at work and can be seen to be at work – there is no pretence that the law is a system of 'rules' applied by the Court. Yet that which 'can be seen' is not simply 'out there'. White's image of a 'momentary incarnation' may be another person's image of an invisible hand, another's rhetorical usurpation, and yet another's black letter. In identifying Marshall as having adopted a 'role . . . like that of a priest as well as that of a trustee', White perhaps can be taken to be reaching for the Marshall within him and adopting a role like that of a priest as well as that of a trustee. We who have reread and reread and reread the Constitution's first seven words – 'We the People of the United States' – can now do so again with modified ears. Who are we becoming?

Reimagining South Africa's 'Transformative Constitution'

In an essay in the *South African Journal on Human Rights*, Karl Klare uses the phrase 'transformative constitutionalism' to refer to 'a long-term project of constitutional enactment, interpretation, and enforcement committed . . . to transforming a country's political and social institutions . . . in a democratic, participatory, and egalitarian direction' (Klare 1998: 150). He takes the imagination* seriously: 'The Constitution invites a new imagination and self-reflection about legal method, and reasoning consistent with its transformative goals' (156). In order to invite reflection on *what* 'the Constitution' *is*, Klare might have done well to talk about the imagination at work during the apartheid regime. Here he could have identified possibilities under very constrained conditions, and used these possibilities as a ground upon which future legal criticism can rest. In addition to Fischer (*Justice), Mandela comes immediately to mind, especially his statement from the dock in the

Rivonia Trial, in which he admitted that he was the leader of Umkhonto we Sizwe (The Spear of the Nation) and had planned sabotage. White engages with his statement in *Acts of Hope*. By way of a summary:

> Mandela's task in this speech as a whole is to justify the acts of violence engaged in by Umkhonto and approved by him. He does this . . . by a process of transformation so profound as to become an inversion: he describes the history and motivation of the A.N.C. and Umkhonto, and the responses of the government, in a way that both strips the government of the claim to be a supporter of civilization, which normally goes with an appeal against violence, and transfers it to the A.N.C. and Umkhonto. The government is not on the side of the law, or justice, or order, or civilization, or democracy; it is lawless, violent, barbaric; it rules by terror, with no claim whatever to the sort of moral standing usually assumed by those who oppose violence. On the other side, Mandela and Umkhonto are the embodiment of civilization—including a large element of Western European civilization—defending itself against barbarism. Sabotage is thus not an instrument of terrorism, as one might at first be inclined to think, threatening the dissolution of civilization; it is a sensible and moderate step taken to prevent a further slide into moral and political degeneration. The state has become the criminal: the criminal the statesman.
>
> (White 1994a: 291–2)

That which White identifies as 'a process of transformation so profound' is an extreme example of what is commonplace, for '[a]ll of us transform our languages all the time' (226). The question is not whether linguistic-cultural transformation happens: it does. Instead, the question concerns its quality and direction. There is thus a sense in which South Africa has always had a 'transformative constitution', not merely since the formal efforts to break away from apartheid. Failure to attend to this sense could lead South Africans to neglect or forget some vitally important transformative moments as a basis for comparing present and future efforts.

Conversation

'A Game with Some Hard Rules': David Tracy
'The Power of Conversation': Jane Austen's *Persuasion*
'The Longer Conversation': The Waitangi Tribunal
'By Challenging Your View of Economics': Peter E. Earl

'As civilized human beings,' writes Michael Oakeshott, 'we are the inheritors . . . of a conversation, begun in the primeval forests and extended and made more articulate in the course of centuries' (1962: 199). He imagines this 'conversation' as a 'meeting-place' in which different forms of expression, such as 'science' and 'poetry', engage with each other. This place has an important form of equality*: 'voices which speak in conversation do not compose a hierarchy'. Put differently, 'different universes of discourse meet, acknowledge each other and enjoy an oblique relationship which neither requires nor forecasts their being assimilated to one another' (198–9).

The readings in White's *The Legal Imagination* readily connect to Oakeshott's imagery. They include not only legal materials but also excerpts from novels, philosophical dialogues, plays, treatises, literary criticism, and histories. Why the extraordinary diversity?

> [M]y purpose is . . . to establish a way of looking at the law from the outside, a way of comparing it with other forms of literary and intellectual activity, a way of defining the legal imagination by comparing it with others. The non-legal readings are meant to give us a common sense (if an incomplete one) of what legal literature leaves out, of what others do that the law does not, and to define a context out of which judgments can begin to be drawn and against which they can be tested.
>
> (White 1973: xx)

We might say that White invites his reader to exercise her analogical 'imagination'* with a view to enriching the conversation of humankind, including the law.

In an assignment in *The Legal Imagination*, White asks his reader to '[g]ive an account of a . . . conversation . . . which you regard as a good conversation' (952). To whom might we turn for help for composing a response?

'A Game with Some Hard Rules': David Tracy

For several decades, Tracy addressed the question of pluralism as it concerns the many diverse religious traditions. He actively sought to learn from other traditions, believing that he could enrich his own tradition by doing so. Along with 'imagination'*, 'conversation' became one of his key words. His 'fundamental aim' in *The Analogical Imagination* 'is to suggest how the strategy of an analogical imagination may serve as a horizon for the genuine conversation open to all in our pluralistic present' (Tracy 1981: xii). Such conversation is a method* for attaining self- and mutual understanding*:

> A religion like Christianity . . . should be willing to enter into the conversation among the religions which the emerging future of global humanity demands. Each self-identity . . . will find itself anew by releasing itself to a self-exposure of conversation with others. . . . For all those who cannot share either the easy answer of a relaxed pluralism or the hard answer of a brittle univocity, the reality of an analogical imagination becomes a live option . . . . That option recognizes as well that each of us understands each other through analogies to our own experience or not at all. What little, painfully little, I understand of the Buddhist notion of compassion, I understand through my own experience of compassion—an experience formed through my concrete involvement in my religious and cultural heritages. I recognize that my focal meaning for compassion is likely to receive a liberating transformation through genuine contact and conversation with the Buddhist traditions. I cannot predict . . . the results of that conversation in advance. . . . [C]onversation occurs *only* where the conversation partners allow the subject matter to take over. Conversation occurs only when we free ourselves for the common subject matter and free ourselves from the prison of our vaunted individualism . . . . [T]he analogical imagination . . . can become a clearing wherein we may finally hear each other once again.
>
> (450–55)

That passage can serve as an analogical resource for a reader of *The Legal Imagination*, helping her to 'hear' White, especially his interest in 'defining the legal imagination by comparing it with others'. We might say: The tradition of the law (or, rather, traditions of the law, for there never has been a single tradition) will find itself anew by releasing itself to a self-exposure of conversation with the others. Lawyers and judges and economists and poets and others understand each other through analogies to our own 'experience'*, and White's readings seek to facilitate this understanding. Whatever his reader might understand about legal justice*, she has been provided with materials that may offer a liberating transformation through genuine contact and conversation with the legal traditions. Neither he nor we can predict the results of the conversation in advance. Conversation of the kind he invites ('transformative') is by definition unpredictable. Such conversation involves creative acts of the analogical imagination, with each party willing to risk her or his self-understanding by engaging with the other. We can expect to become different than we were.

Conversation is a central theme in Tracy's *Plurality and Ambiguity*. Here he is interested in 'how [conversation] may function as a model for all interpretation' (1987: ix). When addressing the 'interaction' between 'the text and the interpreter', he exercises his analogical imagination:

> To name the heart of this process of interaction as interpretation by the word *game* may seem too lighthearted a description. And yet the peculiar kinds of interaction called games are worth puzzling about. Every interaction includes some movement. A game enhances that interaction by emphasizing that the movement itself must take over if there is to be a game at all. . . . The players are there not to play their own game, but to lose their usual self-consciousness in the movement of the play itself. . . . If we allow some claim upon our attention from any game, . . . we can free ourselves from ourselves, however briefly. . . .
>
> Conversation . . . is a game where we learn to give in to the movement required by questions worth exploring. The movement in conversation is questioning itself. . . . A conversation is a rare phenomenon, even for Socrates. It is not a confrontation. . . . It is questioning itself. It is a willingness to follow the question wherever it may go. . . . Conversation is a game with some hard rules: say only what you mean; say it as accurately as you can; listen to and respect what the other says, however different or other; be willing to correct or defend your opinions if challenged by the conversation partner; be willing to argue if necessary, to confront if demanded, to endure necessary conflict, to change your mind if the evidence suggests it. These are merely some generic rules for questioning. . . .
>
> We converse with one another. We can also converse with texts. If we read well, then we are conversing with the text. No human being is simply a passive recipient of texts. We inquire. We question. We converse. Just as there is no purely autonomous text, so too there is no purely passive reader. There is only that interaction named conversation. . . . In conversation we find ourselves by losing ourselves in the questioning provoked by the text. We find ourselves by allowing claims upon our attention, by exploring possibilities suggested by others . . . .
>
> (16–19)

How are we to 'converse' with Tracy's text? Can we 'listen to and respect' what he says? How might we judge our 'movement'*-orientated performance*? If we pay 'attention'*, might we 'lose' our 'usual self-consciousness'? (Might we, to use a common phrase, get 'carried away' by the life of the conversation?) Might we find ourselves asking questions about the neglected foundational position of 'questioning'*? Concerning the 'interaction' with which Tracy is concerned, we cannot adequately talk about it using the opposition of active versus 'passive'. Transcending the opposition is called for, in play'*.

Tracy's image of conversation as 'a game with some hard rules' brings to mind White's image of 'the heart of law'. This, to recall, is 'the open hearing in which one point of view, one construction of language and reality, is tested against another' (White 1984: 273). When one language/reality is placed against another in the spirit of a game worthy of the name, we may find that we have a resource with which 'we can free ourselves from ourselves' (Tracy). This is a resource for acts of justice*.

'The Power of Conversation': Jane Austen's *Persuasion*

Persuasion, to recall (*Character), cavorts with the opposition of 'firm' versus 'weak', an opposition associated with in-equality* in relationships between men and women. Captain Frederick Wentworth, who uncritically accepts the opposition, discovers his self-ignorance, learning that 'my enemy' has been 'my own self' (Austen 1817/1998: 232). The discovery took place at Lyme, where, to recall, the 'determined' Louisa Musgrove takes a knock to her head. (That event revealed the 'weakness' of Frederick's nut analogy.) Frederick becomes free from his unintended commitment to Louisa, for she and Captain James Benwick get engaged. In the penultimate chapter, the conversational action is at Bath's White Hart Inn. When Anne enters, Mrs Musgrove and Sophie Croft are talking with each other, and Captain Harville and Frederick are starting to write a letter to James. Sophie speaks about 'uncertain engagements': 'To begin without knowing that at such a time there will be the means of marrying, I hold to be very unsafe and unwise, and what, I think, all parents should prevent as far as they can'. Anne senses in this a rhetorical resource (*Rhetoric[1]): she 'felt its application to herself, felt it in a nervous thrill all over her' (217). As for Frederick: his 'pen ceased to move, . . . he turned round . . . to give a look—one quick, conscious look at [Anne]' (218).

Harville leaves Frederick to complete the letter, which concerns a painting of James originally intended for Fanny, his previous fiancée who died. He speaks to Anne about the shift of James's affections: 'Poor Fanny! she would not have forgotten him so soon!' After Anne agrees, Harville says, 'It was not in her nature. She doted on him' (219). This particular claim about 'her nature' offers a resource with which to move to the general and back again. Anne makes a claim for the constancy of women, a claim that indirectly expresses her constant love for Frederick.

> 'It would not be the nature of any woman who truly loved.'
>
> Captain Harville smiled, as much as to say, 'Do you claim that for your sex?' and she answered the question, smiling also,
>
> 'Yes. We certainly do not forget you as soon as you forget us. It is, perhaps, our fate rather than our merit. We cannot help ourselves. We live at home, quiet, confined, and our feelings prey upon us. You are forced on exertion. You have always a profession, pursuits, business

> of some sort or other, to take you back into the world immediately, and continual occupation and change soon weaken impressions.'
>
> (219)

It would seem likely that on hearing the words 'weaken impressions', Frederick will remember his nut analogy, particularly his concern about 'a good impression being durable'.

Harville then moves the interchange from the general back to the particular, a move that invites a distinction to be made between men (namely Frederick and James):

> 'Granting your assertion that the world does all this so soon for men (which, however, I do not think I shall grant), it does not apply to Benwick. He has not been forced upon any exertion. The peace turned him on shore at the very moment, and he has been living with us, in our little family circle, ever since.'
>
> 'True,' said Anne, 'very true; I did not recollect; but what shall we say now, Captain Harville? If the change be not from outward circumstances, it must be from within; it must be nature, man's nature, which has done the business for Captain Benwick.'
>
> (219)

Harville may have initially wanted to make an assertion about his sister, but we might say that he is now falling into conversation, especially if he takes up her question. Might he cavort with the two categories 'outward' and 'within'?

In response to Anne's move away from the particular ('Benwick') and her return to the general ('man's nature'), Harville exercises his analogical imagination: 'No, no, it is not man's nature. . . . I believe in a true analogy between our bodily frames and our mental; and that as our bodies are the strongest, so are our feelings; capable of bearing most rough usage, and riding out the heaviest weather' (219). Anne does not challenge his analogy; she accepts it as a possibility. She responds with a different analogy and possibility:

> 'Your feelings may be the strongest,' replied Anne, 'but the same spirit of analogy will authorise me to assert that ours are the most tender. Man is more robust than woman, but he is not longer-lived; which exactly explains my view of the nature of their attachments. Nay, it would be too hard upon you, if it were otherwise. You have difficulties, and privations, and dangers enough to struggle with. You are always labouring and toiling, exposed to every risk and hardship. Your home, country, friends, all quitted. Neither time, nor health, nor life, to be called your own. It would be hard, indeed' (with a faltering voice), 'if woman's feelings were to be added to all this.'
>
> (220)

Let us, as Frederick might well do, move from the general to the particular: did Frederick give much thought to Anne's 'feelings' when she broke the engagement?

At this point, there is a disturbance in the room: 'a slight noise called their attention to Captain Wentworth's hitherto perfectly quiet division of the room.' Frederick's 'pen had fallen down'. Anne and Harville direct their 'attention'* to what may be a shift in Frederick's attention. 'Anne was . . . half inclined to suspect that the pen had only fallen because he had been occupied by them, striving to catch sounds' (220). He has caught Anne's analogies and, in doing so, has dropped the pen. (This fragment connects well to Gadamer's work on 'play'*.[2]) He has experienced a loss of 'self-consciousness in the movement of the play' (Tracy).

Returning to converse with Anne on the topic of gender relations, Harville invokes the authority of books. Anne 'will not allow books to prove anything'. She makes a claim that celebrates similarity *and* difference:

> 'I hope I do justice to all that is felt by you, and by those who resemble you. God forbid that I should undervalue the warm and faithful feelings of any of my fellow-creatures! I should deserve utter contempt if I dared to suppose that true attachment and constancy were known only by woman. No, I believe you capable of every thing great and good in your married lives. I believe you equal to every important exertion, and to every domestic forbearance, so long as—if I may be allowed the expression, so long as you have an object. I mean while the woman you love lives, and lives for you. All the privilege I claim for my own sex (it is not a very enviable one; you need not covet it), is that of loving longest, when existence or when hope is gone.'
>
> (221–2)

Not just all men are created 'equal' (*Equality)! Moving beyond what we might call 'win-rhetoric' (Booth – *Rhetoric), Anne here has transformed an *us against them* (men versus women) story to a *we* story, in which there are 'fellow-creatures'. This is an act of hope centring on an expression of 'hope' about the activity of doing 'justice'*.

Anne's act of hope leads to a constitutional silence*. She 'could not immediately have uttered another sentence; her heart was too full, her breath too much oppressed'. (She has a white heart at the White Hart.) The play of question and answer has also given Harville a limit-experience*, and he is persuaded by what he has heard: 'There is no quarrelling with you.—And when I think of Benwick, my tongue is tied' (222).

Harville has shown in this conversation that he is willing to open himself, his pre-judgments and beliefs, to refutation. If he had been 'totally unconvinced and unbending' (31) – as Frederick may have been with Anne over her decision to end their engagement – they would have had not conversation but parroting of blind prejudice.

Harville and Frederick depart. Frederick hands Anne a letter, in which a constitutional 'silence' of a different kind is broken:

> 'I can listen no longer in silence. . . . You pierce my soul. I am half agony, half hope. . . . I offer myself to you again with a heart even more your own than when you almost broke it eight years and a half ago. . . . I can hardly write. I am every instant hearing something which overpowers me. You sink your voice, but I can distinguish the tones of that voice, when they would be lost on others. . . . You do us justice indeed. You do believe that there is true attachment and constancy among men.'
>
> (223–4)

Frederick has actively got passive and gifted an ear. In doing so, he has attuned himself to her tonal distinctions and to her 'justice' talk (*Attunement). His capacity for 'hearing', we may hear Austen suggest, is part of Wentworth's 'worth'. They reunite at Union Street, beginning a 'gravel-walk, where the power of conversation would make the present hour a blessing indeed' (226).

In *The Legal Imagination*, White includes a passage from Plato's *Republic* and from Richard Hooker's *Of the Laws of Ecclesiastical Polity*. After the passages, White asks these questions about the character of justice*:

> It might be suggested that both Hooker and Plato define justice not by stating certain rules or doctrines or principles of public life, but by demonstrating certain ways of reasoning and conversing about important matters. . . .
>
> 1. Do you agree with this interpretation of what Hooker and Plato are saying? How can you define the processes of reasoning and conversation which each one celebrates?
> 2. Does the view attributed to Plato and Hooker have any validity as applied to modern law? How would you define the processes of reasoning and conversation which constitute the heart of modern justice?
>
> (White 1973: 682)

Those questions could help us frame questions about *Persuasion*. It might be suggested that Austen defines justice . . . by demonstrating certain ways of reasoning and conversing about important matters. How can you define these ways? Can you make any connections to modern law?

'The Longer Conversation': The Waitangi Tribunal

After asking for an account of a 'good conversation', White asks his reader for 'an account . . . which you regard as a failure' (1973: 952). Here goes.

A key moment in the colonization of New Zealand was the signing, in 1840, of the Treaty of Waitangi (*Understanding). The Treaty, according to the translator, the Reverend Henry Williams, was 'an act of love' towards the indigenes 'on the part of the Queen, who desired them to secure their property, rights and privileges' (quoted in Carleton 1874: 313). This 'act of love', perhaps fittingly, was given little written detail. Soon after 1840, however, a project of cultural imperialism was underway. The Queen's representative and other colonial officials unilaterally took control of the politico-legal process by which differences over the meaning of the Treaty were worked out – the feigned *Symonds* case was a means to getting control (*Understanding). (There was no 'hearing' for the parties to the Treaty to negotiate its meaning.) With the colonists controlling the 'government', they dispossessed indigenes of lands and other resources. In an act of dis-integration*, the ethnocentric *Wi Parata* case (*Justice) helped enable the dispossession by separating 'the law' from questions of justice. One does not need to be an Austen reader to know that the 'love'-talk turned out to be hollow.

In recent decades, following the establishment of the Waitangi Tribunal, the Crown has acknowledged historic injustices and has engaged with indigenes to work out reparations and new relationships. The process, however, has not been harmonious.

In the 1990s, Ngati Apa and seven other Maori tribes expressed frustration and concern about the impact of marine farming on what they considered to be their customary rights. The tribes took a case to the Maori Land Court, claiming that areas of the foreshore and seabed in the Marlborough Sounds were 'Maori customary land'. The Crown challenged the claim, arguing that the Court had no jurisdiction. In 2003, the Court of Appeal unanimously held that the Maori Land Court did have jurisdiction to hear the claims.[3] Not content to leave the large stakes to the uncertain play* of conversation in courts, Prime Minister Helen Clark expressed a will to statute: legislation would ensure 'absolute Crown title' over the foreshore, and thus to remove the liberty of the tribes to approach the Maori Land Court for rights claims of this nature. Sensing foul play, a number of tribes turned to the Waitangi Tribunal, which responded with a call for a 'Longer Conversation':

> Maori really want . . . the opportunity to sit down with government and properly explore the options that are genuinely available. As we have said, they consider that they have not had the opportunity. . . . It may be that the conversations would be long ones, and would take place over an extended period. We think it is appropriate. The issues are complex. . . . Although Maori clearly prefer the path through the courts to the one proposed by the Government, the subtleties of each are almost certainly imperfectly understood. It is also very doubtful that the Government really understands where Maori are coming from. The adversarial way in which the issue has developed has led to people taking positions rather than really communicating. In our hearing, we heard from some

> outstanding people about their perspectives of where the Maori interests lie . . . . We think that the government needs to hear [them].
>
> (Waitangi Tribunal 2004: 139–40)

Here is a call for a basic principle of justice*: a hearing. In claiming that it is 'very doubtful that the Government really understands where Maori are coming from', the Tribunal may be heard as promoting the principle of 'hearing the other side'.

Who was listening*? Was the Government willing to converse with the Tribunal about the proposed 'conversation'? Might the subject matter eventually take over, allowing for the establishment of some genuine conversation partners?

Elsewhere the Tribunal suggested that the proposed legislation is contrary to 'the rule of law' (129). Deputy Prime Minister Michael Cullen responded to that fragment and denounced the 'rule of law' talk, especially 'the implicit rejection of the principle of parliamentary sovereignty' – the 'power of Parliament to change the law', he said, 'is central to the exercise of sovereignty and therefore to the contemporary exercise of Article One of the Treaty' (Cullen 2004). Seemingly oblivious to more complex images of sovereignty (consider, for example, Perry Dane's 'Maps of Sovereignty' – *Imagination[4]), which could take the sting out of the S-word, and showing no explicit interest in questions of justice, he echoed this absolutist talk leading up to the enactment of the *Foreshore and Seabed Act* 2004, a purpose of which included 'vesting the full legal and beneficial ownership of the public foreshore and seabed in the Crown'.[5] In brief, the Crown, unwilling to play the risky game of conversation, refused the Tribunal's invitation for a hearing, and failed to move from 'taking positions' to 'really communicating'.[6] This was a lost moment for a productive attunement* toward a mutual understanding*.[7]

With the enactment of the *Foreshore and Seabed Act*, many people suggested that law and justice were apart. What could they have done to try to unite them? What questions could they have asked? I suggest that they might have done well to ask questions about the nature of the relationship between law and justice. One such question could include this: Does the law cease to be law when it is unjust? We might hope that the activity of questioning* can serve as a constructive pressure that takes us in the direction of 'a coalescence between law and justice' (Mahomed – *Justice). We might hope that we can make an imagined 'longer conversation' a reality.

'By Challenging Your View of Economics': Peter E. Earl

Earl works on the interface of economics and psychology. He does not conform to certain orthodox ways – an economist who is immersed in such ways classed his 'behavioural' economics as 'not scientific . . . but economic poetry, not real economics' (quoted in Earl 2000: 38). In *The Economic*

Imagination, Earl composes a response to such a claim. (Like a lawyer, Earl has imagined what another economist might say in refutation of his position, and prepared to meet it – 'If I say this, he may say that; and then I . . .') Some details are as follows.

Earl's composition is a 'dialogue' (1983: 4). The dialogue is between 'The Critic', who makes claims that encapsulate a likely reaction (of an orthodox economist) to Earl's book, and 'The Proponent', who responds as Earl himself would. Part of the way through the dialogue, Critic has this to say:

> But your psychological material, for all its jargon, still seems to me to be rather imprecise. A lot of time you speak of people having 'world views' which 'blinker' them and make them behave in particular ways. You claim that there exists a method of mapping a person's world view but I find it difficult to believe that one can really pin down such a fuzzy concept.
>
> (16)

Here we could ask about the fittingness of the ocular metaphors 'view' and 'blinker' and about the nature of a 'concept', but this might get us unnecessarily bogged down.

Proponent seeks to persuade Critic that one indeed can map a person's 'world view'. Proponent begins by outlining a 'method' for doing so, one that involves several sets of questions that invite 'our subject to compare and contrast several features related to our particular context' (16). Proponent works with books:

> Since we're presently arguing about whether of not *The Economic Imagination* is a contribution to economics, it might be appropriate for us to consider how I might discover your own set of 'economic perspectives'. I would probably start by asking you to describe the likeness and difference you see between, say, this book, Debreu's (1959) *Theory of Value* and Kelly's (1955) *Psychology of Personal Constructs*. If you have only seen and not actually read Kelly's book, this does not matter. You might at least be able to say that, compared with the first two books, Kelly's work is: 'long' (since it runs to two volumes); 'lacking in mathematical notation'; 'older'; and 'heavier'. If you said that Kelly's book was 'about psychology, not economics', I could then ask you to compare and contrast these two disciplines as best you can. This would bring out other things and dimensions to interrelate. For example, you might talk about 'economics' and 'psychology' in terms of 'science/non-science'; 'what I do for a living'; and so on. . . .
>
> The data obtained by this technique can be arranged as a matrix – the 'things' which have been compared and contrasted on one axis and the dimensions used to describe them on the other. . . . The matrix . . .

> enables one to see which things you view as similar and the number of dimensions you can use for describing differences between things. (16–17)

We might wonder how we could contribute to the dialogue. We might start by asking Proponent to describe the likeness and difference he sees between *The Economic Imagination* and *The Legal Imagination* and to compare and contrast the disciplines of economics and law. With Earl's use of reasoning by analogy (albeit for making sense of books rather than cases), we may detect in the discourse of economics a resemblance to 'thinking like a lawyer'.

Since every 'thing' is similar and different to every other 'thing' in potentially infinite ways, this technique enables Proponent to work out a sense of a person's 'world view'. For constructed similarities and differences about 'things' in the world arguably tell us as much about the constructor as they do about the world. Speaking generally, Proponent goes on to say: 'Having discovered the dimensions in terms of which a person views the world, one can work out how she will be disposed to see particular things, how she will behave when confronted with them' (17). Now getting specific and personal (and play*-full, given the professional fetish of Proponent for increasing her or his capacity to make accurate predictions):

> [I]f I discover that you see yourself as both a scientist and an economist, and if the factor analysis reveals that you see 'science' as synonymous with 'formal model-building and testing', I predict that you will not be able to see as an economic scientist someone who comes along and attempts (as I have attempted) to show that henceforth it is important that 'economics' should involve the use of non-mathematical ideas from subjectivist psychology. By challenging your view of economics in this way, that person will by implication be challenging your view of yourself as a scientist unless you can begin to separate 'science' and 'formal model-building and testing' into genuinely independent constructs. You, in turn, will then attempt to challenge that person's claim to be contributing to economics. (17)

We can read these fragments from an imagined dialogue to be part of Earl's efforts to claim meaning for his own experience* of engaging with economists who habitually use the word 'science' (another S-word?) in a narrow sense and in a mechanistic (a series of propositions) way. (Earl resembles a good judge to the extent that he is listening out for an inarticulate and unconscious judgment* behind what could be a lapse of judgment). Resistance to Earl's efforts to use 'science' in a broader sense could place him beyond the pale of the community of power: his 'psychological' study is 'not economics'. Earl could counter such a claim by asking, 'Surely what you call "economics" could include more than just a particular variant of "neoclassical economics"?' His next task might be to keep Critic talking, for the stakes are high.

In line with deliberate efforts to shift out of dualistic thinking, Earl seeks to integrate the 'personal' and the 'academic' (*Integration), as suggested in this remark by Proponent: 'At the end of the day, one must have faith in the ability of a theory to serve the ends for which it was designed. One chooses a theory according to some personal criteria and should use it with caution' (19). In this appeal to 'faith', Earl's language overlaps the language of 'religion', which is commonly imagined to be the opposite of 'science' and which is one of the ultimate conversation-stoppers. But why should this be? Could not this be an opening for continued play with 'compare and contrast'? Concerning certain forms of economics, for example, could we not talk of, say, 'the gospel of efficiency', or 'the priests of efficiency'?

Earl's 'dialogue' ends with Proponent reclaiming 'science' and talking about the importance of questions (*Questioning): '[I]f we look for alternative explanations and question ourselves continually, we may be less likely to end up proposing unhelpful policies. If that is science, then this book, for all its lack of mathematical precision and empirical work, is a scientific work, and a contribution to knowledge' (20). How might Critic respond? Earl leaves this to our own imagination*. Might Critic, through this dialogue, come to sense her own 'blinkers', and thus experience what we commonly call 'self-discovery'? If so, what kind of experience* would this be? A liberating transformation? Disturbing? Both? Whatever the experience, we might say that the 'dialogue' placed her at the edge of composition. This is a place where habitual modes of thought about the world and the self and others in it become unsettled. That is to say, language* doesn't connect the self and the world in quite the same way as it did before. A self-conscious imaginative reordering is called for. Such a reordering may well begin with a question such as, 'Shall I compare thee to . . . ?'

One of the first lessons that I learned at law school was this: there are at least two sides to every argument. Another early lesson was this: on one side, certain analogies are invoked, whilst different analogies are invoked on another side. Economics teachers would do well to consider teaching both lessons, not the least to help them attend to unrecognized analogies in themselves and in those with whom they disagree. Earl offers to teach the lessons in *The Economic Imagination*.

Yet another early lesson at law school was this: reasoning by analogy is at the heart of 'thinking like a lawyer'. It seemed to me then that connections can be made: is not reasoning at the heart of 'thinking like an economist', or at least one who seeks to avoid the sanction of exclusion from the discourse of power?

My own experience of reading Earl's 'dialogue' for the first time was liberating in the sense that it helped me to identify inadequacies of the language I was given to speak as an economics student, who had teachers resembling not Proponent but Critic. This language was used as if it functioned like a mirror, reflecting 'reality', and like a tool for communicating 'ideas' that can be conveyed from one person to another without loss. Earl's dialogue helped me acquire a stronger sense that this so-called 'scientific' language gave rise to a 'world view' – and thus a 'view' of oneself and of others – that was incomplete and problematic.[8]

Shall we compare Earl to . . . ? In 1984, White contributed a paper at a conference titled 'The Rhetoric of the Human Sciences', one aim of which was to bridge disciplines through rehabilitation of the R-word (*rhetoric). The paper was published in a volume (with the same title) that emerged from the conference. With reference to economics, White offered some remarks on the relation between 'science' and 'rhetoric':

> The tendency to think of rhetoric as failed science is especially powerful in the present age, in which such determined attempts have been made to elevate, or to reduce, virtually every discipline to the status of true science. The idea of science as perfect knowledge has of course been recently subjected to considerable criticism, both internal and external. It is now a commonplace that scientific creativity is imaginative, almost poetic; . . . and that science is a culture that transforms itself by principles that are not themselves scientific. Yet the effort to make the language and conventions of science the ruling model of our age, our popular religion, lives on in the language and expectations of others, especially of those who are in fact not true scientists. Much of economic discourse, for example, is deformed by the false claims of the discipline to the status of perfect science, which leads to the embarrassing situation in which economic speakers representing different political attitudes couch their differences in scientific terms, each claiming that the other is no true economist. This not only confuses the observer but renders the field of economics less intelligible than it should be, even to its participants, and it reduces important political differences, which might be the topic of real conversation, to the status of primary assumptions.
>
> (White 1987b: 301–2)

I once saw two economists have a hostile 'exchange', in which one asserted that the other was 'not a real economist'. The word 'real' here was associated with a use of the word 'science', which sounded as if it was capitalized – Science. The user of the word was using it as if it contained a plain meaning. (I am reminded here of Cullen's use of the word 'sovereignty'.) Between the lines, there seemed to be this one: 'Science is mathematical – your qualitative "political" work is obviously not science.' White suggests that what is to be imagined as 'economic' could well integrate a 'political' element. Would he have 'economics' reclaim the name 'political economy'? Raising questions about a change in name might prod an identity crisis for some in the discipline, an experience* about which they could 'science', in the sense of dealing with experience with an orderly method*. There is room for a 'real conversation' here.

Culture

'Talking Past Each Other': Joan Metge
'The Tribe of Economics': Arjo Klamer

In an essay in the *South African Journal on Human Rights*, Karl Klare used the phrase 'transformative constitutionalism' to refer to 'a long-term project of constitutional enactment, interpretation, and enforcement committed . . . to transforming a country's . . . institutions . . . in a democratic, participatory, and egalitarian direction' (Klare 1998: 150). He claims that lawyers would do well to take 'culture' seriously. By 'legal culture', he means 'professional sensibilities, habits of mind, and intellectual reflexes' (166). Attending to culture opens up a line of questioning*:

> What are the characteristic rhetorical strategies deployed by participants in a given legal setting? . . . What counts as a persuasive legal argument? What types of arguments, possibly valid in other discursive contexts (e.g., in political philosophy), are deemed outside the professional discourse of lawyers? What enduring political and ethical commitments influence professional discourse? What understandings of and assumptions about politics, social life and justice?
>
> (167)

Klare's turn to 'culture' may be read as contributing to the rehabilitation of rhetoric* – away from the image of ignoble trickery and toward the image of a potentially noble art by which communities are reconstituted in the pursuit of 'justice'*.

'Talking Past Each Other': Joan Metge

In the late 1960s and in the 1970s a collection of social movements occurred in New Zealand that mark what some people identify as the beginning of 'the Maori Renaissance'. The phrase 'Maori culture' became increasingly used, but there was evidence of misunderstandings, especially between Maori and Europeans (or 'Pakeha') over its meaning. In *The Maoris of New Zealand*, the anthropologist Metge writes:

> If asked what Maori culture means to them, most Pakehas begin by mentioning the Maori language and the distinctive Maori arts and

> crafts – action songs, wood carving, . . . and weaving. Then, after some thought, they add certain 'customs' that are demonstrably from pre-European ('Classic') Maori culture: the . . . use of carved meeting-houses, mourning wakes . . . . This view of Maori culture sees it as belonging to the past rather than the present, and to the private, leisure-time sector rather than the whole of life . . . . Most Maoris intuitively reject this view of Maori culture with its emphasis on the past and a few 'occasional' activities. For them Maori culture is a matter of present experience, a living and lived-in reality either for themselves or for others well known to them.
>
> (Metge 1976: 18)

When Metge was writing, the word 'culture' had a distinctively different place in Maori culture than it did in Pakeha culture. Through a process of enculturation in Pakeha culture, a Pakeha might be expected to use the word 'culture' for talking about 'them', not 'us'. We can be sure that new uses of the word by someone 'probing for common ground' (Booth – *Rhetoric) between the two cultures could complicate Us–Them boundaries in the service of a WE story, one of non-assimilative integration*.

Metge offers an image of 'culture' that can contribute to such integration. She defines culture as 'a system of symbols and meanings in terms of which a particular group of people make sense of their world, communicate with each other, and plan and live their lives' (45). Expressing this idea in 'an extended metaphor', she describes a culture 'as a "language" consisting of "words" together in patterns which "say something".' Culture is not an independently existing object but a process:

> It stresses that culture is . . . not a thing-in-itself with an independent objective existence, but a complex 'idea' in the minds of people. It is essentially a group possession, produced and maintained by interaction between members over many generations. Individuals learn and use it largely unconsciously and with varying degrees of mastery. Like the group itself, a culture never attains a fixed or perfect form but is always in the process of change and development, as it is inherited, employed, re-worked, amplified and transmitted, individually and collectively. The elements of a culture are of many different kinds, ranging from the material and directly observable to the abstract and invisible . . . [T]he meaning of each part lies not in itself but in relation to other parts in the mind of the people. . . . What is distinctive about a culture is not its elements taken separately but the way they are related to each other – their arrangement in a unique configuration.
>
> (45–6)

For Metge, culture is concerned with the production and transmission (and transformation) of 'meanings' between the members of a group. We might say that two people belong to the same culture if they make sense of the world in roughly the same way and that there is a high degree of mutual understanding* when they talk to each other about their thoughts and feelings about the world (Hall 1997: 2). Given the actuality of an inescapable personal dimension of meaning, there can never be 'perfect' mutual understanding. Attending to differences may help us notice the ways in which each of us contributes to the reconstitution of language and culture when we communicate.

In order to get a meaningful cross-cultural conversation* going, we need a great deal of creative effort in overcoming a low degree of mutual understanding – in moving from 'talking past each other' to 'talking together' (Metge and Kinloch 1978; Metge 2001). A lack of a will by one or more of the parties to learn about where the other or others are 'coming from' may lead not only to trouble (associated with imperialism) but also to a form of self-deprivation:

> When we are totally immersed in our own culture we live in it like a fish in water: it is only when confronted with possible alternatives that we become aware of ourselves and of the cultural milieu we formerly took for granted. This growth in self-awareness has been largely thrust upon the Maoris. Pakehas who, lacking this sort of pressure, honestly attempt to learn about the Maori point of view should find a bonus in increased understanding of themselves.
>
> (53)

To understand one's culture well, one must understand other cultures. What Metge calls 'increased understanding' is not the acquisition of additional information about the world, but a transformation in one's sense of the world and of one's place in it. Self-understanding and mutual understanding, as Metge suggests, are connected.

We can connect what Metge says about learning and using a culture with varying degrees of mastery to law students. In *When Words Lose Their Meaning*, when introducing his 'way of reading'*, White describes the activity of becoming a lawyer:

> [T]he way in which law students learn to read cases [is] a way of learning about the world in which they will have to live . . . . On his first day in school, the law student is given a case, or set of cases, just as they appear in the reports, . . . and is asked to reconstruct them from the beginning. His job is to live over in his imagination the experience of the parties and of the lawyers, asking why this choice or that one was made, what he would have done, and how he would have explained himself. . . . His primary way of giving attention to a case is by arguing it in his head, by examining the resources for making appeals and claims on each side that constitute what we call the law. . . . 'What would I do in this case?' is his constant question, and it is a complex one for it is a way of asking simultaneously about

> many things: about the nature of the resources he is offered by his world; about the way he and others can put them to use; about the facts of a particular case; and about his capacity to imagine or to invent new ways of talking that will work in the world he lives in. When he has done, he has mastered the set of persuasive resources that his culture makes available for dealing with a particular situation, and in doing that he has defined their limits. Together, the arguments made on each side establish in the world an idealized conversation in which the resources of the legal culture for claiming meaning and arousing sentiment are at once defined and exhausted and, in this way, exposed to analysis and criticism.
>
> (White 1984: 9)

That passage could serve as a resource for lawyers who unconsciously live by an image of the law, such as a system of rules, to become aware of themselves and of the cultural milieu they take for granted. White offers an image of the law as a 'culture of argument' (231), keywords in which include: attention*, conversation*, experience*, and imagination*. The activity of attunement* to this image may require much effort. For one who is immersed in another subculture in the law, it will be helpful if she constantly asks, 'What is White doing?', for he is engaged in an activity that seems to be beyond the horizons of some lawyers. Her task is to imagine White's way of imagining the law, including his 'way of giving attention to a case'. If she does this well, she will appreciate why White imagines the lawyer as rhetorician, who is centrally concerned with 'the set of persuasive resources that his culture makes available for dealing with a particular situation'. She will also appreciate why White imagines law at its best to be driven by noble rhetoric*, for an 'idealized conversation' will be realized. The parties to it will experience a release from habitual modes of thought and expression. This experience will resemble the experience of attunement to White's image of the law as a culture of argument.

'The Tribe of Economics': Arjo Klamer

In an essay on 'rationality' in economics, Klamer sets out to think ethnographically about the activity* of being an economist. He begins by attending to a move that many economics textbooks make, often without much discussion. The move resides in the use of a 'model' (outsiders might call it a story) that adopts 'the rationality assumption', which maintains that an individual knows her or his own ends and acts to pursue them. In a commentary on Varian's textbook, he writes:

> Economists are clearly captivated by the idea that economic agents are rational in their decisions. But note that Varian talks of a technique—the optimization technique. This suggests that the assumption of rational economic behavior entails a modeling strategy . . . . It tells the economists how to model behavior in any conceivable situation, under any constraints.

> . . . Varian . . . does not bother justifying it in any way; he simply sets to work with it. Such an approach is customary among economists, but I propose that we stop them right at the point at which they formulate their rationality assumption, *before* they get to work with it. For it is at this point that major problems of communication between economists and noneconomists, and even between economists themselves, begin.
>
> (Klamer 1987: 170)

Between the lines, we may detect questioning* that will be familiar to a reader of Klare's 'transformative constitutionalism' essay: What are the characteristic rhetorical strategies deployed by textbook writers? What types of arguments are deemed outside the professional discourse of economists? What enduring political and ethical commitments influence economic discourse? We can be sure that such questions are beyond the pale for many orthodox economists, especially those who imagine economics as a Science (not 'mere story), which is supposed to be beyond the realm of 'political and ethical commitments'.

In his effort to rehabilitate the ordinary, Klamer attends to the act that is central to mainstream economics, namely, 'exchange':

> If someone in an ice cream shop asked, 'Can I have a large ice cream cone?' most of us would be surprised if the person took the cone, said, 'Thank you,' and walked away. Clearly, we interpret the question as a *sign* that signifies a request to exchange money for an ice cream cone. The literal interpretation might make sense to an alien, but to those who 'know,' it is strange . . . . The knowledge that allows us to interpret a sign comes from past experience – in this case the experience that in a shop economic transactions take place, transactions that can be initiated with a friendly question. Such a question, therefore, is to be interpreted within the context of such experiences: the interpretation fills in what the articulated form leaves out.
>
> (174–5)

Ask a good question (one that is ordinary and extraordinary), get a good answer. Klamer here offers some distance on what we do not only when we enter into an 'exchange' but also when we 'interpret'. What he says about the importance of 'experience'* in 'interpretation' brings into economics what many orthodox economists speaking in the name of Science want to leave out. 'That's not objective but merely subjective', they might say.

The kind of knowledge with which Klamer is concerned offers to complicate the objective–subjective opposition. He suggests as much when drawing attention to issues about how economists might talk about the rationality assumption:

> Because articulated signs are necessarily incomplete, as we cannot say everything in words, there are problems with the proper use and understanding

> of signs. Let us consider the statement under examination: 'Economic agents are rational.' Understanding a sign requires knowing how to use it. In the words of Ludwig Wittgenstein: 'Try not to think of understanding as a mental process at all – for *that* is the expression that confuses you. But ask yourself, in what sort of case, in what kind of circumstances do we say "now I know how to go on"?' He suggests that we look at the way an expression is used in the context of what he calls a language game. Knowing how to use the assumption is knowing the rules of the game. However, these rules cannot normally be articulated: they must be learned through example and practice. Michael Polanyi speaks of the tacit dimension of knowledge, using the example of a bicyclist who knows how to keep her balance but does not think about why she can. This is analogous to economists' view of the rationality assumption as a technique: they know how to use it after extensive practice through problem sets in graduate school, but they do not reflect on why it works. They take most of their language game for granted and do not talk about the context in which the statement that 'economic agents are rational' becomes significant.
>
> The student of the rhetoric of economics faces the challenge of speaking about the unspoken, filling in the 'missing text' in economic discourse. The context of the rationality assumption is what allows the assumption to work for some and not for others.
>
> (175)

We might wonder why economists might neglect to reflect on 'why it works'. Does the culture suppress or devalue the 'why' question? For the reflective Klamer, an economics teacher will do well to acknowledge the 'tacit'-ness of economic knowledge. A good teacher will imagine a student's difficulty in 'understanding'* the rationality assumption not as a defect in the student's cognitive abilities but as a defect of her own instruction. Teachers who desire to advance self-awareness among economists will take 'rhetoric'* seriously, including the rhetoric of the 'unspoken' (Silence*). They might do well to begin work on an economics of attention*, which could address questions about the costs and benefits of taking a 'language game for granted'.

Klamer's 'game'-talk brings to mind White's engagement with 'the language of economics', an engagement that provides a resource for a productive alienation* from it. Consider the following passage:

> [E]conomics is . . . a culture shaped in part by the implications of its intellectual and verbal habits. Suppose you decide to study the way wealth is created by exchanges, and for purposes of analysis you posited a set of actors, of equal age and competence, each with some control over the material of the universe—called resources—and you assumed as a psychological principle an unlimited acquisitiveness on the part of each, and therefore, with respect to resources, a severe structural scarcity.

> Suppose further you assumed that each agent was interested in its own welfare only, and thus perceived itself to be in permanent competition with all other agents . . . . Next you assumed a medium in which surplus could be accumulated without limit. Then you began to see what flowed from these assumptions and tried to analyze real world events in these terms.
>
> If you did this you would find yourself caught in a game, perhaps a fascinating game, testing your capacity to draw certain kinds of logical conclusions from the premises stated, a game with a force and life of its own. You would become a player, an economist; you would inhabit a world with its own values, its own realities, its own rewards. From such simplicity, such complexity! And such fun, too, though for me rather of an empty kind (at least until an attempt was made to connect the economic language and its culture to others). For good or ill, the language and its practices would gradually start to shape the way you saw the world and felt about it, your sense of yourself and of others. . . . [D]espite its claims to be merely hypothetical, economic theory becomes a culture of its own and can be studied and judged as such. My present point is not to criticize economics . . . but to suggest how habits of thought and language have tendencies, pressures of their own, that can perhaps be checked or controlled, but ought certainly to be reckoned with: how language has real power over the mind that uses it, even the mind that contributes to its reformulation.
>
> (White 1987a: 1967–8)

The image of doing economics and being 'caught in a game' challenges the dominant individualistic image of a world of autonomous human actors. In White's 'play'*-full world, in which we cannot avoid the play of language*, the 'player' is also the played. (White's reader may find that his language is starting to shape the way she sees the world. 'What *game* are we playing?') Due to the force of a culture that neglects culture, many economists dismiss, devalue, or ignore talk about it. They habitually imagine language as a transparent tool for pointing to objects in the world. Following from this, they pay no serious attention to large dimensions of human knowing that centre on experiencing and understanding and judging – that is, to what Lonergan calls 'transcendental method'*. They fail to explicitly address questions such as: What does this game feel like? Is it a worthy game for me and for others? In doing so, no invitation is made to become attentive to one's experience, an intelligent reader of one's experience, and a sound judge (*Judgment). One may come to resemble a cyborg, made in the dominant mechanistic image of *Homo economicus* (*Character).

Equality

'Economic Power': John R. Commons and *Holden v. Hardy*
Speaking Truth to Power: Nelson Mandela
Socratic Questioning in the Classroom: Clark D. Cunningham

'[A]ll men are created equal', the American Declaration of Independence says. What can that phrase come to mean? More broadly, what is to become of the word 'equality'? What meanings might be worthy of respect?

'Economic Power': John R. Commons and *Holden v. Hardy*

In 1896, the state of Utah passed a health-related statute limiting the hours of work in underground mines to eight per day. Sheriff Hardy arrested an employer named Holden for employing someone to work for ten hours per day. Holden's lawyer argued that since the worker had 'voluntarily' engaged his services the statute violated his 'liberty' to make contracts protected by the Fourteenth Amendment. The United States Supreme Court sustained the statute as a legitimate exercise of the police power:

> The legislature has . . . recognized the fact which the experience of legislators in many states has corroborated, that the proprietors of these establishments and their operatives do not stand upon an equality and that their interests are, to a certain extent, conflicting. The former naturally desire to obtain as much labor as possible from their employees, while the latter are often induced by the fear of discharge to conform to regulations which their judgment, fairly exercised, would pronounce to be detrimental to their health or strength. In other words, the proprietors lay down the rules and the laborers are practically constrained to obey them. In such cases self-interest is often an unsafe guide, and the legislature may properly interpose its authority.
>
> (*Holden v. Hardy* 1898: 391)

An Adam Smith reader might think that the 'invisible hand' does not apply in this case.[1] While the 'hand' may 'frequently' harmonize 'self-interest' and the public interest, the conditions required for this to happen in this particular case may not exist. A key word in the *Holden* opinion is 'constrained'. While all economic actors are 'constrained' in their choices, not all are equally constrained. If the number of available workers declines, an employer will become more 'constrained'. If employment opportunities increase, 'the fear of discharge' for a worker may become inconsequential. New circumstances thus may change the point at which 'the legislature may properly interpose'.

The *Holden* case has an important place in Commons' *Legal Foundations of Capitalism*, which identifies 'the visible hand of the court' in the transformation from feudalism to capitalism and in the ongoing evolution of capitalism (1924/1995: 204). Here he defines property rights as relative capacities and constraints among people arising from scarce resources. The capacities are 'rights' and 'liberties', and the constraints are 'duties' and 'exposures' (6). Let us use these terms to talk about the *Holden* decision.[2] In sustaining the statute fixing maximum hours of work in mines, the Supreme Court held that the employer, Holden, had *no right* to require his employees to work more than eight hours per day. As such, the employees had *no duty* to work more than eight hours per day if Holden commanded. That is to say, the employees were granted the *liberty* to refuse to work more than eight hours per day without 'fear of discharge'. This reduced their *exposure*. Had the Court deemed the statute to be unconstitutional, the employees would have been exposed to the liberty of Holden to discharge them if they refused to work more than eight hours per day.

Commons used the word 'reciprocity' to refer to a situation in which 'parties are clothed each with a similar outfit of rights, exposures, duties and liberties':

> Both modern economic theory and legal theory are founded on doctrines of equality as well as liberty. But the meaning of equality is being gradually changed to that of reciprocity. If all individuals were exactly equal in physical, economic and persuasive powers, then there would be no reasonable purpose in placing any limits on their liberties, since no one could harm or mislead another anyhow. But, since the real fact is one of astounding inequalities, limits are placed somewhat on the liberties of the more powerful under the name of duties, such that a more reasonable degree of equality may be maintained. These duties create correlative rights on behalf of the inferiors which are equivalent to reducing the exposure of the weaker parties by reducing the liberty of the stronger. Conversely, a reduction of duties on the part of inferiors increases their liberty while reducing the rights and enlarging the exposures of the stronger. According to the degree to which these determinations are carried is there constructed a reciprocal exposure to each of the liberty of the other and a reciprocity of rights and duties.
>
> (130)

Commons sought to develop an economics – or, rather, 'the art of political economy' (379) – that addressed questions about 'degree'. (Along with other political and legal economists, such as Robert Lee Hale, he contributed to the critique of so-called 'laissez-faire constitutionalism'.[3]) Such an economics could also make a place for words having their 'meaning' 'changed', with a 'reasonable purpose'. His own work offers a contribution to this change. His 'reasonable purpose' is to reconnect economics to questions of 'justice'* (276).

Today, the large majority of economists live by mechanistic metaphors and have no place for lines of questioning* opened up by Commons. The image of the independent economic actor reigns supreme. White has suggested that the 'ideologically charged version of economics' is impoverished:

> The institution of the market is celebrated by its proponents because in their view it is democratic—each person brings to the market his own values and can 'maximize' them his own way—and because it is . . . open, leaving the widest room for individual choice and action. . . . The market is further justified . . . [on the] ground . . . of its fairness. This claim has two versions: the first rests upon the ethical standing of voluntary action and holds that the results of the market process are justified with respect to every actor because the choices by which it works are voluntary. The second version becomes the affirmative celebration of autonomy or liberty: whether or not it is efficient, the market is good because it gives the widest possible range to freedom of choice and action. . . . The obvious trouble with this line of defense . . . is that it assumes that all exchanges are for all actors equally voluntary and equally expressive of autonomy, a position that common sense denies.
>
> Let us begin with the 'voluntariness' of the exchanges studied, which is essential both to the 'welfare' and to the 'autonomy' justifications. . . . Obviously most human choice is greatly constrained, some of it cripplingly so. It may be true that I sell my labor for the minimum wage, working at a noisy, ugly, demeaning, boring, and perhaps dangerous, job, but only because that is the best I can do. I do not want *that* choice to be given the sort of standing that an investor's choice to go for stocks rather than bonds, or my own choice to spend Saturday afternoon on the river or at the museum, should be given. . . .
>
> The incapacity of economics to reflect degrees of voluntariness is actually a particular instance of a larger feature of the discourse, one that derives from its quasi-mathematical character. Its use of labels is inherently binary. One either is or is not 'competent,' an action is or is not 'voluntary,' because the formulas that are the stuff of economic thought require that a particular person, object, or event either be, or not be, an 'A' or a 'B' or whatever other label is used. . . . Of course, our actual experience is not of binary or dichotomous phenomena but of degree and of change. Our ordinary language, in its imprecisions and overlappings, reflects that fact.
>
> (White 1990: 62–5)

Commons built a line of inquiry on 'degrees of voluntariness' – especially on the reality that 'choice is greatly constrained, some of it cripplingly so'.

Conventional economics centres on 'choice' within a *given* pattern of 'freedom', but ignores the factors and forces shaping the pattern. (Commons sought to talk about and judge patterns of freedom – as he did in his discussion of the *Holden* case.) Commons suggested that the conclusions of such economics relating to 'freedom' (or 'efficiency') are not independent of its premises. He questions the value of the premises as they concern the *purpose(s)* of law. White would have economists give a privileged position not to abstract concepts but to 'experience'*. Here we have unsettled moments in which we might be inclined to ask questions such as 'What is "the market" and where can you find it?' Like 'the law', that which we call 'the market' is not an identifiable thing. Real-world markets with real-world individuals are evolving institutional processes, or patterns of experience, and our talk should reflect this fact. Conventional economists talk about the 'autonomy' of the individual, but they do not seem to sense that they themselves are engaged in a 'real-world' relation with their reader in which autonomy is itself an issue (*Reading). White directs attention to a linguistic prison in which they place their reader, a prison that permits no talk of 'degree' and 'change'.

Speaking Truth to Power: Nelson Mandela

In 1961, Mandela called for a National Convention to begin composing a non-racial constitution. The authorities might have heard him, especially the part about a possible three-day strike, but they were not listening*. Whilst underground, he contributed to the writing of Umkhonto we Sizwe's constitution. In 1962, Mandela was arrested and put in jail. He was charged with incitement to strike and with leaving the country without a passport. 'It was indisputable – and in fact I did not dispute – that I was technically guilty of both charges', says Mandela in his autobiography (1994: 313). Rather than dispute, he made a plea in mitigation, which touched on the matter of deaf ears:

> Throughout the fifty years of existence the African National Congress . . . has done everything possible to bring its demands to the attention of successive South African Governments. It has sought at all times peaceful solutions for all the country's ills and problems. . . . [W]hen Mr. Strijdom became Prime Minister of this country, my leader, Chief A. J. Luthuli, then President of our organization, made yet another effort to persuade this Government to consider and to heed our point of view. . . . Chief Luthuli's letter was not even favoured with the courtesy of an acknowledgement from the Prime Minister's office.
>
> This experience was repeated . . . . Here we, the African people, and especially we of the National Action Council . . . were faced with this conflict between the law and our conscience. . . . [W]hat were we to do? Were we to allow the law, which states that you shall not commit an

> offence by way of protest, to take its course and thus betray our conscience and our belief?
>
> (in Karis and Carter 1977: 737–8)

This is an 'experience'*-centred story about a failure to respond to the call of another, one that included basic questioning* about the nature of 'the law', especially its relation with justice*. 'The white power', Derrida comments, 'does not believe itself required to respond, does not hold itself responsible before the black people' (1987: 31). There is no communication that can form a real community: 'The blacks cannot assure themselves, by return mail, by verbal exchange, by any look or sign, that any image of them has been formed on the other side, which might return to it in some way.' The 'other side . . . does . . . worse' than 'not answering': 'it does not even acknowledge receipt.' (We might call this deliberate non-attunement*.) This is a serious failure: 'Not to acknowledge receipt is to betray the laws of civility' (31). Mandela's story cavorts with the distinction between the inside and the outside: 'Those who one day made him an outlaw just did not have the right: they had already placed themselves outside the law' (32). What would they have needed to do to listen justly? After hearing the sound of silence* here, we may have a renewed appreciation for the value of the legal hearing.

In *Acts of Hope*, White engages with Mandela's statement from the dock in the Rivonia Trial. His engagement includes these words about equality:

> The cultural force of the ideals of democracy and law to which he appeals is demonstrated . . . by the government's own reluctance to be seen to abandon them entirely. The condition of Mandela's speech is a public trial, presided over by a judge and attended by journalists. The government could simply have murdered him, or tried him in private, or turned the proceedings into a show trial. But they did not, and their decision had consequences against their immediate interest, for it enabled Mandela to speak and be heard. The trial created a moment of rhetorical equality between state and accused, and as such enacted a political value inconsistent with the regime of oppression of which it was a part. To admit such a hearing into one's system is to scatter seeds of possibility whose growth the government cannot entirely control.
>
> (White 1994a: 293–4)

Given that the word 'rhetorical' is commonly used to point to contemptible tricks with words (*Rhetoric), White might have done well to work with a better name. However, our encounter with White here may persuade us to join him in rehabilitating it. In doing so, we can join him in his basic concern, namely, integration*. White's integrative spirit includes putting together the 'cultural' (*Culture), the 'political', and the 'rhetorical', at the heart of the legal – the 'hearing'.

In the early 1960s, when Mandela became an outlaw, White was thinking about going to law school. He went to hear a moot court argument involving a question of state tax and administrative law. The experience 'probably closed the decision' for him (White 1973: xxxiii). It was an experience that ran counter to his expectation:

> I had expected this to be resolved in a technical and uninteresting manner, by a dry-as-dust reading of some rules found in an old book with yellowing pages, but I quickly saw that instead it required argument about the most interesting and important things: about the meaning of language, including the way language means; about the purposes of the tax laws; about the relations between the citizen and government; about the kind of respect that one agency of government owes to judgments reached by another; and so on. The argument always had justice—and whatever justice could be made to mean—as its subject, and it seemed to me to involve everything, to call upon every capacity of mind and imagination. And it had to be shaped, in time as spoken, on the page as written, and directed to a particular audience or a set of audiences; in those ways at least, perhaps more, it had to be a work of art. I was entranced, and went back to hear other arguments, struggling to follow them, imagining myself making them.
>
> Here was a profession that was set up on the idea that each side would have equal time to talk; that the judge or other audience would hear you out; that you could make whatever arguments seemed to you right; that you could do whatever you could to reformulate the language to make it say the truth from your perspective; and to do all this in the interests of people who could not adequately speak for themselves.
>
> (White 2001: 219)

White stresses throughout his writings that what is commonly objectified as The Law is not a set of rules but a collaborative enterprise of making meaning, an 'art' combining relativism (insofar as we can talk about 'truth from your perspective') and idealism, giving a place to pursue 'justice'*. Also concerning idealism, this place takes our 'we' seriously, for 'each side would have equal time to talk'. This place offers a non-trivial and much neglected form of equality. It can help one to speak truth to power.

Socratic Questioning in the Classroom: Clark D. Cunningham

In *The Legal Imagination*, White seeks to establish a classroom in which 'we are all colleagues' (1973: xxii). What might this mean?

In an essay 'Learning from Law Students', Cunningham reflects on a course that he taught, 'Law as Language, Law as Literature', which uses White's book as a textbook. He contrasts White with the 'Socratic' law teacher Charles Kingsfield, who became (in)famous through the book, movie and television series *Paper Chase*. Centring on the activity* of questioning*, Cunningham writes:

> [T]he Kingsfield method does not indicate to the student that the professor expects to learn something new from the student or to have her own understanding effectively refuted. Indeed, there seems to be a fundamental epistemological difference between Socrates' dialectical approach and the Kingsfield method. Students who enter a Kingsfield classroom are given the message implicitly—and sometimes explicitly—that their minds are to be wiped clean of whatever knowledge and methods of thinking they had acquired before law school. Learning to 'think like a lawyer' is a whole new mode of thought, and an important part of the teacher's task is to show students the deficiencies of their previous forms of analysis and discourse. . . . The purpose of Kingsfield's questioning is not a sincere effort by the teacher to learn . . . from the student, but rather a rhetorical device to expose the inadequacies of the previous answer.
>
> In contrast, Socrates' dialectic method is founded on the belief that the conversational partner is a source of fundamental knowledge and, indeed, that true education is a process of recalling what one already knows at a deeper level. Socrates described his role as that of a midwife, bringing other men's thoughts to birth . . .
>
> I have taught [my course] four times, each time using *The Legal Imagination* as the core textbook. My experience has been that the relation between law teacher and student (and among students) can change when we sit down to read literary texts together. The Kingsfieldian teacher is always suspected of 'hiding the ball': she knows the right answer already and is just waiting until the interrogative process either narrows the options to that answer or exhausts student imagination, at which point the teacher pulls the answer out of a hat. But even law professors are not expected to know all of the answers to how to interpret a Shakespearean sonnet or an essay by Proust. More importantly, the conventions of the discourse are different. Students know that they can draw upon their pre-law-school knowledge and experience and their own good sense.
>
> (Cunningham 1994: 200–2)

Here is an 'experience'*-centred story that is concerned with making a judgment* about different modes of teaching. Cunningham suggests that Socrates' basic question is something like this: What can I learn from my 'conversation partner'? That question differs from Kingsfield's basic question, which is something like this: How can I prove that I am correct and that they are wrong? Kingsfield's question has no place for him to engage in the activity of 'learning', ultimately of attunement* to the language* of another person. The central relationship in the Whitean classroom is the 'conversational' relationship in which self and other engage in a joint inquiry into self and other. (Resisting a Kingsfieldian mindset of an *us versus them* (teachers versus students) mentality, Cunningham takes the 'we' seriously – 'when we sit down to read literary texts together'.) This relationship is one of 'rhetorical equality' (White – *Rhetoric). The heart of the conversation is 'sincere' 'questioning', one that proceeds from a collective perception of common humanity.

Cunningham goes on to suggest more about an egalitarian classroom and a Socratic education worthy of the name:

> As fellow literary critics, my seminar students teach me; but my most exciting learning experience is when students become authors in their own right. The invitational approach of White's textbook encourages students to venture their own experiences and insights . . . . I am struck by the tragic loss in law school when students are treated as blank slates. Not only do law students bring to the school a variety and depth of life experiences (and academic training), necessarily well beyond the range represented by their teachers, but their very state of mind in law school is an invaluable resource. They are aware of something that their teachers have forgotten, of the opacity of legal language: what is visible to them . . . has become transparent to law-school graduates. Their capacity for thoughtful critique and dialogue may, therefore, exceed in important ways what can be found in the faculty lunchroom and at academic conferences. A mode of teaching that makes possible learning from law students, then, seems more truly Socratic than the approach that widely bears the name.
>
> (202–3)

After experiencing the Whitean classroom, a student may feel the desire to do some comparative law-classroom research on, say, the nature of 'tragic loss', or on 'the opacity of legal language'* in law teachers. A student with a background in economics may feel the desire to re-work Smith's invisible hand metaphor*. Here goes: By pursuing his own questions, a student frequently promotes collective well-being more effectually than when she really intends to promote it – she is led by an invisible hand to render translucent the metaphors that are 'transparent' to her teacher, metaphors that can hinder an authentic joint inquiry in the direction of justice*.

Experience

'OE' is a term commonly used in New Zealand to refer to a young adult's 'overseas experience'. Many people who have been on OE suggest that it was their first real education. These remarks on the institution are suggestive:

> Once away, the young New Zealander stops being an insider in a taken-for-granted culture, and becomes an outsider somewhere else. On OE there is the liberty to reconstruct themselves. OE transcends the intellectual and spiritual limitations of staying in a small New Zealand town, or an over familiar city. A huge world of options and experiences has suddenly opened. During their absence they also develop an 'outsider' view of New Zealand. They can now claim a far larger vision than those who stayed at home.
>
> (Bell 2002: 147)

We might wonder how OE-ers 'reconstruct themselves'. How might an OE-er go about making a judgment* about their own performance*? To whom could a person turn for preparatory help before departure?

'Beyond Our Own Circle': Jane Austen's *Persuasion*

Early on in *Persuasion*, the heroine Anne Elliot moves from her family's ancestral home, Kellynch-hall, to temporarily reside at nearby Uppercross Cottage, where her sister and brother-in-law live. Soon she reflects on her displacement:

> Anne had not wanted this visit to Uppercross, to learn that a removal from one set of people to another, though at a distance of only three miles, will often include a total change of conversation, opinion, and idea. She had never been staying there before, without being struck by it, or without wishing that other Elliots could have her advantage in seeing how unknown, or unconsidered there, were the affairs which at Kellynch-hall were treated as of such general publicity and pervading interest; yet, with all this experience, she believed she must now submit to feel that another lesson, in the art of knowing our own nothingness beyond our

> own circle, was becoming necessary for her; . . . She acknowledged it to be very fitting, that every little social commonwealth should dictate its own matters of discourse; and hoped, ere long, to become a not unworthy member of the one she was now transplanted into.—With the prospect of spending at least two months at Uppercross, it was highly incumbent on her to clothe her imagination, her memory, and all her ideas in as much of Uppercross as possible.
>
> (Austen 1817/1998: 43–4)

Unlike open-minded Anne, the 'other Elliots' do not recognize the value of learning from others and of 'a total change of conversation, opinion, and idea'. In being 'transplanted', Anne gets to occupy different positions from which to read histories and events. In the process the familiar (including her family) become strange, and the strange becomes familiar – a movement* that we might call a productive alienation* from the commonplaces by which she lives. In making sense (exercising her 'imagination'*) of her 'experience', she is able to develop her capacity for critical judgment*, which for her is an important character* strength.

Persuasion can be read as an addition to the genre of *Bildungsroman* (novels of character formation). A careful *Persuasion* reader will be equipped well to catch the drift of White's course book *The Legal Imagination*, especially these prefatory remarks:

> [T]his book is . . . formally addressed to a 'law student,' but I trust you can take that as the sort of fiction that it is – a bit as though this were an epistolary novel, perhaps, in which the reader is one of the characters – and I hope that you may even take some pleasure and interest in what happens to this 'reader' as the text progresses. My object in this book is to make a place for myself and to help my reader do likewise, a position from which the world, and our contributions to it, can be seen and judged in a new way. This book is meant to lead the law student away from the law to such a position, which must be largely of his or her own making. For other readers, it does not seem to matter much whether they approach it from the legal side or from some other direction: from that of literary criticism, for example, or certain sorts of anthropology or sociology, or philosophy or history, or indeed, perhaps most fruitfully of all, from the experience of ordinary life.
>
> (White 1985b: xi)

We might say that White invites his reader to move beyond her own circle. For the purpose of developing her critical judgment, White's reader will do well to engage in the activity of clothing her imagination, her memory, and all her ideas in as much of the beyond as possible. 'Where is "the law"?', she may ask as 'the text progresses', not knowing if she is moving 'away' from it (whatever 'it' is).

'Every Freshman a Phoenix': Composition and Literary Criticism at Amherst

When White was 18 years old, he went to Amherst College. Its freshman composition course, English 1–2, directed by Theodore Baird, was a 'radical immersion in the waywardness of language' (Poirier 1992: 180). With an interest in the nature and significance of language*, let us do a little immersion.

In *Living Speech*, White talks about an assignment that Baird gave to his students. Here is the assignment:

> You are now a member of a community, a social organization, or rather a number of communities (Amherst College, the freshman class, a particular dormitory, etc.). This world is often described as artificial and secluded, an Ivory Tower. (The origin of this metaphor is obscure.) You may yourself believe, you may feel, that you have left behind the Real World. After all this is 'only' a college, you are 'only' a college student, this is 'only' a course.
>
> In the form of an essay deal with the following questions:
>
> 1. What is real about the Real World?
> 2. How do you know when you really are in the Real World?
> 3. If you have been in the Real World, why did you get out of it?
> 4. If you are outside the Real World, how did you get into it?
>
> Finally, define 'The Real World.'
>
> (quoted in White 2006: 68)

Here we have an example of Baird's lines of questioning* that offer an experience of confusion. One task for the student is to learn to cope with the confusion, and possibly even transcend ('get out of') it (whatever 'it' might be). The form of Baird's first question will be familiar to a Brecht reader (*Alienation), who will appreciate the significance of a question that seeks to make the familiar (in this case a cliché) strange. Baird shared with Brecht and others an image of art as a means of productive reorientation.[1]

In a study of Baird's course, the author included a section titled 'Every Freshman a Phoenix'. Here is a fragment from it:

> Few first-term freshmen . . . know what the course is all about; and . . . the initial assignments are specifically designed to jolt the freshman into recognizing that he doesn't know even what he does when he draws a line. . . . The jolt to the freshman's command of language is startling. . . . English 1–2 doesn't stop with the destruction of the freshman's control of language and meaning. The Amherst instructors believe that from these ashes . . . the whole freshman command of communicable meaning

> will gradually rise anew, mysterious and awkward and capable of staring directly into the sun.
>
> (Broderick 1958: 51)

At the outset of the course, a student might imagine that language is merely a neutral tool in communicating about the world. After a 'jolt', the student may come to appreciate that language is an evolving cultural artefact for making and remaking ourselves and our world – the real world. While the 'jolt' that contributes to 'the destruction of the freshman's control of language and meaning' may sound painful, the 'rise' that follows may sound like an invaluable act of self-transcendence.

In *The Edge of Meaning*, White talks about Baird's course as it concerned the student's relationship with language:

> [T]his course invited us to see our world as made up of languages, of different ways of talking; to see our college, for example, not as a thing or a structure, but as a set of more or less shared expectations as to how to talk and live, and much the same could be said of other institutions, from country clubs to the law. Each of these languages consisted of patterns of response and action, which could be learned, and learned well or badly. If one learned them by rote, unreflectively, one might become too much shaped by these patterns, by social and moral cliches, and perhaps never be capable of independent thought and action. The task of life was therefore a writing task, to learn to use our various languages reflectively, in such a way that we controlled them rather than they us; to use them to express our own experience, or to attain our ends; and this meant learning to have both experience and ends worthy of the name in the first place.
>
> (White 2001: 131)

Baird empowered students by enabling them to imagine how languages 'control' (what's in that metaphor?) them – *are* them to a significant extent – and that they have choices concerning how to respond to this 'control' – choices about who they are becoming (*Character). In being invited 'to express our own experience', White was invited to imagine himself not as Anystudent conveying memorized information to Anyteacher but as a composer of language speaking in an authentic voice* with a fellow composer. With the invitation comes a prod to make authority a subject of conscious thought. The kind of authority that interested Baird was not so much official capacities and roles but a certain form of talk, a form that is living and authentic. We can be sure that the kind of experience that Baird valued was not the repeatable kind but the unique, which transforms us for the better, opening us to new experiences.

The first chapter of White's course book begins with a section titled 'Learning the Language of the Law'. Here is a foundational line of questioning*:

> What are the 'limits' on what can be said in technical legal language? . . . What is meant when your friend at the cocktail party calls you 'legalistic' and gives up in disgust? Can you stand outside the legal language system and look at it? Can you stand far enough back from your legal education to ask, 'What am I becoming?'
>
> (White 1973: 8 and 10)

In attempting to find a place to 'stand' (might there be a more fitting metaphor*?), White's reader will be concerned with working out the 'limits' of 'the legal' and of her self. She might do well to ask: How will I know if I am 'outside the legal language system'? Is not the 'legal language system' in a certain sense 'inside' me, or at least one of my many selves?

We can imagine White's *The Legal Imagination* as a reconstituted version of Baird's course, with many challenging assignments. Speaking generally about his course, White says this in the penultimate chapter:

> You might sum up the experience this course offers by saying that it is an experience in the collapse of language under strain . . . . You have experienced what could be called the central frustration of writer and lawyer, the perpetual breaking down of language in your hands as you try to use it. None of our languages . . . can bear the stresses of our demands for truth and order and justice. Such, it seems to me, are the conditions of our existence.
>
> (White 1973: 760)

The 'experience' of 'frustration' can readily lead to a confident judgment* that mechanistic metaphors for the phenomenon of language do not do it 'justice'*, metaphors that can readily turn humans into objects and that can get in the way of an attunement* to the 'conditions of our existence' (760).

'Genuine Limit-Situations': David Tracy

In *Blessed Rage for Order*, Tracy draws from the language of Bernard Lonergan (*Method) for developing a method for theologians. One aim is to develop and fashion a language for talking about experience. Tracy has 'come to believe that . . . "limit" can be used as a key . . . category for describing certain signal characteristics peculiar to any language or experience with a properly religious dimension' (1975/1996: 92). Here is a key passage:

> The . . . limit-situation . . . refers to those human situations wherein a human being ineluctably finds manifest a certain ultimate limit or

> horizon to his or her existence. . . . More exactly, limit-situations refer to two basic kinds of existential situation: either those 'boundary' situations of guilt, anxiety, sickness, and the recognition of death as one's own destiny, or those situations called 'ecstatic experiences'—intense joy, love, reassurance, creation. All genuine limit-situations refer to those experiences, both positive and negative, wherein we both experience our own human limits (limit-to) as our own as well as recognize, however haltingly, some disclosure of a limit-of our experience. The negative mode of limit-situations . . . ('boundary-situations') allow and, when intense, seem to demand reflection upon the existential boundaries of our present everyday existence. When an announcement of a serious illness—whether our own or of someone we love—is made, we begin to experience the everyday, the 'real' world, as suddenly unreal: petty, strange, foreign to the now real world. That 'limit' world of final closure to our lives now faces us with a starkness we cannot shirk and manages to disclose to us our basic existential faith or unfaith in life's very meaningfulness.
>
> The positive mode of limit-situations can be described . . . as 'ecstatic experiences.' Undeniably, such experiences (love, joy, the creative act, . . .) are authentically 'self-transcending' moments in our lives. When in the grasp of such experiences, we all find, however momentarily, that we can and do transcend our usual lackluster selves and our usual everyday worlds to touch upon a dimension of experience which cannot be stated adequately in the language of ordinary, everyday experience. Authentic love, both erotic and agapic, puts us in touch with a reality whose power we cannot deny. We do not work ourselves into a state of love . . . . We 'fall,' we 'are' in love. While its power lasts, we experience the rest of our lives as somehow shadowy. The 'real world' no longer seems real. We find ourselves affirming the reality of ecstatic experience, but not as something merely decided upon by us. In all such authentic moments of ecstasy, we experience a reality simply given, gifted, happened. Such a reality, as religious mystics remind us, may be a taste of that self-transcending experience of a 'being-in-love-without-qualification' familiar to the authentically religious person.
>
> (105–6)

Here is a resource for thought and expression about our movements* in and out of the so-called Real World. If we are *out*, the passage may help us to get in or to understand how we got out. If we are *in*, the passage may help to get out or to understand how we got in. If we are both *in* and *out* at the same time, it may help us to make sense of our perhaps normal schizophrenic experience.

The passage from Tracy could help us to frame some questions about White's basic questions in *The Legal Imagination*. For example: Does his inquiry into the nature of the 'legal' resemble an inquiry into the 'religious'? If so, might we have to re-imagine what the 'legal' and the 'religious' are? How will we

do that? Who might we become in the process? Might we become more fully equipped to do justice* to *The Legal Imagination*?

Might we hope to have a 'self-transcending' experience whilst making sense of those questions? This experience might be an 'aha' moment that accompanies the feeling that one has fittingly placed the questions in the universe, say by connecting it to the questions of a theologian. In placing White's questions one might feel that one has found a place to stand in the world.

'I Jettisoned Chicago Economics': Leonard Rapping

In the early 1980s, Arjo Klamer undertook a collection of 'conversations' with economists, with the aim of attending to 'the more personal and communicative aspects of economics' (Klamer 1984: x). In the book that emerged, 'Leonard Rapping occupies a special position, partly because of his . . . conversion from conventional to radical economics' (xi). Reflecting on the 'conversion', Rapping remarked:

> Friedman's book *Capitalism and Freedom* was very important to me. I believed in it. The thing that impressed me most about Friedman was his emphasis on freedom. . . . I must say that I did feel free until the late 1960s.
>
> I became . . . increasingly involved in the anti-war movement. In all my training at Chicago there was no serious mention of the global system. . . . I jettisoned Chicago economics. But it left me in an intellectual vacuum. . . . I tell you, the reconstruction of a worldview is a long, slow process. It is also a wrecking experience. The process is never completed.
>
> I [was] offered the chairmanship of the Economics Department [at the University of Massachusetts] in 1971. . . . Later, when the department hired several radicals and anti-war activists, I felt it was the right environment for me. The department was ecumenical. Ideologically diverse points of view were represented. It was the perfect environment to inquire about the world. This was the beginning of a profound education for me. Without the experience of changing values I would not have grown intellectually and morally.
>
> (in Klamer 1984: 222, 226–8 and 228)

That passage can help direct attention to the reality that economics is diverse – comprising much more than one school of thought (or social commonwealth). There are various ways of imagining the processes of valuation that we call 'the economy'. These different ways have emerged out of different beliefs, cultures and experiences. (Economists would do well to learn the art of knowing their own nothingness beyond their own circles.) Some economists, including Klamer and Rapping, promote diverse ways of doing economics. It seems tempting to say that they take intellectual freedom seriously. We might wonder what character* strengths they could give to *Homo economicus*, who is commonly defined as an isolated individual that transcends culture. At the very least, we may suspect that they may promote the image of a unique individual who emerges from an evolving culture and who is capable of a rich experience.

What might Rapping mean when he says that he 'believed in' Friedman's book *Capitalism and Freedom*? What exactly did he do when he 'jettisoned Chicago economics'? Does being an economist (of whatever school) somehow irreversibly transform a person? White's book on learning to read the poet Herbert, *'This Book of Starres'*, offers food-for-thought for those and similar questions. White is centrally interested in the experience of reading* Herbert, an experience that he likens to travel. When talking about the topic of belief, he exercises his analogical imagination*:

> [T]o read Herbert is like spending a year, say, in Morocco or Bangkok. Having lived that way for a time it becomes part of one's experience, part of what Kenneth Burke called one's 'equipment for life.' To protect yourself by staying in the Hilton Hotel would be simply to insulate yourself from that experience and to give yourself another, that of hotel life. To engage with a text or a culture means to accept something other, provisionally but really, and this works changes on the self. Suppose, to take the analogy one further stage, that your travels take you to a place where you learn the local language, not only intellectually but actually, by which I mean that you learn to use it to make the gestures, to engage in the practices, that constitute life in that world. Belief is now no longer an issue. Language and practice are things people do, and we have done them: prayed for the gods to bring rain, exorcised a witch, built our house with a barrier at the door to exclude demons, bowed low to a holy man, and so on. To say we disbelieve the meaning of all these things is a somewhat thin remark against the actuality of our conduct and experience, our engagement with a way of imagining the world and ourselves. To speak a language is in an important sense to believe it.
>
> What I say is of course not only true of Christian language, or theological language, but of any. The language of the Talmud, for example, to one who has actually engaged in its processes of thought and imagination, will always have a kind of reality that cannot be erased by an assertion of disbelief; the same is true of the language of modern law, or of Homer's poetry.
>
> Outside the field of religion we are so comfortable with this fact as not even to notice it; but religious belief is such a charged topic for many of

> us that we want to deny it. Here I want only to say—or to warn— . . . that to engage with this poetry is to engage with the language in which it is written, and this requires a momentary acceptance of it, an acceptance that will in some sense live in the mind thereafter, even if one ultimately rejects it wholeheartedly, as disgusting or vile, just as the experience of Morocco or Paris lives in the mind even if it is later rejected. But one cannot reject it while one is reading it, for that is no longer reading. We must engage with the mind and imagination on the terms that it offers us, or not at all; and even if we later reject these terms, our experience of them will nonetheless have been a real one.
>
> (White 1994b: 44–5)

How are we to 'engage' with White's text? What do we need to 'do' that will be worthy of being called 'a momentary acceptance of it'?

In light of our reading of Rapping, let us put White's words to 'use'. To read Friedman or any of the Chicago economists/priests is like spending a year, say, in a different culture. To *really* read a text or a culture involves an encounter with an other (with a different cultural horizon), an encounter that changes that which we call the self. To say as much is to offer an image of the individual that differs markedly from the image of the autonomous individual at the base of Chicago economics. The image of autonomous individual assumes that language is a transparent tool for pointing to reality (such as 'the field of religion') and conveying information to another autonomous individual. In the real world, however, language is a medium with which we constitute self and other and a relationship between them. It is important to add, however, that the linguistically constructed image of the autonomous individual using a transparent language is also part of our real world, which shapes how we experience the world and ourselves in it. This image is a powerful one, which we will believe as we put it to work in the world. It is impossible to simply jettison it in the way that a pilot can drop fuel from an aircraft. One can hope to establish a different relationship with a language, such as being able to productively control it rather than being controlled. The process of establishing a different relationship, to be sure, can be a wrecking experience. It may, however, be a necessary one in the activity of attunement* to the language of another person.

Imagination

'Play I in One Person Many People': William Shakespeare's *King Richard II*
'Maps of Sovereignty': Perry Dane on the Cherokee Nation
Images of Images: Kenneth Boulding's *The Image*

There is a long history of deprecating the imagination, frequently by setting it in opposition to reality. Beginning with *The Legal Imagination*, White joins those who would complicate the imagination–reality relationship. This is his central 'thesis': 'the activities which make up the professional life of the lawyer and judge constitute an enterprise of the imagination, an enterprise whose central performance is the claim of meaning against the odds: the translation of the imagination into reality by the power of language' (1973: 758). How might we imagine the imagination?

'Play I in One Person Many People': William Shakespeare's *King Richard II*

In the opening act of Shakespeare's history play, King Richard banishes Henry Bullingbrook ('Bolingbroke' in some editions), Duke of Hereford, from England. Bullingbrook's father, John of Gaunt, Duke of Lancaster, encourages his son to 'imagine' his exile in a way that will make it less of a 'sorrow' (*c.*1595/1990: I.iii.285 and 291). Bullingbrook responds:

> Oh, who can hold a fire in his hand
> By thinking on the frosty Caucasus?
> Or cloy the hungry edge of appetite
> By bare imagination of a feast?
> Or wallow naked in December snow
> By thinking on fantastic summer's heat?
> Oh no, the apprehension of the good
> Gives but the greater feeling of the worse.
> (I.iv.293–300)

Bullingbrook, and perhaps also Shakespeare's imagined audience, will soon learn that the relationship between 'imagination' and reality can differ from that suggested here.

At the end of Act I, King Richard expresses the unbecoming hope that his uncle, Gaunt, will die, so that he might seize his estate for use in putting down a rebellion in Ireland. The Duke of York is disturbed, not the least because Bullingbrook will be deprived of his inheritance. York later offers King Richard an image of the foundations of his authority. With the fealty of Magna Carta between the lines ('fealty' being a reciprocal relationship – with the barons granted certain rights in return for service and loyalty), York claims that the sovereign's powers and rights are limited:

> Was not Gaunt just? And is not Harry true?
> Did not the one deserve to have an heir?
> Is not his heir a well-deserving son?
> Take Herford's rights away, and take from time
> His charters and his customary rights.
> Let not to-morrow then ensue today.
> Be not thyself. For how art thou a king
> But by fair sequence and succession?
> Now, afore God – God forbid I say true! –
> If you do wrongfully seize Herford's rights,
> . . .
> You lose a thousand well-disposèd hearts,
> And prick my tender patience to those thoughts
> Which honour and allegiance cannot think.
> (II.i.189–208)

In pursuing a line of questioning* about the 'just' (*Justice), York has attempted to genuinely persuade King Richard to reconsider his proposed action. York, however, having earlier remarked that 'all in vain comes counsel to his ear' (II.i.4), would not have much hope of persuading him. '[D]eaf' (II.i.16) King Richard, who seems completely unmoved by York's speech, ignores his uncle's warning. Perhaps with little capacity for listening*, he shows no interest in responding to York's justice talk.

Support rises for Bullingbrook, and he senses an opportunity to 'challenge law'. When King Richard is in Ireland, Bullingbrook tells York, who is now Lord Protector in King Richard's absence, that he has come to 'lay my claim / To my inheritance of free descent' (II.iii.134–5). York and King Richard lack the capacity to resist him with force. Bullingbrook sets himself up to take the crown in Parliament. When he asks, 'Are you contented to resign the crown?' (IV.i.199), King Richard responds:

> Aye – no. No – aye, for I must nothing be,
> Therefore no 'no', for I resign to thee.
> Now, mark me how I will undo myself.
> I give this heavy weight from off my head
> And this unwieldy sceptre from my hand,
> The pride of kingly sway from out my heart.
> With mine own tears I wash away my balm;

With mine own hands I give away my crown;
With mine own tongue deny my sacred state;
With mine own breath release all duteous oaths.
(IV.i.200–9)

With this 'mine . . . mine . . . mine . . .', King Richard has taken charge of the performance*, setting out to 'undo' his identity, leaving little or no place for Bullingbrook. We might wonder at what point King Richard becomes just plain Richard. A Brecht reader (*Alienation) might readily imagine Shakespeare, behind the lines, asking his audience, 'Have you ever really looked carefully at The Crown?' Shakespeare thereby renders the familiar strange, offering the experience* of words losing their meaning and the opportunity to become a self-conscious composer of meaning.

When the crown is transferred, Richard reflects on his name: 'I have no name, no title' (IV.i.254). There perhaps is no surer sign of an identity crisis than having 'no name'. He then seeks a 'mirror', wanting to see whether he has changed: 'it may show me what a face I have / Since it is bankrupt of his majesty' (IV.i.265–6). His customary denunciation follows: 'Oh flattering glass, / Like to my followers in prosperity / Thou dost beguile me' (IV.i.278–80). Richard throws the mirror to the ground, possibly shattering much more than a mirror. This performance marks the formal dissolution of a self cum institution. 'King Henry' lacks the imagination to put the pieces together.

Alone in prison, Richard has to re-imagine himself: 'if I turn mine eyes upon myself / I find myself a traitor with the rest, / For I have . . . / Made glory base, a sovereignty a slave, / Proud majesty a subject, state a peasant' (IV.i.246–51). Talking alone, he continues re-imagining himself:

I have been studying how I may compare
This prison where I live unto the world,
And for because the world is populous
And here is not a creature but myself
I cannot do it. Yet I'll hammer't out.
(V.v.1–5)

Richard here is talking to himself about his own thought process. One of the common consequences of a traumatic experience is a disrupted relationship with language, ultimately with the terms with which one's past experiences have been negotiated and worked out. Richard begins to work through a disrupted language that he can use only in fragments. He shows an impulse to analogize with the aim of forming order out of chaos. He has to work hard at recomposing himself. With his multiple use of 'I', we may sense a 'self' searching for an identity. We are witnessing an activity, an impulse for making a resemblance. He goes on to say:

. . . play I in one person many people,
And none contented. Sometimes am I King,

> Then treasons make me wish myself a beggar,
> And so I am. Then crushing penury
> Persuades me I was better when a king,
> Then am I kinged again, and by and by
> Think that I am unkinged by Bullingbrook,
> And straight am nothing.
>
> (V.v.31–8)

This talk, the activity of an internal conversation* between several voices, is about Richard's experience of turning from one role to another and about his effort to make sense of this experience. Sometimes he is Sovereign, until a self within him says otherwise. To say otherwise is to become a traitor, until a self within says otherwise. Can his many selves work out a harmony?

King Richard II has a place in *The Legal Imagination*. White suggests that the play offers an inquiry into the imaginative foundations of authority:

> It seems to be part of the notion of authority that it is unquestioned, an obvious fact, not a judgment: 'Not all the water in the rough rude sea / Can wash the balm from an anointed king,' says Shakespeare's Richard II, defining the attitude which regards what happens in that play – the deposition of a king – as unthinkable. . . . Does a lawyer ever have such authority? Can he somehow manufacture it for himself, or for his arguments?
>
> How is the authority of a proposition, a source, or a person to be established, and once established, how questioned? . . . The essence of a language of authority is that it shall not be questioned but accepted as necessary; and, as Shakespeare's *Richard II* demonstrates, when such a language is taken as open to question, it loses its peculiar force at once.
>
> (White 1973: 815 and 817)

Here is a resource with which to ask what it can mean 'to question' (*Questioning). When 'a language . . . loses it peculiar force', its users will find that their way of imagining the world collapses. The desire for some sort of coherence requires them to imaginatively create a new way of imagining the world.

White reads the play in *Acts of Hope*. After presenting King Richard's decision to give up the crown to Bullingbrook, White identifies two people with different imaginative capacities:

> I think we should take it that Richard sees what Bolingbroke does not, that once the crown has become the subject of effective threat and negotiation it is no longer the crown at all. From the moment his imperious display is disregarded by Bolingbroke, kingship, as he has known it, becomes impossible and therefore valueless. There is nothing except unconditional submission that Bolingbroke can give him. If Bolingbroke

> is not going to give him that, Richard will not keep the crown—not be part of that kind of degradation of himself and it—but will resign it.
> (White 1994a: 68)

Bolingbroke, who is no poet, simply takes the crown, 'the meaning and value of which he has himself destroyed' (69). He is given the opportunity to learn that the activity of law deeply involves reality-creating symbols that can become meaningless without due exercise of bare imagination.

With the dynamics of deposition imagined that way, White goes on to identify the nature and significance of the loss of 'the language of kingship':

> Henry . . . is not—and in some sense cannot be—king and cannot call upon the resources and language of that office. When at the chaotic ending of the play Henry learns that Richard has been murdered . . . he has no way of talking about his situation at all, except to undertake a crusade to the Holy Land by way of expiation.
> (73)

When a king is not a king, we are offered the potentially disturbing experience of key words losing their meaning. Shall we compare Henry to Huck Finn, who sought not to 'undertake a crusade' but to 'light out for the Territories' (*Language)?

Just as Richard ends his life self-consciously exercising his analogical imagination with respect to his place in the world, White ends his reading of the play exercising his with respect to the place of the play in the world:

> Shakespeare's work . . . has affinities with Chaucer's *Canterbury Tales*, . . . comprehending at once . . . the immense and the minuscule. This way of writing, by poetic comprehension, unites the concerns of beauty and truth alike, because beauty can be thought of, as Coleridge suggested, as the comprehension of contradictions within an order and because on these understandings the truth of any utterance lies not in itself but in its relation to another; and the concerns of justice too, for justice can be seen to be a way of giving each voice, each possibility for speech, its widest and fullest range.
>
> This kind of work has obvious similarities to law, for, like law, it is a way of seeing what can be said on both sides; but not only both sides of an existing question, the very statement of which defines the language that can be used to respond to it, but 'both sides' in a deeper way: seeing how competing languages can be framed and put to work, entailing as they do competing ways of imagining and acting in the world. Here these possibilities are arranged not at haphazard but in such a way as to lead us to accept first one, then another, and in the process undo ourselves.
>
> The effect of the whole is rather like a Socratic *elenchus* at work on the main terms of the discourse—treason, loyalty, crown, etc.—which are so

> deeply undermined that they can never be used again by the attentive reader, or at least not with the old naive confidence they once enjoyed. The effect of the play is to leave us in a position of greater uncertainty than ever before about our languages, with an increasing sense that we can have nothing to say upon which we can lean without question. Its movement is one of intellectual and moral affliction, as we are brought to the limits of our imaginations and understandings; like the characters in the play we come at the end to a kind of silence, but a silence that is itself a way of facing our situation in the world.
>
> This suggests that the ethics and politics of the play is Socratic too, for it locates us in a position of increased responsibility and decreased certainty, expanding our knowledge of the way in which valid forms of thought and speech erode each other. The position Shakespeare brings us to share is in a deep way paradoxical, for in one sense it is all icy objectivity and detachment—this is the way the world is, the play is saying, this is how people talk, one poised against the other; I am the analyst or surgeon who can see one, then another, each in its fullness; sympathy would blur the picture—yet, in another, it is the grandest affirmation of our common humanity, of the multiplicity of languages that define us; it is work belonging in the same class . . . as the great poems of Homer. (78–9)

The image of the 'position' that 'Shakespeare brings us to share' is helpful for thinking about the 'position' that White brings us to share in *Acts of Hope* and in his other books. We may not be able to hear the ancient principle 'hear the other side' in quite the same way any more, for we might be inclined to 'question' what is meant by 'side'. (There are many 'sides' for talking about 'sides'. Should we not be trying to hear 'voice'* against voice against voice?) How are we to imagine the experience of being 'brought to the limits of our imaginations and understandings'? Is this not a 'religious' 'limits'-experience, one with which Tracy is centrally concerned (*Experience)? Might we feel a 'blessed rage for order' (Tracy), and for 'justice'*? What are we to think of White's claims about Shakespeare's ontological claims ('this is the way the world is')? Does not the vertiginous simultaneous 'icy objectivity and detachment' and 'the grandest affirmation of our common humanity' call for 'a kind of silence'*. The 'paradoxical' image suggests to me that Shakespeare establishes a place that is at once outside and inside life with language, a place that will be of interest to theologians. There is a place for economists too: the reality of 'competing languages' should be of interest – 'Which language is more efficient?' Perhaps that question could lead to an 'economics of language', in which the main term of the discourse, *economics*, is so deeply undermined that it can never be used in the conventional way by a reader who is *paying* attention*? Theologians and economists could get together to talk about how to 'undo ourselves'. With 'many people in one person', the question might be: which selves?

'Maps of Sovereignty': Perry Dane on the Cherokee Nation

In 1828, the Legislature of the State of Georgia passed a statute to assert control over Cherokee lands supposedly protected by the United States of America in the Treaty of Hopewell, signed in 1785. The Cherokee turned to the United States Supreme Court for protection against this unilateral act of incorporation. In the second of the two Cherokee Cases, Chief Justice John Marshall, talking about the relationship between the Cherokee and the United States of America, offered this by way of context:

> [T]he settled doctrine of the law of nations is, that a weaker power does not surrender its independence – its right to self-government, by associating with a stronger, and taking its protection. A weak state, in order to provide for its safety, may place itself under the protection of one more powerful, without stripping itself of the right of government, and ceasing to be a state. Examples of this kind are not wanting in Europe.
>
> (*Worcester v. Georgia* 1832: 561)

Marshall, speaking for the Court, held the Georgia statute in question to be void. And he held that Indian 'nations' were distinct peoples with the right to retain independent political communities. Georgia's effort to impose its law on the Cherokee was deemed to be an illegitimate 'extra-territorial' act.

Marshall's opinion stimulated various questions relating to politico-legal identity in his time. Such questions have continued to flow. Dane asks these: 'How would Marshall have drawn a . . . cartographer's map [of Georgia]? Would it have included the lands of the Cherokee nation? Or would Marshall have drawn the Georgia state lines around the Cherokee nation?' (1990: 990). Dane responds as follows:

> I suspect that Marshall might have insisted on drawing two maps. In one, Georgia and the Cherokee nation would be separate states. In the other, they would not. To say that the Cherokee were 'extra-territorial' was, I think, for Marshall both an exercise in the imagery of state exclusivism and, also, a transformation of that imagery. The Cherokee could be both inside and outside Georgia. They can (I am less certain that Marshall would agree with this) be both inside and outside the United States. That willingness to draw two maps, or three maps or four maps is, as much as anything, the surest sign of sovereignty-talk at its most mature, its most expansive, its most real. Indeed, I would be willing to generalize from Marshall's procedure: Sovereignty-talk, at its best, comprehends the willingness and the ability to hold, in tandem, apparently contradictory images of the relationship between self and other. It is the ability to insist on absolute dominion, and yet also recognize the dominion of others, or to comprehend the possibilities of equality even

> while comprehending a relationship of hierarchy. It is an exercise of craft – legal craft – in which these different images all find their respective places and their appropriate contexts. It is the epistemic courage to see that these images need not be reduced one to the others, or to some single compromise position that is unfaithful to them all.
>
> (990–1)

Dane here identifies an act of constitutional transformation – a 'transformation' of 'the imagery of state exclusivism'. Also, Dane himself performs the same act, cavorting with the orientational metaphors of 'inside'/'outside' and 'hierarchy'/'equality'*. After reading Dane, we may never hear the word 'sovereignty' – at least when it is used with 'naive confidence' (White) – in quite the same way again. How are we to judge Dane's judgment* about different kinds of sovereignty-talk? Might we do well to use the language of character* virtues, especially his word 'courage'?

The subtitle of Dane's essay is 'A Meditation'. What connection does meditation have to do with the activity* of being a lawyer? Is not meditation some sort of religious activity, and thus outside the law? Against those questions, however, does not Dane sound like a lawyer, confidently speaking the language of sovereignty? Is he not writing from inside the law? In his own sovereignty-talk, he seems to be offering the 'contradictory images' that are his subject. He is mixing genres, and in doing so bringing together parts of our culture* that are commonly imagined to be apart. This is a constructive act of integration*, which could be a source of hope for those on the margins, such as the Cherokee, and for those who desire to act justly toward them.

Dane's talk about sovereignty is a response to a basic line of questioning*. He is thinking in particular about relations between 'Native Americans' and other Americans. The particular, however, flows from the general:

> 'Who are these people?' is, for any legal order looking at the world, the great question of existential encounter. . . . [T]he process of recognition . . . has certain important common elements. One is the willingness to ask the sort of questions that open up the possibility of encounter, questions like 'who are we to tell them what to do?' or 'what is going on out there?' Another is the willingness to answer these questions through multiple, even apparently contradictory images.
>
> (1004–5)

What kind of character* takes 'the great question of existential encounter' seriously? Shall we compare Dane to . . . ? How shall we set about providing an 'answer' to those questions? What method* could help us?

Dane's reading brings to mind White's 'thesis' in *The Legal Imagination* – to recall: 'that the activities which make up the professional like the lawyer and judge constitute an enterprise of the imagination'. Let us turn to White's efforts to elaborate:

> The demands on your imagination start outside the legal language system, perhaps outside all language, when you first face a client or a judge or a juror and ask yourself 'Who is this person?' in a way that recognizes that he may be different from you. What is called for here is a social and narrative imagination, a capacity to envision different versions of the future. . . . 'Who is this person, and how shall I address him?' is a constant question in the life of the lawyer, and you will not think it a simple one. The imagination here is a faculty of sympathy as well as intellect.
>
> (758)

Who is this author, and how shall I address him? Who is my reader, and how shall I address her?

The 'radical question of justice', says White, is this: 'Who are we to each other?' (1990: 233) That 'justice' question is at the heart of this book, and can be heard throughout it, mostly between the lines, so to speak; it is 'a constant question' not only 'in the life of the lawyer', but also in the rest of life. It is a very familiar question, perhaps too familiar and in need of a productive alienation* from the commonplaces we live by.

Images of Images: Kenneth Boulding's *The Image*

'For especially valuable work on the way we imagine the world', White (1994c: 29) directs his reader to Boulding's *The Image*. We might hope that Boulding's book can help us to constructively imagine White's work.

Boulding seeks to establish a 'new science' founded on 'the image', a science with 'remarkable unifying power' (1956: 148). He sets out 'to discuss the growth of images, both private and public, . . . in society at large'. His principal reason for doing this is to 'develop a really adequate theory of behavior'. For him, 'behavior depends on the image' (18). Some remarks on the nature of 'the image' are as follows:

> The image is built up as a result of all past experience of the possessor of the image. . . . From the moment of birth if not before, there is a constant stream of messages entering the organism from the senses. At first, these may merely be undifferentiated lights and noises. As the child grows, however, they gradually become distinguished into people and objects. He begins to perceive himself as an object in the midst of a world of objects. The conscious image has begun. . . . Every time a message reaches him his image is likely to be changed in some degree by it, and as his image is changed his behavior patterns will be changed likewise.
>
> (6–7)

We might do well to imagine how we might be 'changed' as we read *The Image*. How might different degrees and forms of change among different people be associated with their different 'past experience'*?

When 'a message' hits an image, Boulding says that 'one of three things can happen.' (I) '[T]he image may remain unaffected.' Here he invites us to 'think of the image as a rather loose structure, something like a molecule', and 'we may imagine that the message is going straight through without hitting it' (7). (II) A message 'may change the image in some rather regular and well-defined way that might be described as simple addition'. Here he speaks of looking at an atlas and 'finding out exactly the relation of Nyasaland to Tanganyika'. The significance: 'I will have added to my knowledge, or my image; I will not, however, have very fundamentally revised it. . . . Something that was a little vague before is now clearer' (7–8). (III) '[A] revolutionary change.' Here: 'a message hits some sort of nucleus or supporting structure in the image, and the whole thing changes in a quite radical way.' A classic example is a conversion: 'A man, for instance, may think himself a pretty good fellow and then may hear a preacher who convinces him that, in fact, his life is worthless and shallow, as he is at present living it. The words of the preacher cause a radical reformulation of the man's image of himself in the world, and his behavior changes accordingly' (8).

When can someone say that she has acquired knowledge that has the quality of 'truth'? What is the place of 'science' in Boulding's image talk?

> Most epistemological systems seek some philosopher's stone by which statements may be tested in order to determine their 'truth,' that is, their correspondence to outside reality. I do not claim to have any such philosopher's stone, not even the touchstone of science. I have, of course, a great respect for science and scientific method – for careful observation, for planned experience, for the testing of hypotheses and for as much objectivity as semirational beings like ourselves can hope to achieve. In my theoretical system, however, the scientific method merely stands as one among many of the methods whereby images change and develop. The development of images is part of the culture or the subculture in which they are developed, and it depends upon all the elements of that culture or subculture. Science is a subculture among subcultures.
>
> (16)

Like Lonergan's 'transcendental method'*, Boulding's 'system' is open. For those who live by an image in which the words 'culture'* and 'science' point to distinct realms, his 'theory' of 'the image' offers a challenge. *The Image* could change someone's image in a 'revolutionary' way. The book could even lead to the formation of a subculture that contributes to a radical transformation of other subcultures, including both law and economics.

Boulding offers a series of chapters about 'the image' in various aspects of life, including: 'in the theory of organization' (19); 'at the biological level' (32);

'of man and society' (47); 'the sociology of knowledge' (64); 'in economic life' (82); and 'in the political process' (97). He imagines his work on 'the image' as providing a 'foundation [for] a new science'. He proposes a name: 'Eiconics'. Whilst 'eiconics' may get 'confused with the study of icons', some 'confusion . . . and the subtle overtones of half-remembered associations are all part of the magic of the name' (148). Here he suggests what we users of language may all know at some level: the use of a new word has no meaning to a hearer until she connects it with some aspect of her own experience. Different people will have different experiences, and thus the meaning of the word will differ from person to person.

Boulding makes the basic point that as human beings we ceaselessly image and re-image the world. A discipline called eiconics would help make our ways of imaging the world, and our action within it, the matter of critical thought and expression. Eiconics has the potential to integrate every discipline (*Integration). This seems to me to be an extraordinary act of the imagination.

Shall we compare Boulding to . . . ? If anyone gets a new edition of *The Image* published, she or he could connect to White and imagine how Boulding might have imagined the law. White's reading, in *Acts of Hope*, of Justice Harlan's dissent in *Poe v. Ullman* readily connects to Boulding's image of images. Here is a fragment:

> On Harlan's view, the idea that the Constitution should be regarded as speaking in plain English and saying just what it means is dispensed with, just as it was by Brandeis, and for much the same reason: that the Constitution is meant to serve the highest purposes of government and collective life and that these cannot be reduced to a code. Instead, the Court must accept responsibility for judgment, which for Harlan means a responsibility to educate itself at the hands of its own past. His image of the cultural process that is wider than any person, yet entails principles of its own transformation, is familiar to us from Hale; and as Harlan himself sees, the extraordinary duty and privilege of the judge is to reconstitute this source of authority in his own prose. The line between self and world is in this way blurred, as the mind of the judge is partly made by the very material it transforms.
>
> (White 1994a: 160)

Any dogmatic claim that 'the Constitution should be regarded as speaking in plain English' would have no meaningful place for the activity of comparing our images of 'the Constitution', nor for acts of 'judgment'* about their appropriateness in situations of conflict. Such a claim, that is, would have no place for the activity of attunement*.

Centring on the White image of the hearing as 'the heart of law' (we engage with this image above in the opening section of the Introduction), we might say in an effort to connect White and Boulding, the law provides a subculture in which two or more rival images of certain events in our culture can be placed against each other. In doing so, it makes our construction and reconstruction of images conscious and creates a moment at which controlled change of images and culture becomes possible. In this regard, the law lends itself as an example for other discourses (such as economics) for the management of their own cultural change, which takes place with the continuous construction of new images.

One feature of White's work to which I am attracted is its self-reflexivity. This feature is notably absent from the work of economic imperialists, who seem to avoid turning their theories on themselves. In *Justice as Translation*, White suggests as much:

> Whatever its merits, the language and practice of economics cannot be justified in its own terms . . . . When the economist speaks to us, he is acting not as an economic actor himself, engaging in arms-length exchanges designed to increase his utility, but as one mind speaking to another, seeking to persuade to particular conclusions, to a language, to a view of life. He speaks as a person asking to be believed. He is engaged, that is, in the rhetorical and communal practices of conversation in which he asks to be listened to as one who seeks the truth, and these are activities for the description and criticism of which his own language as an economist is wholly inadequate.
>
> (White 1990: 79)

The economist who promotes a certain image of *Homo economicus* will do well to attend to its limits, especially as it concerns the place of the economist in it. In doing so, she may feel inclined to modify the image so that she can have a meaningful place in it. This could transform *Homo economicus* into a language producer and chooser, one who can participate in linguistically enabled ex-changes, becoming other to themselves, and equipping themselves to do justice*.

Integration

'An Integral Reality': Lon Fuller's Jurisprudence
Modern Constitutional Diversity: James Tully's *Strange Multiplicity*

'Since the opinion must make sense as a whole, the ultimate demand is one of integration.' So says White in a passage on the 'rhetoric and poetics of the law' (1985a: 241), a passage that is one of the epigraphs to this book. Elsewhere, White defines the word 'integration' more broadly as 'the putting together into coherent wholes of what would otherwise be fragmentary or broken' (1985b: xiv). Like White's books, this book as a whole is intended as an act of 'integration'.

'An Integral Reality': Lon Fuller's Jurisprudence

Before studying law, Fuller studied economics, which is concerned with choosing under conditions of scarcity. As implied in his *Law in Quest of Itself*, economics is of relevance to the legal philosopher:

> Though there are no doubt many permissible ways of defining the function of legal philosophy, I think the most useful is that which conceives of it as attempting to give a profitable and satisfying direction to the application of human energies in the law. Viewed in this light, the task of the legal philosopher is to decide how he and his fellow lawyers may best spend their professional lives.
>
> (Fuller 1966/1999: 2)

The scarcity that mattered to Fuller was 'human energies'. In this regard, he concerned himself with basic questions of human existence. How might he define 'profitable and satisfying'? Who might he become in doing so?

Many legal philosophers have spent a great deal of time asking questions about the nature of 'the law *that is*' and its relationship with '*a good law*' (10). In response to such questions, Fuller exercised his analogical imagination*:

> Common sense tells me that there is a clear distinction between a thing's being a steam engine and its being a good steam engine. Yet if I have a dubious assemblage of wheels, gears, and pistons before me and I ask, 'Is this a steam engine?' it is clear that this inquiry overlaps mightily with

> the question: 'Is this a good steam engine?' In the field of purposive human activity, which includes both steam engines and the law, value and being are not two different things, but two aspects of an integral reality. (11)

What at first may seem like a 'clear distinction' may soon seem murky with a suggestive line of questioning*. Fuller's word 'activity'* is an important term for connecting what might seem unconnected, for offering 'an integral reality'.[1]

Fuller presents various images of law in his classic work of imaginative legal literature, 'The Case of the Speluncean Explorers'. Five cave explorers are trapped after a landslide. With the certainty of death by starvation coming before rescuers, one of the explorers is killed and eaten, and the survivors are convicted of violating a law making it a crime, to be punished with death, to 'willfully take the life of another' (1949: 618). There is an appeal in the Supreme Court of Newgarth. The five Justices clash. Justice Tatting, who claims that he is 'usually able to dissociate the emotional and the intellectual' (626), becomes swamped:

> The more I examine this case and think about it, the more deeply I become involved. My mind becomes entangled in the meshes of the very nets I throw out for my own rescue. I find that almost every consideration that bears on the decision of the case is counterbalanced by an opposing consideration leading in the opposite direction. My brother Foster has not furnished to me, nor can I discover for myself, any formula capable of resolving the equivocations that beset me on all sides.
>
> I have given this case the best thought of which I am capable. . . . Since I have been wholly unable to resolve the doubts that beset me about the law of this case, . . . I declare my withdrawal from the decision of this case. (631)

Tatting would have done well to jettison the intellectual/emotional split and go on to think and talk like a whole person, who does not need the security of a 'formula' to generate a univocal right answer and who is willing and able to take on an authentic existence. With the remaining four Justices equally divided on the status of the conviction, Fuller's disorientated reader may feel compelled to compose a judgment* worthy of the name.[2]

White's *Justice as Translation* can help equip Fuller's reader to make such a judgment. Here White seeks to identify possibilities in the judicial opinion that can serve as a ground for criticism. He places the character* strength of 'openness', which connects to the topic of equality*, high among the 'virtues' of a judicial opinion. Consider this:

> A common view of the judicial opinion is that it is a kind of brief, a mobilization of all the arguments that can colorably be made on behalf

> of the result chosen, with somewhat less superficial acknowledgment of what can be said on the other side than one finds in a lawyer's brief. But it might be thought that the task of the judge in writing an opinion is to expose to the reader the grounds upon which her judgment actually rests, with as full and fair a statement of her doubts and uncertainties as she can manage. Such an opinion would establish a relation of fundamental equality with the reader, who might follow the whole argument, consider himself enlightened by it, but come to the opposite conclusion. I think no Justice has consistently written out of such an understanding; Harlan comes closest, but one can see instances of such authenticity of mind in the work of others as well, including Holmes, Jackson, Black, and Douglas.
>
> This kind of openness, if it could be achieved, would not only establish an admirable relation with the reader, it would enact an important intellectual virtue, perhaps the central virtue for the lawyer, namely, the suspension of judgment. If the lawyer knows anything at all, he knows that when he has heard one party's story he has heard only half the case; that when he feels a reaction or response leading him one way, it is likely to be matched by one tugging in the opposite direction as well; and that the art of law is not that of linear reasoning to a secure conclusion, but an art, fundamentally literary and rhetorical in kind, of comprehension and integration: the art of creating a text—a mind and a community—which can comprise two things at once, and two things pulling in different directions. In speaking for one side as a lawyer, or for one result as a judge, that is, the legal mind should recognize (implicitly in the lawyer's case, explicitly in the judge's) what can be said for the other, thus by an art of integration creating a world in which differences can coexist.
>
> (White 1990: 224–5)

That passage brings to mind the Joint Opinion in *Planned Parenthood v. Casey* (*Judgment), in which the Justices speak as people confronting a difficult issue (on which reasonable people, including judges, can expect to have 'differences') within an evolving tradition. What White calls 'authenticity' is the expression of a person speaking in good faith and meaning what she says; in the legal context she is taking responsibility for reconstituting a complex web of authorities, none of which can neatly (in a 'linear' movement*) dispose of the issue at hand. This responsibility, from which Tatting fled, involves the judge not just simply finding the law (as if it is an object that is 'out there') but also creatively *making* it. Out of this flows a polyphonic 'judgment'*, one that enriches the life of the ancient principle of justice, 'hear the other side'.

Modern Constitutional Diversity: James Tully's *Strange Multiplicity*

'Can a modern constitution recognise and accommodate cultural diversity?' That is the question with which Tully opens *Strange Multiplicity* (1995: 1).

In asking it, he is resisting any suggestion that 'culture is irrelevant, capable of being transcended, or uniform' (63). In responding to it, he offers 'a play of the imagination' (201), a phrase familiar to a reader of *The Legal Imagination* (*Play). Like White's course book (and his other books), *Strange Multiplicity* brings together fragments from diverse texts, including Sophocles *Antigone*, Hale's *A History of English Law*, The Québec Act of 1774, the *Federalist Papers*, and Wittgenstein's *Philosophical Investigations*. This collection, which Tully weaves together with an engagement with Bill Reid's sculpture *The Spirit of Haida Gwaii*, makes up a 'strange multiplicity', about which the book speaks. The sculpture, a picture of which is at the front of Tully's book, is a canoe with a crew of 13. The travellers are from Haida mythology:

> *Xuuwaji*, the bear mother, who is part human, and bear father sit facing each other at the bow with their two cubs between them. *Ttsaang*, the beaver, is paddling menacingly amidships, *qqaaxhadajaat*, the mysterious, intercultural dogfish woman, paddles just behind him and *Qaganjaat*, the shy but beautiful mouse woman is tucked in the stern. *Ghuuts*, the ferociously playful wolf, sinks his fangs in the eagle's wing and *ghuut*, the eagle, seems to be attacking the bear's paw in retaliation. *Hlkkyaan qqusttaan*, the frog, who symbolizes the ability to cross boundaries (*xhaaidla*) between worlds, is, appropriately enough, partly in and out of the boat. . . . *Xuuya*, the legendary raven – the master of tricks, transformations and multiple identities – steers the canoe as her or his whim dictates. Finally, in the centre of this motley crew, holding the speaker's staff in his right hand, stands *Kilstlaai*, the chief or exemplar, whose identity, due to his kinship to the raven (often called *Nangkilstlas*, the One who gives orders), is uncertain. Bill Reid asks of the chief, 'Who is he? That's the big question.' So the chief has come to be called 'Who is he?' or 'Who is he going to be?'
>
> (17–18)

For Tully, the sculpture, with its 'motley crew', is a fitting 'symbol of the spirit of a post-imperial age of cultural diversity' (17), an age that resists the claim that '[d]iversity leads to disunity' (196). As for 'the big question', Tully invites his reader to ask a similar one in the context of contemporary constitutionalism. Let us ask: Who are we? Alternatively: Who are we going to be?

Let us connect the 'motley crew' with what is familiar to us. We might imagine the frog as a lawyer, who has an 'ability to cross boundaries . . . between worlds'. In particular, to use White's words, 'in her conversations with her client', the lawyer has to move between 'the language of the law' and 'the ordinary language of the citizen' (White 1990: 261–2). As such, the lawyer is in a basic sense a translator, who 'lives in the space between two languages' (260). Is not the life of the lawyer constantly 'partially in and out of the [law] boat'? Or perhaps the lawyer resembles the raven? What about the judge? The Supreme Court? Who is the Court going to be?

Connecting the crew that way, however, may be an obstacle to an equitable reading*. After an initial introduction to the sculpture, Tully writes:

> Approaching *The spirit of Haida Gwaii* in the right spirit does not consist in recognising it as something already familiar to us and in terms drawn from our own traditions and forms of thought. This imperial attitude is to be abjured. Rather, recognition involves acknowledging it in its own terms and traditions, as it wants to be and as it speaks to us. No matter from which direction you approach the canoe, the crew members manifestly seem to say that, after centuries of suppression, they are here to stay, in their own cultural forms and ways. Hence, if there is to be a post-imperial dialogue on the just constitution of culturally diverse societies, the dialogue must be one in which the participants are recognized and speak in their own languages and customary ways. . . . This world reversal, from a habitual imperial stance, where one's own customary forms of reflection set the terms of the discussion, to a genuinely intercultural popular sovereignty, where each listens to the voices of the others in their own terms, is the most important and difficult first step in contemporary constitutionalism.
>
> (23–4)

The primary sense of justice*, Tully suggests, is hearing. Might our 'customary forms of reflection' be an obstacle to hearing Tully's voices (*Listening; Voice)? If so, how can we distance ourselves from them? Tully shares with others an image of art as a medium for estranging the 'familiar' (201–6). In this potentially productive alienation*, there is also a familiarizing of the strange. This image of art is at work here in the present book. We can imagine ourselves reading Tully as part of our attunement* to White's work – not 'recognising it as something already familiar to us and in terms drawn from our own traditions and forms of thought'. We might hope that in reading Tully's unusual text we will have a transforming presence for justly placing and reimagining the 'strange multiplicity' of White's work.

White's efforts to estrange the familiar and to familiarize the strange are carried out through the familiar activity of 'conversation'* (or 'dialogue'). The same can be said of Tully. As part of Tully's conversational turn, he says this about *The Spirit of Haida Gwaii* as 'a constitutional dialogue, or multilogue, of mutual recognition':

> The passengers are squabbling and vying for recognition and position each in their culturally distinct way. . . . The narratives of the thirteen *voyageurs* tell of how their identities have been shaped and formed through millennia of overlapping interaction together. They exist as they are, in all their distinctiveness, not in spite of, but in virtue of, their interdependency over time and history. These aspects are embodied in

> the endless ways in which they overlap and crisscross without losing their identities in their astonishing arrangement in the canoe.
>
> (24–5)

Here we have imagery that strongly resembles White's use of the word 'integration' in *Justice as Translation*: 'a putting together' of 'elements' that when 'combined do not lose their identities but retain them, often in clarified form; yet each comes to mean something different as well, when it is seen in relation to the other' (1990: 4). We might hope that, in reading Tully, we come to a new image of White's work, especially his 'law and literature'. White's aim here is 'not to "connect fields" . . . but to try to transform our sense' of two similar *and* different activities (17). The activity of attunement to White involves doing a version of what he does: putting together elements, such as economics and theology, to try to transform our sense of each.

Let Tully continue to talk about *The Spirit of Haida Gwaii* as it concerns the multidimensional activity of transforming constitutions:

> The questioning, contestation and renegotiation of their cultural identities seems plain for all to see. . . . *Xuuya*, the raven steering the canoe, . . . is forever changing his or her identity and so illustrating that things are not always as they appear – that our habitual forms of recognition are often stultifying forms of misrecognition which need to be upset and reversed from time to time. . . .
>
> Now the ability to change perspectives – to see and understand aspectivally – is acquired through participation in the intercultural dialogue itself. By listening to the different stories others tell, and giving their own in the exchange, the participants come to see their common and interwoven histories together from a multiplicity of paths. Nurturing a reflective awareness of the diversity of cultural perspectives is a major function of Aboriginal storytelling at public festivals and constitutional negotiations. *The spirit of Haida Gwaii* is designed to awaken and stimulate this dialogical capacity for diversity awareness. As you walk around the canoe you soon realize that it is impossible to take it in from one comprehensive viewpoint. It defies this form of representation. Rather, you are drawn to see it from the perspective of one passenger after another, and their complicated interrelations guide you to see the whole now under one aspect, now under another.
>
> *The spirit of Haida Gwaii* also depicts in a striking manner a specific concept of equality as equity. All members are equally recognised and accommodated, as far as possible, in terms of their own cultural identity. The members make up an association more akin to the irregular arrangement of an ancient, custom-based constitution than to a modern, uniform constitutional association. The overall cultural diversity is a thing of justice and beauty, analogous to ecological diversity . . . . However, . . . it offends against a powerful norm of uniformity in modern constitutionalism

> and provides one of the major objections to the politics of cultural recognition.
>
> How do the citizens tell if the constitutional arrangement they have reached at this point in their journey is equitable and just? There is no transcendental standard beyond the discussion in the canoe from which it can be measured. This Platonic viewpoint is . . . unavailable. The answer would seem to be that they practise the spirit they embody.
>
> (25–7)

By 'listening'* to Tully's story, and giving our own story in exchange, we can come to make connections from a 'multiplicity of paths' – as we are doing here in this alphabetical lexicon. Both White's and Tully's storytelling seeks to cultivate a 'reflective awareness of the diversity of cultural perspectives' – that is, to help us pay attention to different spheres of attention*. As you pick up and open, for example, *The Legal Imagination*, you soon realize that it is impossible to take it in from one comprehensive viewpoint (our ways of imagining the world are transformed as we read it). The same can be said for *Strange Multiplicity*. Both books have much to suggest about the relation between style and substance, for both 'practise the spirit they embody'. We may hope that in connecting White and Tully any 'habitual forms of recognition' within us that give rise to 'stultifying forms of misrecognition' have been 'upset and reversed'.

Judgment

When We Think About New Cases: Linda Ross Meyer
'The Source of This Court's Authority': *Planned Parenthood v. Casey*

At the beginning of *The Human Condition*, Hannah Arendt identifies her 'very simple' aim as 'to think what we are doing' (1958: 1). There is a sense in which White's work is written out of the same aim. Like Arendt, he seeks to become more conscious of our acts of judgment. In *When Words Lose Their Meaning*, White inquires into 'ways in which we can criticize and judge the cultures and texts we read' (1984: 13). He presents his point of departure as follows:

> [M]any of the judgments invited in this book are akin to the judgments one regularly passes on literary or musical or other artistic works or to judgments traditionally made in legal or historical criticism. . . . All these are judgments, after all, about what is better and worse in civilization; they are not scientific and cannot be reduced to rules or criteria, yet they make up an immensely important part of our shared life. We make such judgments all the time, sometimes tentatively, sometimes with confidence. We share and elaborate these judgments with others and, in the process, often complicate or change them. We recognize that some of our judgments are better than others and that some of our friends are better judges than others. We have a sense of fallibility and an eagerness to improve. In this sense we are all critics of civilization already and we are engaged in teaching each other how to be critics; our aim here is to learn more about something we already do.
>
> (14)

What 'judgments' might we make about that passage? Does his line of thought sound sensible? For White, in our lives we are continuously making 'judgments' (including in the choice of language*), and we will do well to attend to this activity* with the hope of becoming better judges. That the judgments he is concerned with are not 'scientific' does not make them unworthy of serious consideration. We may find that consideration in this direction may lead to better 'science', if by that word we mean reflective inquiry.

When We Think About New Cases: Linda Ross Meyer

During an evening in 1928, two people went to a café in Glasgow, Scotland. One of them bought a bottle of ginger beer for the other to drink. The bottle was dark, which concealed a decomposing snail. The snail came out after one glass of the ginger beer had been consumed. The famous case *Donoghue v. Stevenson* began. Before the courts, the consumer, May Donoghue, alleged shock and gastroenteritis. In the House of Lords, Lord Atkin put the issue as follows: 'Whether, as a matter of law in the circumstances alleged, the defender owed any duty to the pursuer to take care' (*Donoghue*, 579). Lord Atkin concluded that there was a duty:

> My Lords, if your Lordships accept the view that this pleading discloses a relevant cause of action you will be affirming the proposition that by Scots and English law alike a manufacturer of products, which he sells in such a form as to show that he intends them to reach the ultimate consumer in the form in which they left him with no reasonable possibility of intermediate examination, and with the knowledge that the absence of reasonable care in the preparation or putting up of the products will result in an injury to the consumer's life or property, owes a duty to the consumer to take that reasonable care.
>
> (599)

That passage is important for talking about the case's *ratio decidendi* (or 'holding'), which, according to one textbook, is 'the principle of law arising from the case which is applicable to subsequent cases and states the law for all future parties to similar disputes' (Scragg 2005: 20). Determining the *ratio* is not a simple process, for our sense of what might count as 'similar' may well vary. This will become apparent when we think about new cases. Does *Donoghue* apply when, say, a manufacturer of underwear leaves bisulphate of soda in them, causing dermatitis? (This question emerged several years later in *Grant v. Australian Knitting Mill.*) We confront this question: 'is a hidden chemical in clothing analogous to a decomposing snail in a bottle?' (Scragg 2005: 18). In short, when a new case arises, we have to deal with 'analogical relevance' (23), and in so dealing we can interpret an earlier case in a new light. 'It is for a subsequent court to determine what the *ratio decidendi* of a prior decision is' (21).

'What are the *relevant* considerations?' That is a question that Linda Meyer, in *The Justice of Mercy*, asks when talking about legal reasoning as it concerns the topic of justice* (2010: 31). Let her outline what is involved:

> Deciding which . . . factors are 'relevant' and matter and which are 'not relevant' and do not matter is a complex judgment of pattern finding, more perception than deduction. . . . [T]he common law reaches back into the tradition for guidance and, in trying to find a pattern to fit the

> new case, . . . changes how we articulate the 'holding' of the old case as well as the one we are currently deciding. The tradition both guides and morphs at the same time. The newly articulated holding, of course, is itself subject to a new understanding when we confront yet another case and reflect on whether a previously unexamined element of an old case is 'relevant' or not in the new situation.
>
> (31)

> Common-law reasoning *is* the attempt to know how to respond to the unique case from where we stand in our own imperfectly applicable past experience. But what we often forget is that the call of the particular infuses the decision regarding whether or not the past is relevant or irrelevant and, either way, changes our experience (our past law, rule or practice) in the encounter. Law cannot contain others in logical boxes, because the others shift the boundaries of the boxes in the course of law's 'application.' Because common-law reasoning strives to remember the cases narratively . . . and not just the 'rules' of the case, injustice can poke out of the past as a chafing lack of fit that may be retrofitted long after the case is 'past.' We often repudiate old decisions in the course of making new ones, because they no longer 'fit' the pattern we see. We repudiate state-mandated prayer, Japanese internment, slavery, . . . even as we base decisions today on our sullied past experience. . . . Justice is the 'fittingness' of what we do . . . .
>
> (42–44)

In the echo of our reading of Brecht (*Alienation), we might hear Meyer asking her fellow lawyers this question: Have you given much thought to the case method* of law? She among lawyers who are articulate when explaining legal 'know how'. Key components of legal reasoning are 'experience'* and 'understanding'*. Such reasoning has a place for the 'new', the 'other', the 'particular'. In reasoning with analogy in a particular case, we move from what is familiar to what is unfamiliar. The movement* is not linear but cyclical or spiralling, placing a case in a shifting 'pattern' – 'tradition both guides and morphs at the same time'. Here we can talk about acts of 'justice' in terms of the 'fittingness' of a 'judgment'.

Meyer is in tune with claims from various disciplines that analogical reasoning is integral to human thought. When talking about the case method, she exercises her own analogical imagination:

> It is no mystery that the common-law case-by-case reasoning works this way when we reflect that language itself works this way, giving voice to the new by reference to the old and simultaneously changing the connotation of the 'old' words, as is the case with the terms *cell phone*, *facsimile*, *Internet*, *Web site*, *surfing*, *skyping*, *texting*, and so on. . . . Heidegger's insight is that the basis of human thought is not deductive reasoning but experience,

> connectedness, in-touchness, ability to . . . 'see' things *as* like and unlike, connected with each other in some relation of relevance or irrelevance from the past into a future.
>
> (32–3)

> In the comfortableness of judgments of the . . . fitting, we tend to forget that our past traditions are given, because, as Heidegger might put it, when we use our past cultural 'case law' as 'tools' of judgment, their Being as a giving retreats from view. . . . We simply do our judging without thinking about how we are doing it, moving from 'No late papers' to 'No late papers except in cases of sudden serious illness' or from 'innkeeper' to 'landlord' without even noticing that we made a judgment of 'fit.'
>
> But when an individual case threatens to overturn our comfortable sense of fit, we are struck afresh by our responsibility for the other. We experience this judgment often as one of 'compassion' because of its emotional attunement to the singular. It is, as yet, inarticulate, incapable of being articulated in the traditions or case law we have at our fingertips. Before it can come to language, however, it comes to presence as a body slam of emotion, as an overwhelming need to act against established law.
>
> (46)

A Meyer reader who imagines that the common-law case-by-case reasoning lacks coherence and integrity may 'experience' that passage as 'a body slam of emotion'. 'How' might he go on to judge Meyer? Will he be just or unjust? We might say that justice begins in a certain sort of attention*, namely the 'noticing of a judgment' with regard to 'fit'.

How might we 'fit' Meyer into this book? Might she be of help to us in attuning to the activity of 'attunement'*? Let us now return to our efforts to hear White. These are the opening words in the Preface to *The Legal Imagination*:

> The task of telling the reader what sort of book he has in his hand is unusually difficult in this case, for this book does not fit easily into any existing category. Since it might be said to have as its purpose the definition of a new subject, or at least a new way of addressing one, it cannot be classified by identifying its subject matter in traditional terms, and any introductory remarks can be at best only suggestive.
>
> (White 1973: xix)

A Meyer reader will know that much is at stake in the task of 'fit'-tingly placing White's book. To do justice to it, we might do well to begin reasoning from book to book. Shall we compare *The Legal Imagination* to . . . ? What about *The Justice of Mercy*? We might hope that in the process of determining 'like' and 'unlike', White's unfamiliar book becomes familiar.

Like *The Justice of Mercy*, *The Legal Imagination* resists rule-centred law. Much legal discourse concerning rules assumes the sufficiency of its own language, with language imagined as a mere tool for pointing to 'things'. White resists such imagery. In talking about the 'intellectual structure of the legal rule', he claims that '[t]here is a sense in which the very structure or syntax of the rule – the way it works – makes it a radically fictional expression' (229). He identifies several 'characteristics of the statutory rule that . . . contribute most to this effect', including 'the simple process of naming'. On this process, he says, using Wittgenstein's key term 'language game' (*Activity):

> Reduced to its simplest terms, the rule can be said to operate this way: a label is applied to experience, and a consequence determined by the label is imposed. The rule seems to reduce all experience to a single descriptive term: one is or is not 'married' or 'domiciled in Nevada' or 'inducted,' and from this everything flows. We lawyers know that a great deal of thought and argument of a most interesting kind lies behind the statement of the issue and application of the label, but no hint of that appears in the rule itself. Rules such as 'an arrest is valid where based on probable cause' . . . seem to call for nothing more than a simple glance at reality to see if the name fits or not. We know – but are not told – how false that is. . . . The phenomenon can perhaps best be stated by saying that the rule appears to be a language of description, one that works by a simple process of comparison, but it is in truth a language of judgment, working in ways that find no expression in the rule itself. . . . [O]ne might wish to trace this misleading usage to some congenital dishonesty or stupidity on the part of lawyers, but I think it is better regarded as one manifestation of a common misunderstanding of how language works: the view that all language always operates by naming, that what words do is stand for things or ideas in the world. Thus when I say, 'Put the milk on the table,' it might be said that I engage in the process of naming, and indeed naming is part of what I do. But you know very well that the notion of naming does not exhaust what can be done with language; it is only one language game out of many. . . . The apparent syntax of the legal rule is a syntax of simple 'naming,' but this appearance is seriously misleading because it hides the truth that the use of the rule requires a process of judgment – of argument and thought – of a most difficult kind. There are those, for example, who speak as if they believe that what the Constitution requires is perfectly plain, and that deciding constitutional cases is simply a matter of looking and seeing; but such a view – whatever the merits of the proposed results in particular cases – can only debase the process by which constitutional decisions are made and explained.
>
> (229–31)

What is White suggesting when he says, 'you know very well that the notion of naming does not exhaust what can be done with language'? In what sense do you and I 'know'? After reading Meyer, we might say this: we can fail to bring to life what we know, our 'knowing-how', for our 'tools' of 'judgment' can 'retreat from view'. Those who speak as if 'what the Constitution requires is perfectly plain . . .' are failing in this way. They are, for the moment at least, living by simplistic visual metaphors for imagining language, thought, and communication – metaphors frequently not recognized as such (*Metaphor). (Working with legal and other rules requires much 'more than a simple glance at reality to see if the name fits or not', for 'naming' contributes to the 'constitution' of a person's imagined 'reality', which can be contested in court.) In distinguishing 'a language of description' from 'a language of judgment' (or of 'argument'), White can be read as making a contribution to legal literacy with the hope of enriching legal discourse, centring on judgment worthy of the name.

'The Source of This Court's Authority': *Planned Parenthood v. Casey*

White's reading, in *Acts of Hope*, of the United States Supreme Court case *Planned Parenthood v. Casey* (1992) may be of value to those who think that 'there may simply be no way to "integrate" the dazzlingly different perspectives of the "pro-choice" and "pro-life" adversaries in the abortion debate' (Levinson 1991: 1865). White's reading, which readily connects to the key word integration*, may also be of value to a reader of *The Legal Imagination* who seeks 'a legal passage' in which 'the contemplator becomes the contemplated' (1973: 100) – in which, that is, there is a dramatic shift in attention*.

Casey concerns a woman's constitutional 'liberty' to choose to terminate a pregnancy. The authority of the well-known case *Roe v. Wade* (1973) is at issue, and this had some considerable significance given that the Court now had four justices who had been nominated by Presidents Reagan and Bush, both of whom had sought to appoint justices who would overrule the case. The Court explicitly addresses the doctrine of *stare decisis* ('the decision stands'), providing a base for one of the most extraordinary judicial opinions in the history of American constitutional law. This is the Joint Opinion of Justices Kennedy, O'Connor, and Souter, all of whom were nominated by either Reagan or Bush. The Justices make an authentic judgment, at least in the sense that they resist any suggestion that no other decision was possible. They stress '[t]he inescapable fact . . . that adjudication of substantive due process claims may call upon the Court in interpreting the Constitution to exercise that same capacity which by tradition courts have always exercised: reasoned judgment. Its boundaries are not susceptible of expression as a simple rule' (*Planned Parenthood* 1992: 849). In resisting overruling *Roe*, the Justices touch on the issue of what it means to believe in the rule of law:

> Our analysis would not be complete . . . without explaining why overruling Roe's central holding would . . . seriously weaken the Court's capacity to exercise the judicial power and to function as the Supreme Court

> of a Nation dedicated to the rule of law. To understand why this would be so it is necessary to understand the source of this Court's authority, the conditions necessary for its preservation, and its relationship to the country's understanding of itself as a constitutional Republic.
>
> (865)

With these words, the Justices invite their readers to ask some basic 'authority' questions that are beyond questions relating to the merits of the case. The basic questions may facilitate a productive alienation* from the slogans that citizens may live by, an alienation that can promote a move from dead speech to living speech.

With an interest in contributing to talk about 'authority', White takes up the Justices' invitation. Here is one fragment:

> In a final section of its opinion, before reaching the particular provisions of the Pennsylvania statute before it, the Court expands on what it thinks is at stake in its decision: the legitimacy of the Court itself, and its capacity to perform its essential and unique role in our democracy. To discharge its responsibilities and maintain its position the Court must seek to decide cases on the ground of principle, or what it earlier called 'reasoned judgment,' and it must be seen to do so. 'The Court must take care to speak and act in ways that allow people to accept its decision on the terms the Court claims for them, as grounded truly in principle, not as compromises with social and political pressures having, as such, no bearing on the principled choices that the Court is obliged to make.' Essential to this goal is respect for the decisions of the past; frequent overruling of its own decisions would be a statement by the Court itself that they were not entitled to respect.
>
> Where, as here, the Court decides a matter intensely divisive of our polity, it is especially important to respect the choices that have been made in the past. 'Only the most convincing justifications' could demonstrate that an overruling in such a case was 'anything but a surrender to political pressure.' Once the decision is made, it is essential to live with it unless it is plainly wrong. This is the point where the Court comes closest to acknowledging the existence of the enormous forces at work in our country on this subject, referred to above, making it a focus of opposition that has some of the characteristics of a civil war itself. The extraordinary character of the issue makes principled judgment, and adherence to prior authority, all the more important. To reverse oneself under pressure will give the impression, perhaps correctly, that the Court is nothing but another vehicle for political life—and that, though they do not say so, the appointment of new justices can properly rest on purely political and result-orientated judgments rather than qualities of mind and character traditionally thought essential to the judicial role.
>
> (White 1994a: 176–7)

White here works hard to distinguish what we call 'the legal' from 'the political'. Of course 'the legal' has a 'political' element in the sense that judges are not neutral machines working with fixed rules, but there are, as White suggests, different kinds of 'politics' that can and should be judged. He is resisting those who would use the word 'politics' to stop what he considers to be a vitally important conversation* (including talking about how we 'speak and act'), one that IS 'the law' and that can and should distinguish and judge different kinds of politics.

At the beginning of the passage just quoted, White uses the words 'perform' and 'role' for talking about the Court. This brings to mind the image of courts as theatre (*Alienation). Let White continue with his reading of the *Casey* 'drama':

> There follows now an extraordinary moment in the history of American law. The Court turns its mind to the way citizens respond to its decisions, especially those they disagree with. Of course it is easy to support the Court when it comes out your way, and of course many people who disagree respond with simple and continuing opposition or resistance. It is not with either of these groups that the Court concerns itself but with those who disagree with the result, yet 'struggle to accept it, because they accept the rule of law.' To them the Court must keep its promise; for if it does not, but reverses itself too easily, in the end 'a price [will] be paid for nothing.' The Court does not explicate this point further, but what they mean, I think, is this: they are imagining the moral drama that occurs when a person is opposed to a law yet respects it, a drama in ordinary life that is in fact the parallel of the one they are experiencing as judges. This drama is seen as a painful but also a good thing, good especially for the character of the person in question and for any community of such people. The reason it is good is that only at such moments is the commitment to the rule of law a meaningful one: when you agree with the law, there is no problem; when you resist and oppose, you are refusing to accord the law respect. Only when you disagree on an important matter are you given the opportunity to learn what respect for the law means and to engage in the moral practice of respecting it. Such a moment is a stage in the development of an essential ingredient of civic character; it is part of an education, not purely practical or intellectual or a matter of training but an education of the whole self. In this it would be recognizable by Plato and Aristotle, both of whom saw education as the development of the character through testing and the development of habit. A person who has been through the struggle the Court describes will know, as no one else really can, the importance of the rule of law itself; and having respected it against his own inclination, he will be in a position to insist that others respect it against theirs.
>
> (177–8)

Every 'role' in a 'drama' connects to other roles. The judicial role cannot exist without 'citizens', who cannot escape judging the judges. How are they to do so? What kind of 'character'* do they create? The image of 'a painful but . . . good' process of 'struggle' brings to mind the cliché 'No pain, no gain'. For one who might find it difficult to get beyond the sense that abortion is murder (I am not claiming that abortion is not murder), hearing the slogan may make the difficulty even greater. However, we can find value in the common. 'No pain, no gain' brings to mind *activity*. Both the Court and White are at pains to direct attention to 'the law' (in the phrase 'the rule of law') not as an object but as an activity*. This activity is an educational one. Their image of education is against the mechanical and the routine.

'What is *really* meant by "commitment to the rule of law"?', some might now ask. After further comment on those who contributed to the Joint Opinion, White says: 'The rule of law they describe is enacted in the process in which they engage both themselves and their reader; it is in this mode of thought and life, not on mere statements or commands, that they imagine the law's authority' (181–2). The rule of law, that is, is in a process of becoming through our hope-full efforts to 'imagine' and re-imagine it. This may be disturbing to a person who imagines the imagination* to be a faculty that is at odds with rational thought. White invites such a person to re-imagine the imagination.

White's friend and colleague Milner Ball, whom we met above (*Alienation), found himself unable to join him in expressing approval for the Court's opinion in *Casey*. In a 'dialogue' between the two, published in the *Yale Journal of Law & the Humanities* (Ball and White 1996), White offered a resource with which they might understand why they disagreed:

> I would like to begin with a question: Can you imagine an opinion coming out with the result that *Casey* reached that you would admire and respect? If not, I think you are saying that abortion is an issue on which there is for you only one tolerable answer. So read, your question is an eloquent and passionate defense of the woman's right to choose whether or not to terminate the existence of a fetus within her.
>
> The problem the law faces is that there are other people who maintain the opposite position with equal passion and eloquence, namely that abortion is the murder of an unborn child and that it should never, or almost never, be permitted. I think we cannot expect the two sides to agree on what they regard as the merits of the case. What the law can hope to do is offer them something else on which they can agree, namely that decisions made by certain lawmakers, under certain conditions should be granted respect and obedience, even if one disagrees with the choice they have made.
>
> (487)

We will do well to pursue a line of questioning* about our questioning. This could include: What questions are we asking? What questions should we ask? Those two questions might help us to identify the specific activity* in which we are engaged, such as advocating for one 'side' rather than judging 'the two sides'. If the issue of '[w]hat the law can hope to do' is addressed first, then we may more readily come to understand why we disagree.

Before a case is decided, it may be easy to get 'the two sides to agree' that 'under certain conditions' a decision by a Court 'should be granted respect and obedience'. Difficulties may come afterwards: in getting the party for whom the Court did not give the desired result to remember and recommit to the agreement. Hopes are not static entities to which we can point but, rather, evolving processes that shift with our evolving expectations and experiences.

Justice

'The Sole Arbiter of Its Own Justice': *Wi Parata v. Bishop of Wellington*
'The Just Man Justices': Gerard Manley Hopkins
'When the Laws Themselves Become Immoral': Bram Fischer
'A Coalescence between Law and Justice': Ismail Mahomed

In Plato's *Crito*, Crito tries to persuade Socrates to escape from prison in order to avoid his death sentence. In response, Socrates imagines the arguments that the Laws of Athens would make against him escaping. The arguments include the following:

> [I]f you go to one of the neighbouring states . . . , [w]hat subjects will you discuss, Socrates? The same as here, when you said that goodness and justice, institutions and laws, are the most precious possessions of mankind? Do you not think that Socrates and everything about him will appear in a disreputable light? . . . If you leave . . . , returning injustice for injustice and injury for injury, breaking your agreements and covenants with us, . . . then you will have to face our anger while you live.
>
> (Plato *c.*360 BCE/1993: 90–91)

These words have weight for Socrates. He rejects the plan to escape, and he goes on to prepare for death.

In *Acts of Hope*, White reads the *Crito*, attending closely to Socrates' response to Crito. After discussing the decision by Socrates to obey the Laws, White writes:

> [T]his end, unlike escape, does not require Socrates to give up the major purposes of his life. Indeed, it is a way of fulfilling a major part of that purpose, which is to establish . . . the legitimacy of discourse about the nature of the just community. . . . If he escaped to Megara or Thessaly, he could pursue questions of justice, if at all, merely as a theoretical matter, without the engagement with the actual that can make the pursuit real. For in his life Socrates has constituted Athens as an idealized dialogic partner, a moral actor for whom justice can be as central a concern as it is for an individual. It is this fictive creation partly of his own making that he would rather die than deny; especially when the death, like this one, would do so much to make this fiction real.
>
> (White 1994a: 33–4)

That passage can help us attend to the reality that in many important circumstances the line between imagination* and reality is an imagined one. An important question is this: What 'fictive creation' is worth pursuing? That question overlaps this 'character'*-related question: Who are we becoming in doing so? The topic of 'justice' overlaps that question, for justice is concerned with relations between characters.

'The Sole Arbiter of Its Own Justice': *Wi Parata v. Bishop of Wellington*

In 1848, eight years after entering into the Treaty of Waitangi (remarks on which reside above in the section 'The Longer Conversation' – *Conversation), the tribe Ngati Toa gifted land to the Anglican Bishop of Wellington for the building of a school. Several years later, Governor Grey issued a grant that included the gifted land. The school, however, did not get built. Wi Parata eventually challenged the grant, basing a claim on the Treaty. The challenge came before the Supreme Court of New Zealand. If Parata was hoping to start a productive conversation about the meaning of the Treaty, the Court dashed those hopes. The Court deemed the Treaty to be 'a simple nullity':

> On the foundation of this colony, the aborigines were found without any kind of civil government, or any settled system of law. There is no doubt that during a series of years the British Government desired and endeavoured to recognise the independent nationality of New Zealand. But the thing neither existed nor at the time could be established. The Maori tribes were incapable of performing the duties, and therefore assuming the rights, of a civilised community. . . . [T]he Crown was compelled to assume in relation to the Maori tribes, and in relation to native land titles, these rights and duties which, *jure gentium*, vest in and devolve upon the first civilised occupier of a territory thinly peopled by barbarians without any form of law or civil government. . . .
>
> On the cession of territory by one civilised power to another, the rights of private property are invariably respected, and the old law of the country is administered . . . by the Courts of the new sovereign. . . . But in the case of primitive barbarians, the supreme executive Government must acquit itself, as best it may, of its obligation to respect native proprietary rights, and of necessity must be the sole arbiter of its own justice. Its acts in this particular cannot be examined or called in question by any tribunal, because there exist no known principles whereon a regular adjudication can be based. Here, then, is one sufficient reason why this Court must disclaim the jurisdiction which the plaintiff is seeking to assume. . . .
>
> The existence of the pact known as the 'Treaty of Waitangi' . . . is perfectly consistent with what has been stated. So far as that instrument

> purported to cede the sovereignty – a matter with which we are not directly concerned – it must be regarded as a simple nullity. No body politic existed capable of making cession of sovereignty, nor could the thing itself exist. So far as the proprietary rights of the natives are concerned, the so-called treaty merely affirms the rights and obligations which, *jure gentium*, vested in and devolved upon the Crown under the circumstances of the case.
>
> (*Wi Parata* 1877: 77–8)

Readers familiar with the historical context against which the Court spoke might sense that it is completing the wars that began in the 1860s. Having made the apparently obvious distinction between a 'civilised power' and 'primitive barbarians', the Court talks of the necessity ('must') for different treatment with regard to 'rights of private property' and 'native proprietary rights'. The Court asserts that the latter and their relation to the will of 'the supreme executive Government' cannot be a topic of 'justice'-talk, for there were 'no known principles whereon a regular adjudication can be based'. The putative non-existence of any such principles did not prevent the Court from innovating and creating them. But to do so would run counter to what the Court seems to want to do, namely, present The Law as a 'settled system' of rules.

We might do well to ask why the Court addresses the question about the existence of an 'independent nationality'. The indigene parties to the Treaty included 'the Separate and Independent Chiefs of New Zealand'. There was a significant question of the identity of the party before the Court, with complex claims possible, perhaps including talking about Ngati Toa with reference to the 'domestic dependent nation' category given to the Cherokees (this category is treated well in Perry Dane's 'Maps of Sovereignty' – *Imagination). This connects with the question of the meaning of the word 'sovereignty' as used in the Treaty. This question could lead to a volume, but the Court reduces 'sovereignty' to a 'thing', leaving no room for an activity* worthy of the name understanding*. We might do well to question whether 'what has been stated' is indeed 'perfectly consistent' with the Treaty. This will depend on our method* of reading* both the Treaty and 'what has been stated'. To draw from one of the epigraphs to this book, the Court lacked the capacity to 'feel the spectral sadness of the written word without a voice to fill it' (Ortega).

In modern Waitangi law talk, the *Wi Parata* decision is commonly thought to be problematic at the level of rules: the judges 'misunderstood' the doctrine of 'native title'.[1] While in one sense the authority of *Wi Parata* has been undermined, it remains authoritative in that it imagines law as an object, in the form of a system of rules.

The Courts have repeatedly declared that the Treaty is not part of New Zealand's domestic law until 'it has been incorporated in a statute'.[2] What are we to think about the metaphor* 'incorporated' (the root of which is 'in the body')? If we imagine 'the law' not as a body of rules but as a compositional process, then we may imagine that Waitangi law could be turned inside out in the name of justice.

An imagined critic responds with these remarks: 'Law is and ought to be objective – in order to be law. Justice is subjective.' Behind these remarks, and the objective–subjective opposition in them, is a culture that devalues the justice question – and devalues the phenomenon of culture*, a force that lends itself to productively complicating the objective–subjective opposition.[3] Starting with *The Legal Imagination*, White has invited a re-valuation:

> How odd it may seem that law school does not begin with, or perhaps consist of, a course on the subject of justice: what it is and how it can be achieved.
>
> (White 1973: 631)

After reading Brecht (*Alienation), we may imagine that law school is a good place for putting to use the 'alienation effect'. A Brecht reader might begin a line of questioning* with this question: Have you paid attention to the grammar of "justice"?

'The Just Man Justices': Gerard Manley Hopkins

In *Justice as Translation*, White invites us to '[i]magine a language that emphasized the verb instead of the noun' (1990: 272). This might prod us to language* justly.

Hopkins took verbing seriously. In 1877 or thereabouts, he wrote the poem 'As kingfishers catch fire', which contains these lines:

> Selves—goes itself; *myself* it speaks and spells,
> Crying *What I do is me: for that I came.*
>
> I say more: the just man justices;
> Keeps grace: that keeps all his goings graces;[4]

How are we to extract the meaning of those lines? 'Meaning', however, is not an object in the text; it is an experiential process, meaning *to* a self, who 'selves' whilst reading*. Concerning 'justice', how should the 'self', 'I', talk about 'justice'? A better question might be: How might we justly selve with fellow selvers?[5]

In *Justice as Translation*, White talks about how we might talk about justice. The penultimate chapter begins as follows:

> Imagine for the moment that I am speaking to you not in writing but face-to-face, and that in an effort to make a new start, I say: 'I want to talk to you next about justice and translation.'

So I want to begin. But what kind of sentence is that? It makes 'justice' and 'translation' nouns, or nomens, as if they were entities in the world that could be named—pointed out and referred to—by these words, which of course there are not. . . .

And I say 'I' and 'you' with great assurance, as though there were one 'me,' who 'wants to talk,' and one 'you,' who is expected to—to what? 'listen?' 'receive?' 'understand?' Or simply do nothing, not to be there in the discourse at all? . . . Certainly there is no suggestion in my opening sentence that you 'want' anything, that you have a will or a set of desires; and no suggestion either that each of us is actually a set of multiple selves, speaking and acting sometimes in discord, sometimes in harmony. . . .

***

In this chapter and the next I want to say: . . . that translation . . . is a model of law and justice, for these two are at their heart also ways of establishing right relations, both between one person and another and between a mind and the languages it confronts.

But what can it mean for me to try to 'say' such things? For example, will I simply trace out a mechanical analogy between two sets of practices, translation and the law, observing correspondences and differences, as if the whole world could be described in terms of interacting parts, as a kind of machine, in a language that mirrors such a reality—as if language were simply a system for naming? When I come to talk about the art of recognizing another and respecting difference, which is my true subject, will I find a language adequate to the task or will I reduce myself to clichés about 'empathy' or 'diversity'?

***

In this chapter I have been speaking as it were dialectically, saying one thing and then responding to myself in a somewhat different voice, and I shall continue to do this. In talking in this odd and double way, I am trying to direct your attention to a central expectation that we all have about a disquisition of this sort: namely, that in it I will try to 'say' something either in direct propositional form or in the kind of extended analogy that is a set of propositions in another guise. 'I will try to utter propositions that are clear: you will try to apprehend them, so that you may test their validity in your own way.'

But all that is to presuppose a view of language and of conversation I wish to resist, with which indeed my views of 'translation' and 'justice' are inconsistent. So I write and speak against the very force of the language I am using, against the occasion of my writing, against the expectations that bring us for this moment together. The question for me and for you is, then, Can I make a text that will embody or enact the view

> of language—of 'translation' and 'justice'—out of which I function and do so in a way that will be of use to you?
>
> So I want to say: Do not look for propositions here, for conceptual elaborations and extended analogies, for anything stated, but for movement, for shifts in the meanings of words. Listen to the voices: my voices and your own, as you hear yourself respond in different ways to what I say. There, in the music the voices make, whether beautiful and harmonious or raw and ugly, is where the meaning lies; it is to that music that our attention and judgment should above all be directed.
>
> (White 1990: 229–31)

Imagine for the moment that White has just stopped speaking to us face-to-face and that in an effort to continue the conversation, I say: 'Professor White/Jim, I want to do justice to your talk about justice and translation.'

So, one of my 'multiple selves' has spoken – and another self is now saying so.

What sort of sense are you and I to make of that last sentence?

Is this a parody of 'White'? Maybe it is an attempt, in a good cause: '[p]arody trains the ear as almost nothing else can do' (White 1973: 957). 'I' may lack the ability to write a parody that is funny or illuminating. It may even be impossible to make a parody of a person or style that one admires. Perhaps 'you' are like some White critics who do not admire his style and perhaps 'you' find this 'parody' funny?

Which one of 'you'?

Are you trying to get me worried about me possibly having schizophrenia?

I'm trying not to get you worried about anything but to invite you to consider establishing harmonious internal relationships, productive inner face-to-face talk.

Do 'I' really want to try to start talking in the strange way that the many persons lumped together under the name 'White' talks?

Why 'strange'? Don't we talk like that much of the time? Isn't what seems strange really quite familiar? Might this way of talking be an attempt to suggest what it might mean to 'listen' (*Listening)? Might it be a way to direct 'attention'* to 'movement'*, to 'shifts in the meanings of words'?

From where or what is our attention going to shift? Do we need to pay attention to our attention? Are we setting up an inquiry into the economics of attention?

Might this to-and-fro response to White be suggestive of what he might mean by 'the art of recognizing another'? To 're-cognize' is in a sense to 'know again'. White's 'music'-al polyphonic talk perhaps can help us to know our 'multiple selves' again and to let them speak. In letting them speak with White's multiple selves we may hope to have justly spoken, to have become just. 'The just man justices'.

'When the Laws Themselves Become Immoral': Bram Fischer

'The people of South Africa will never forget him.' So said President Mandela in the first Bram Fischer Memorial Lecture (1995/2003: 468). Fischer was part of a well-known family: his grandfather had been prime minister of the Orange River Colony and his father was judge-president of the Orange Free State. 'Although he could have become prime minister of South Africa, he became one of the bravest and staunchest friends of the freedom struggle that I have ever known' (Mandela 1994: 84). Fischer has been described as having 'an integrity which was unbending' (Mahomed 1998: 209). Adequately placing the word 'integrity' on him could be challenging, for he played the roles of lawyer and revolutionary at the same time: he supported the armed struggle by Umkhonto whilst defending its members – including Mandela – in the Rivonia Trial.

In 1964, Fischer and others were charged under the Suppression of Communism Act.[6] During the trial, he went underground. (He had been granted bail to enable him to go to London to argue an appeal before the Privy Council.) In a letter to his counsel, a letter read to the court, Fischer said:

> I wish you to inform the Court that my absence, though deliberate, is not intended in any way to be disrespectful. . . . My decision was made only because I believe that it is the duty of every true opponent of this Government to remain in this country and to oppose its monstrous policy of apartheid with every means in his power. . . . Cruel, discriminatory laws multiply each year, bitterness and hatred of the Government and its laws are growing daily. . . . Unless this whole intolerable system is changed radically and rapidly, disaster must follow. Appalling bloodshed and civil war will become inevitable . . . . To try to avoid this becomes a supreme duty, particularly for an Afrikaner, because it is largely the representatives of my fellow Afrikaners who have been responsible for the worst of these discriminatory laws. . . . If by my fight I can encourage even some people to think about, to understand and to abandon the policies they now so blindly follow, I shall not regret any punishment I may incur.
>
> I can no longer serve justice in the way I have attempted to do during the past thirty years. I can do it only in the way I have now chosen.
>
> (quoted in Clingman 1998: 355–6)

Fischer's use of the word 'regret' here brings to mind Aristotle's claim that a person experiences regret when he fails to be a friend to himself.[7] Being a friend, for Aristotle, connects to the topic of justice: 'Friendship and justice seem . . . to be exhibited in the same sphere of conduct and between the same persons' (Aristotle *c.*350 BCE/1976: Bk. 8 s. 9). 'Do'-ing 'justice' and being a friend to the nation is Fischer's principal concern. He would resist anyone who would separate law and justice. As there is now little or no law worthy of the name, he 'can no longer serve justice in the way' that he has done.[8]

Two days after Fischer went underground, the Johannesburg Bar Council moved to remove his name from the roll of advocates, on the grounds of 'dishonourable conduct'. Fischer believed that the Council was acting unjustly. He wrote this letter to his counsel, who would present it to the Supreme Court:

> I assume that the sole reason for the decision is that I deliberately absented myself from my trial and estreated my bail.
>
> The principle upon which I rely is a simple one, firmly established in South African legal tradition. Since the days of the South African war, . . . it has been recognised that political offences, committed because of a belief in the overriding moral validity of a political principle, do not in themselves justify the disbarring of a person from practicing the profession of law. Presumably this is because it is assumed that the commission of such offences has no bearing on the professional integrity of the person concerned.
>
> When an advocate does what I have done, his conduct is not determined by any disrespect for the law nor because he hopes to benefit personally by any 'offence' he may commit. On the contrary, it requires an act of will to overcome his deeply rooted respect of legality, and he takes the step only when he feels that, whatever the consequences to himself, his political conscience no longer permits him to do otherwise. He does it not because of a desire to be immoral, but because to act otherwise would, for him, be immoral.
>
> Though there have always been persons who have been prepared, by way of protest, to accept such punishment in respect of political crimes as might be imposed by an independent Judiciary, this is not what we face in South Africa today. However independent and fair the Bench in my case, I was facing, if convicted, an 'indeterminate' sentence which would be imposed at the sole and unfettered discretion of the Minister of Justice. We have already seen how this type of sentence has been imposed upon Mr. Sobukwe and we have already seen how European public opinion in this country, to its lasting disgrace, has failed to register any protest against this arbitrary, indefinite incarceration and has complacently accepted this total abolition of the rule of law.
>
> I do not pretend that I was unaware of these factors when I applied for bail. What I do say is that during the trial these and other factors caused me to change my mind as to the effectiveness of the protest upon which I had decided and compelled me to the view that any really effective protest would have to be made in much sharper form—in an open defiance,

> whatever the personal consequences might be, of a process of law which has become a travesty of all civilised tradition: A political belief is outlawed, then torture is applied to gather evidence and finally the Executive decides whether you serve a life sentence or not.
>
> (quoted in *Society of Advocates of South Africa v. Fischer* 1966: 135–6)

Fischer here expresses a commitment to 'the rule of law', which he insists has effectively ceased to exist. (How does one make such a judgment*?) Speaking out of a 'principle . . . firmly established in South African legal tradition', Fischer defines himself as a lawyer, one who seeks to engage in the practice of respecting the rule of law. A reader of Edmund Burke might detect in Fischer a classic conservative reformer – someone 'capable of conserving what is best in what they have inherited and of reforming whatever is defective' (White – *Character). Those South Africans who did not sympathize with Fischer might have been inclined to pick out the phrase 'to change my mind' to make a claim that he lacks 'integrity'. A counter-claim could attend to the changing circumstances to which he points, as Burke might have suggested. Integral to 'integrity', as an Austen reader will know (*Character), is open-mindedness, a trait that readily connects to 'a change of mind'. With his eye on 'all civilised tradition', there is a healthy closure that combines with the openness, for he is not merely doing what appears best to him at the moment. To use Burke's language, Fischer is not making 'a series of unconnected acts'.

The Court attended not to any 'supreme duty' but to 'the unpleasant duty of giving a decision on an application for disciplinary action against the respondent, who is well known to the members of the Court' (134). It attended narrowly to consequences:

> [T]here is a . . . consideration which must not be overlooked: that is the impact of conduct of this nature upon public opinion. If conduct of this nature on the part of a senior and respected officer of the Court were to be overlooked as venial, the impact on the administration of justice would be deplorable. No one released on bail could be expected to regard his undertaking in his recognisance as binding upon him and not lightly to be breached, and judicial officers would be in a quandary in every case where application for bail was made.
>
> (136–7)

But matters overlooked before might now be noticed if the Court 'overlooked' what could be 'overlooked'. One of them is the 'total abolition of the rule of law', which makes a mockery of talk about 'the administration of justice'.

In November 1965, Fischer was arrested. Four months later, he would find himself alone in the 12-man dock that had been constructed for the

Rivonia Trial. He was accused of being a member of the Communist Party that had joined Umkhonto in acts of sabotage. In his speech, Fischer said:

> My Lord, when a man is on trial for his political beliefs and actions, two courses are open to him. He can either confess to his transgressions and plead for mercy, or he can justify his beliefs and explain why he acted as he did. Were I to ask for forgiveness today, I would betray my cause. That course, my Lord, is not open to me: I believe that what I did was right, and I must therefore explain to your Lordship what my motives were; why I hold the beliefs that I do, and why I was compelled to act in accordance with them.
>
> . . . I accept, my Lord, the general rule that for the protection of a society laws should be obeyed. But when the laws themselves become immoral, and require the citizen to take part in an organized system of oppression – if only by his silence and apathy – then I believe that a higher duty arises. This compels one to refuse to recognise such laws.
>
> The law, my Lord, under which I have been prosecuted, was enacted by a wholly unrepresentative body, a body in which three-quarters of the people of this country have no voice whatever. This and others laws were enacted not to prevent the spread of Communism, but, my Lord, for the purpose of silencing the opposition of the large majority of our citizens to a government intent upon depriving them, solely on account of their colour, of the most elementary human rights . . . .
>
> . . . All the conduct, my Lord, with which I have been charged, has been directed towards maintaining contact and understanding between the races of this country. If one day it may help to establish a bridge across which white leaders and the real leaders of the non-whites can meet to settle the destinies of all of us by negotiation, and not by force of arms, I shall be able to bear with fortitude any sentence which this Court may impose on me.
>
> (quoted in Clingman 1998: 409–10 and 415)

In situations 'when the laws themselves become immoral', a 'higher' law comes into operation. For Fischer, laws worthy of the name have an element of aspiration. He insists that his 'conduct' has an element of aspiration, namely, to 'help to establish a bridge across which white leaders and the real leaders of the non-whites can meet to settle the destinies of all of us by negotiation, and not by force of arms'. The metaphor* of his conduct as a 'bridge' is an act of hope in the direction of justice. This bridge could transform South Africa from the un-'justify'-able culture of destructive authoritarian 'silencing' to a culture that is a worthy member of 'the civilized world'. Fischer's words are an act of courage on behalf of South Africans who feel that the 'hideous' apartheid regime is worthy of a deposition.

Whilst deemed to have broken 'the law', there is a sense in which Fischer possibly did not. The law and morality relation is an entry into this sense.

The word 'and' in 'law and morality' here can have a disjunctive effect that Fischer resisted. For him, 'when the laws themselves become immoral', the laws are not laws. His resistance to denying the humanity of 'the large majority of our citizens' might be said to be a product not only of his 'political beliefs' but also his *legal* beliefs, his beliefs about what the law *is* and *ought* to be. Like 'law and morality', 'the political' and 'the legal' are not distinct entities but overlapping processes. He might have done well to say this. At the level of grammar, moving from entities to processes calls for less nouning and more verbing. Doing so can help our languaging contribute to culturing, in and out of lawyering, that has a place for justicing.

Fisher's talk about 'beliefs'[9] brings to mind some fragments in White's *Living Speech*. White here talks about his association with Quakers and the practices in which he participated. After doing so, he goes on to give the word 'belief' new life:

> Ultimately the belief upon which these practices rests cannot be encapsulated in a phrase, or creed, or any other set of statements. It is not propositional in nature but experiential, a discovery or a commitment. This fits with the history of the word 'belief,' which does not etymologically mean what we often take it to mean, namely an assertion of propositions claiming to utter the truth of what cannot be known, but a form of love: its is cognate with the archaic 'lief,' as in 'I would lief,' and with our word 'love' itself. The sort of belief I am speaking of is not an intellectual or conceptual position but something that lies beneath or beyond all such things: a kind of commitment of the self. The quotation from Simone Weil reflected in the title to this book suggests that there is an inherent connection between love and justice. This connection is I think true of the special kind of love we call belief, namely that it is essential to justice, and justice to it.
>
> (White 2006: 214)

How are we to do 'justice' to White's efforts to re-imagine that which we call 'justice'? If we play* the believing game (Weisberg and Peters – Listening*), a game that calls for serious reading* (that which is 'a kind of commitment'?), we may never hear the words 'justice' and 'belief' in quite the same way again. The familiar may have been productively alienated (*Alienation). Like White, we may have a dis-'position' to put the 'propositional' in its due place and to attend to that which 'lies beneath or beyond'.

After talking of his Quaker beliefs, White makes a connection between them and to the activity* of being a lawyer:

> Think of what makes possible the life of the hardworking lawyer: a belief that what he is doing makes sense and has value in itself, as he himself works out the terms of a settlement, say, or a contract for the sale of urban

> real estate, and as he imagines his fellow lawyers, across the country, doing much the same thing. If he lost that belief, and thought that all he was doing was working for money, or that what he himself said had no meaning beyond the instrumental or manipulative, that would make the life in a deep sense impossible. Without a belief in the real value of the conversation about justice that is at the center of the lawyer's life he would be dead at the core. One can imagine a lawyer or a judge suffering a loss of faith almost as easily as one can imagine a priest doing so. In both cases the life led on such terms would become impossible, empty, dead, no longer full of the life and promise that were its essence.
>
> (216–17)

When Fischer went underground, if asked whether the activity of being a lawyer in South Africa 'makes sense and has value in itself', we may suspect that he would have said 'no'. The great problem for him was the absence of 'the conversation about justice that is at the center of the lawyer's life'.

'A Coalescence between Law and Justice': Ismail Mahomed

In 1997, President Nelson Mandela appointed Ismail Mahomed as Chief Justice of South Africa's highest court, the Supreme Court of Appeal. Later in the year, Mahomed spoke at a dinner given by the Johannesburg Bar to celebrate his appointment. His speech attends to the law–justice relationship:

> The Johannesburg Bar . . . has been in effect my life . . . . Many contradictory images . . . flash before me when I recall this life . . . . There is nostalgia and satisfaction—even pride—in the recall, but also much pain and shame; richness and fulfilment, but also humiliation and indignity . . . .
>
> The pain and humiliation were intense. My status was determined by reference not to what I was but was not. I was '*non-white*'. It set about imposing on me a badge of inferiority sought to be written on my forehead. Its dominant consequence manifested itself in rejection and exclusion . . . ; exclusion from the right to occupy any office in chambers for counsel in Johannesburg, leaving me for twelve years to squat from hour to hour and from office to office in the chambers of one or other colleague temporarily in court; . . . exclusion from the right to sleep overnight in Bloemfontein during appearances before the highest court, leaving me to skulk across the border of the Free State before sunset to find accommodation from night to night more than a hundred kilometers away. These exclusions reinforced a multitude of other exclusions which denied my humanity. . . .
>
> There was a special sting about this form of exclusion. The study and practice of law has appealed to my idealism, because the justification for law was its pursuit of *justice* and its capacity to resist injustice. But it was

> through the instrumentality of law itself and the institutions of justice that palpable injustice was inflicted on me and other persons of colour. But this paradox was not without compensation: it enabled me to focus more intensely and consciously on what the philosophical and ethical legitimate ends of justice were, the degree to which they were manifestly inconsistent with the laws which regulated life . . . .
>
> . . . The passion for justice which inspired so many was effectively diverted in many cases into a sterile subculture in which debate on the ethical rationale for just laws became irrelevant, many lawyers retreated into the technicalities of a very constricted legal positivism, which increasingly made recourse to moral values remote in the interpretation and enforcement of fundamental rights and duties. Instead of a coalescence between law and justice, there grew a dangerous distance between the two, and the law and lawyers began to lose much of their legitimacy among people who they were unable to protect against injustice.
>
> (Mahomed 1997: 604–8)

Mahomed would resist those who would eliminate 'idealism' and reduce law to 'technicalities', for to do so would produce a 'sterile subculture'. For the same reason, he would resist those who would keep 'the legal' apart from 'the philosophical and ethical'. The apart-ness can transform an idealizing activity* into an instrument of oppression. The transformation in South Africa was associated with the exclusion of questions of justice from the life of a lawyer. Mahomed would insist that such questions are always legitimate.

Questions of justice are at the heart of White's work. In an interview on the eve of his retirement, he attended to the relationship between law and justice:

> [W]hat I mean by the word *law* is mainly what we teach: a complex inherited language of analysis and argument . . . and a set of intellectual and social practices, again complex, by which that language can be put to use in the world—practices that can be done well or badly, with consequences, small and great. . . . These practices have at their center a perhaps somewhat surprising idealism: the statutes and judicial opinions that bear on a case are not read cynically, or reduced to the motives presumed to underlie them, but read as if they were composed by an ideal legislator, an ideal judge, someone who is saying what he means and meaning what he says. The judge is addressed, in the courtroom and in briefs alike, as if he were an ideal judge, and the lawyers too are spoken of with respect, as honorable advocates. This idealism is, of course, in some sense a fiction: neither judge nor lawyer nor legislator is always wise, always honest, always responsible, and sometimes they are the opposite of these things. But it is a positive fiction, creating a pressure on all parties to become and act better than they might otherwise.

> There is another kind of idealism in the law, crucial both to its methods of change and to its meaning, that resides in the virtually universal but little noted convention that the lawyer and judge alike must credibly claim that the outcome for which they argue, or which they reach, is not only called for by the legal texts in question, but is in an important sense itself just. To say that the law requires an outcome, while admitting that it is unjust, or to claim that justice requires an outcome, while admitting that the law does not permit it, is to make a fatally incomplete and defective argument. The simultaneous insistence upon law and justice produces a constant pressure to think and rethink both what justice is and what the law requires. It is an engine for opening the law to our deepest values.
>
> I have spoken here of the law at its best. Of course it is often corrupted, like any social and cultural form. Sometimes it is very bad: unthinking, conclusionary, authoritarian, erasing the experience of others, bullying, inhuman, not connected in any good way with either reality or justice. But it always has within it the seeds of its own excellence.
>
> (in Gaakeer 2007: 1418–19)

Like the passage from Mahomed, here is 'someone who is saying what he means and meaning what he says' while offering some reflections that unite truths and 'values'. White's truth involves 'fiction'. Whilst some people might suggest or claim that 'fiction' taints our thinking, White insists that it *is* and *ought* to be integral to the activity of thinking as a lawyer. We might say that justice begins with 'a positive fiction'. Without 'idealism', as Mahomed would insist, the law can become 'very bad: unthinking, conclusionary, authoritarian, . . . inhuman'. We will do well, then, to pursue a line of questioning* concerning the nature of the law's 'excellences', 'and what they might be', so that we can bring into 'reality' the law 'at its best'.

Language

'It Most Froze Me to Hear such Talk': Mark Twain's *Huckleberry Finn*
When a Law Student Reads *Huckleberry Finn*: Elizabeth Perry Hodges
When an Economist Drafts Legislation: John R. Commons
'The Legal-Economic Nexus': Warren J. Samuels

In our engagement with the *Cohen* case (*Alienation), we attended to uses of the F-word. It is readily imaginable that Justice Harlan struggled when thinking about how to use 'the four-letter word'. A critic of the case might find Bakhtin to be helpful:

> The word in language is half someone else's. It becomes 'one's own' only when the speaker populates it with his own intention, his own accent, when he appropriates the word, adapting it to his own semantic and expressive intention. Prior to this moment of appropriation, the word does not exist in a neutral impersonal language (it is not . . . out of a dictionary that the speaker gets his words!), but rather it exists in other people's mouths, in other people's contexts, serving other people's intentions: it is from there that one must take the word, and make it one's own. And not all words for just anyone submit equally easily to this appropriation, to this seizure and transformation into private property: many words stubbornly resist, others remain alien, sound foreign in the mouth of the one who appropriated them and who now speaks them; . . . it is as though they put themselves in quotation marks against the will of the speaker.
>
> (Bakhtin 1981: 293–4)

Whenever we language, we have decisions relating to 'own'-ing and disowning 'it'.[1] An awareness of such decisions will help us to form and pursue 'intentions' of our own. Attending to the 'moment of appropriation' – in relation to any word – can help in the activity* of attunement* to the process of transforming constitutions of 'language'.

In *The Legal Imagination*, White talks about 'success' for the lawyer 'as a matter of one's relationship with language' (1973: 49). The achievement of the 'right relationship with . . . the language of the law . . . – a sense that you are saying the right thing in the right way – both from outside your professional life, as you look at what it means to you and to others, and from inside it, as you try to do your job well' (50), is a challenge for White's reader.

'It Most Froze Me to Hear Such Talk': Mark Twain's *Huckleberry Finn*

In the opening chapter of *The Legal Imagination*, White offers some food-for-thought about owning and disowning the N-word. This word appears several times in a passage taken from Twain's *Huckleberry Finn* and in White's questions about it.

In 1895, Samuel Clemens (aka Twain) gave a lecture on ethics centring on a situation in which 'a sound heart and a deformed conscience come into collision'. He drew from *Huckleberry Finn*, in which the hero has a 'conscience' that emerged in 'slave-holding days'. Clemens says this about those days:

> [T]he whole community was agreed as to one thing – the awful sacredness of slave property. To . . . help a hunted slave . . . carried with it a . . . moral smirch which nothing could wipe away. . . . [T]his sentiment . . . seemed natural enough to me then . . . , though it seems now absurd. It shows that that strange thing, the conscience . . . can be trained to approve any wild thing you want to approve if you begin its education early and stick to it.
>
> (quoted in Blair 1960: 143–4)

The novel offers an education about 'the conscience' and 'its education'. It offers the experience* of inhabiting a world in which the 'slave as property' metaphor* is as 'natural' as breathing, a world that becomes full of tension when Huck and hunted slave Jim become friends. Out of this tension, the familiar 'thing' that we call 'the conscience' can become 'strange', and thus the subject of conscious attention*.

Twain's novel begins with Huck up against 'sivilizing' pressures from his foster mother and from her sister, Miss Watson. Huck finds himself running with Jim, who is 'owned' by Miss Watson. The threat of a new owner has led him to run:

> Ole Missus – dat's Miss Watson . . . treats me pooty rough. . . . I hear ole missus . . . gwyne to sell me down to Orleans. . . . [S]he could git eight hund'd dollars for me, en it 'uz sich a big stack o' money she couldn' resis'. . . . I lit out mighty quick, I tell you.
>
> (Twain 1884/1985: 96)

Jim and Huck float down the Mississippi River on a raft. The novel's 16th chapter begins with them talking about nearing Cairo, Illinois, where Jim will be 'free'. A collision occurs within Huck:

> Jim said it made him all over trembly and feverish to be so close to freedom. Well, I can tell you it made me all over trembly and feverish, too,

to hear him, because I begun to get it through my head that he *was* most free – and who was to blame for it? Why, *me*. . . . Conscience says to me, 'What had poor Miss Watson done to you, that you could see her nigger go off right under your eyes and never say one single word? . . .'

Jim talked out loud all the time I was talking to myself. He was saying how . . . when he got to a free State he would go to saving up money and never spend a single cent, and when he got enough he would buy his wife, which was owned on a farm close to where Miss Watson lived; and then they would both work to buy the two children, and if their master wouldn't sell them, they'd get an Ab'litionist to go and steal them.

It most froze me to hear such talk. He wouldn't ever dared to talk such talk in his life before. Just see what a difference it made in him the minute he judged he was about to be free. It was according to the old saying, 'give a nigger an inch and he'll take an ell.' . . . Here was this nigger which I had as good as helped to run away, coming right out flat-footed and saying he would steal his children – children that belonged to a man I didn't even know; a man that hadn't ever done me no harm.

(145–6)

A Bahktin reader may notice that quotation marks surround the first two uses of the N-word. 'Conscience' became disturbed at Jim's aspiring 'talk'. The Huck that uses 'the old saying' is not the Huck that has become a friend to Jim.

With the language of race running through Huck, he paddles ashore with the intention to turn Jim in. Jim then speaks:

'Pooty soon I'll be a-shout'n for joy, en I'll say, its all on accounts o' Huck; I's a free man, en I couldn't ever ben free ef it hadn' ben for Huck; Huck done it. Jim won't ever forgit you, Huck; you's de bes' fren' Jim's ever had; en you's de *only* fren' ole Jim's got now.'

I was paddling off, all in a sweat to tell on him; but when he says this, it seemed to take the tuck all out of me. I went along slow then, and I warn't right down certain whether I was glad I started or whether I warn't. When I was fifty yards off, Jim says:

'Dah you goes, de ole true Huck; de on'y white genlman dat ever kep' his promise to ole Jim.'

Well, I just felt sick. But I says, I *got* to do it – I can't get *out* of it.

(146–7)

Jim's open and sincere 'friend'-talk is a real jolt for the part of Huck that a few moments earlier had only seen 'Miss Watson's nigger'. The jolt may serve as a resource for him to transcend ('get out of') the cultural force of the N-word, if only for the moment.

Somehow, Huck does get out of turning Jim in. Along comes a boat with two men. They are slave hunters with guns. Huck cleverly tricks them to depart without checking the raft. Then we hear Huck:

> They went off, and I got aboard the raft, feeling bad and low, because I knowed very well I had done wrong, and I see it warn't no use for me to try to learn to do right; a body that don't get *started* right when he's little, ain't got no show – . . . . Then I thought a minute, and says to myself, hold on, – s'pose you'd a done right and give Jim up; would you felt better that what you do now? No, says I, I'd feel bad – I'd feel just the same way I do now. Well, then, says I, what's the use you learning to do right, when it's troublesome to do right and ain't no trouble to do wrong, and the wages is just the same? I was stuck. I couldn't answer that. So I reckoned I wouldn't bother no more about it, but after this always do whichever come handiest at the time.
>
> (149)

Huck's rule, 'do whichever come handiest at the time', may sound unsound, lacking moral grounds, but we may do well to resist making such a judgment*.

'When Huck says that he will just do what comes handiest at the time, what does he mean by "handy"?' So asks White at the beginning of a line of questioning* (1973: 25). Here he invites thought about 'the experience of being brought up to say "nigger,"' especially its 'effect . . . on human relationships'. White suggests that the force of the N-word may be getting in the way of Huck becoming an abolitionist:

> It may help you to see Huck's position if you ask what else he could have called Jim than 'nigger.' Exactly what other word in the language he was given might he have used? To say 'my best friend, Jim' would have been an absurdity – 'slave' and 'friend' cannot go together that way, because 'slave' means 'chattel.' It could only be understood in some peculiar or metaphorical way like 'my best friend, Lassie' or 'my best friend, IBM.' Huck makes no verbal response when Jim calls him the 'bes' fren' Jim's ever had,' though he is deeply affected and it is clear the friendship goes both ways. To say something directed to the general social situation, such as 'slaves are really our equals,' would be to attack an institution central to society, imbued with all the values of property, regularity, productivity, the necessary order of things; to speak against it would be to incite to anarchy. As Huck rightly saw, the idea of slavery was intimately tied to the most fundamental ideas of right and wrong, and the untangling was beyond his capacities.
>
> (25–6)

It may help you to see White's position if you ask what he is doing and why. In offering his reader 'help . . . to see Huck's position', he is involved in 'the negotiation of meaning' (Lakoff and Johnson – *Metaphor). White, that is to say, is exercising his metaphorical imagination in the activity of attunement* to Huck's language and reality. White's particular interest is in Huck's horizon, in seeing what Huck cannot see – what is 'beyond' him. He suggests that Huck is experiencing a 'genuine limit-situation' (Tracy – *Experience).

Without the 'capacities' to do the 'untangling', we might imagine that Huck's creative imagination led to the 'handiest' rule. This enables Huck to resist 'the necessary order of things' without stirring up 'anarchy'. This is an impressive achievement.

When a Law Student Reads *Huckleberry Finn*: Elizabeth Perry Hodges

In a contribution to a 1988 *Texas Law Review* colloquy titled *Human Voice in Legal Discourse*, Hodges offers a reading of *Huckleberry Finn*. Hodges senses that in the novel we have a microcosm of a society, 'a system of varied and opposing voices continually developing and renewing itself' (1988: 632). Through its hero, 'Twain illustrates the intricate process by which the human voice in all of its complexity wages battle against stereotyping and sterility' (632–3). With this 'battle' in mind, she believes that the novel can help law students think about thinking and speaking like a lawyer:

> In teaching writing to law school students, I notice a conscious effort on their part to erase any sign of nonprofessional discourse. In their effort to survive the first year, they somehow learn that this is what they ought to do. They come to view the law as a tool for achieving objectivity and even 'truth,' concepts that they perceive to have some absolute and fixed value. Some part of the self, in other words, seems to swallow whole, without recognizing it, the language of 'right' and power with which Huck begins to quarrel.
>
> (633)

In directing attention to the 'conscious effort on their part', Hodges can help empower a 'part of the self' to imagine the law as a medium for 'achieving objectivity' of a relative (non-'absolute') kind.

Hodges suggests that Huck's 'handiest' rule is far from unsound. When talking about the action just after his use of 'the old saying', she says:

> Thinking within the ethical and social terms of his society, he resolves with great difficulty to paddle ashore . . . to turn Jim in. But when Jim says, 'you's de bes' fren' Jim's ever had,' Huck is unmanned: 'it seemed to kind of take all the tuck out of me.' Jim is defining his relation to Huck, not in the context of master-slave or white-black, but in new and non-racial terms. His language momentarily escapes the dominating system

> through which he and Huck had been forced to define themselves. . . . Caught between two different ways of thinking and speaking, he is not quite able to see that the 'right' thing to do is, in his own words, the 'wrong' thing. The labels put him in a bind which he escapes only by changing the words: 'So I reckoned I wouldn't bother no more about it, but after this always do whichever come handiest at the time.' In his struggle to free himself from inherited ways of thinking, he opens up a different linguistic space by using the term 'handiest,' establishing a different standard that could generate a new language, and perhaps, in time, a new social condition. Through his own language, Huck implies a new system of thought that would enable blacks and whites to live together as friends.
>
> (631–2)

Huck's creative use of the word 'handiest' seems to be the nerve of a complex process involving 'language', 'inherited ways of thinking', and a potentially 'new social condition'. The identification of this process, in which the in-'between' is a key place, along with the possibility that Huck (or anyone) can engage in a 'struggle to free himself from inherited ways of thinking', opens up an inquiry into human experience*.

Hodges invites her students to engage in a conversation resembling Huck's internal one. She urges them, 'to hop on a raft and, rather than parrot the worst of legal expression, to examine both their own language and that of other legal and literary authors, exploring the assumptions and preconceptions that underlie these writings'. Such an invitation can be disturbing and challenging: 'The students are, at times, as uncomfortable as Huck, fearful of the prospect of forging a new language and a new order out of a wider range of experiences and voices than is usually expected in a legal context.' Students can expect to develop a new relationship with their language:

> They begin to see that much of what they write is 'wrong,' not necessarily because the content is 'wrong,' but because their language fails to reflect the unavoidable fact of their membership in a larger community from which they derive their fundamental linguistic abilities and to which, as mediators from the world of law, they must communicate. Some failure is inevitable, for like Huck, we inherit ways of thinking that become ways of speaking, and we risk becoming partially blinded by the very formulas we strive to master. But like Huck, too, we need to be alert to the limitations of formulas and to the ideologies buried within them so that we may avoid their potentially rigid grip.
>
> (633)

When a student can 'begin to see' the 'world of law' as a 'language', which has 'limitations', he or she may acquire a sharper sense (or a higher degree of 'alert'-ness) of the possible dangers and rewards of a life in the law. One danger is 'becoming partially blinded by the very formulas we strive to master'. One reward is the opportunity for an authentic professional existence that includes self-consciously transforming the formulas in a constructive direction (justice*?).

Hodges' students will be well equipped to make sense of the opening of *The Legal Imagination*. Here White suggests that 'the legal language system' is more than 'a technical language': 'we can talk about the legal language system . . . to include not only peculiar and technical phrases but habits of thought and conditions of mind' (8). Adopting this broad sense of language sets up these questions:

> Your question, which the course as a whole is meant to elaborate, is this: how will you, you personally, as an independent mind, respond to and attempt to control the pressure of your training in the law?
>
> (9)

> What is meant when your friend at the cocktail party calls you 'legalistic' and gives up in disgust? Can you stand outside the legal language system and look at it? Can you stand far enough back from your legal education to ask, 'What am I becoming?'
>
> (10)

We can be sure that a reading list that includes *Huckleberry Finn* can help a law student respond to the big questions of life. When responding, she should be sure to resist metaphors of stasis (like 'stand') and give life to metaphors of movement*.

When an Economist Drafts Legislation: John R. Commons

In the early 1900s, Commons helped draft a public utilities law and a law establishing an Industrial Commission. The purpose was to ascertain and enforce 'reasonable' prices and 'reasonable' practices. Commons sought to know the point at which courts would declare an unconstitutional taking of 'property' or 'liberty' of employers. (He addressed the Fifth and Fourteenth Amendments.[2]) He began reading numerous judicial opinions with hope of connecting economics and law for intelligible talk about the meaning of the word 'reasonable'. In his autobiography, he remarks that economists expressed doubts about his language:

> Reasonable values and reasonable practices were entirely new words introduced into the theories of political economy. Often my students and sometimes my economist critics said that 'reasonable' was something purely

> subjective, and there were as many meanings of reasonableness as there were individuals. Such a term placed the determination of reasonableness in the arbitrary mind of whatever individual happened to be in authority. But I considered this objection to be an inheritance from the subjective individualism of preceding economic theorists. A collectivist theory of value derived from existing best practices, from custom, the common law, and the decisions of courts, could make reasonableness 'objective' and therefore capable of investigation and testimony, leading to the formation of working rules for collective action in control of individual action.
>
> (Commons 1934b: 156)

Commons sought to escape the hold of influential binary oppositions, including individual versus collective, objective versus subjective and reason versus value. He wrote at a time when the phrase 'the art of political economy' was almost out of circulation, partly due to the power of 'the subjective individualism of preceding economic theorists'.

Commons attended to shifting meanings of numerous key words in his discipline. His inquiry led to an analysis, in his *Legal Foundations of Capitalism*, of the emergence and development of capitalism. A key fragment here is struggle over the meaning of the word 'liberties' in Magna Carta:

> It might mean the 'libertates' of Magna Carta, which were the privileges of the landlords granted by the monarch, or it might mean the liberty to buy and sell, to be free from violence, theft and trespass, derived from approved customs which constituted the common law. The two were inconsistent. One was a contradiction of the other. Freedom, or liberty, in the sense of a grant out of the royal prerogative, stood for a relation of superior to inferior; freedom or liberty in the sense of the common law stood for a relation of equality between members of the same class. The first is more properly to be distinguished as 'freedom,' the second as 'liberty.' Freedom was a grant of power to participate in the privileges of those who were specially favored by a superior. Liberty was the common-law right to equality of treatment among individuals who belonged to the same class whether privileged or unprivileged. Equal liberty was inconsistent with unequal freedom.
>
> (Commons 1924/1995: 50)

Commons' inquiry into the legal foundations of capitalism led him to appreciate how changes in the meanings of words correspond with cultural change. Language and culture*, that is to say, are intimately connected. The transformation from feudalism to capitalism took place in no small part out of new judicial definitions of 'liberty' and 'property' in working out conceptions of reasonableness.

When Commons immersed himself in the activity of drafting legislation, he had to imagine various cases that could arise and how a judge might resolve them. In doing so, he attended to the ways in which the meaning of language is shaped by 'purpose':

> The common mind conceives that a horse is a horse, and that is the end of it. The metaphysical notion abstracts a concept of horseness, and, like Plato, fills the sky with a world of ideas that come down and embody themselves in things; or like Hegel or Karl Marx, finds the 'idea' of 'liberty' or of 'social-labor-power' embodied in primitive society and struggling to unfold itself through the centuries. But the judicial mind perceives that a horse is a horse for some purposes and something else for other purposes, that liberty is good in some circumstances and not in others. For the physiologist a horse is a life process, for the farmer the horse is horse-power, for the lawyer the horse is property, for the business man the horse is the price of the horse. The horse is an object of infinite qualities, faculties, possibilities, and is classified differently for different purposes, with a different *class name*, which is a different definition. Thus definition is a collecting, by the purpose of inclusion, of qualities that are deemed similar, and an eliminating, by the process of exclusion, of qualities deemed dissimilar, always with reference to their fitness in attaining the purpose of the one who does the classifying. In this respect, definition is classification according to the importance of the facts.
>
> (346–7)

Commons here defines himself not as an abstract theorist who is preoccupied with a consistent set of propositions and definitions ('by *idea* I mean . . . ; by liberty I mean . . .', and so on) but as one who is concerned with argument from (and the contribution to) 'circumstances', which is the heart of what has been called 'the common-law mind' (Pocock 1957). The legal case, for Commons, does not arise in a vacuum, upon which a court begins with a blank sheet of paper; it is part of an ongoing activity* in which the court reconstitutes the past, in the form of precedents.

There is an important sense in which the centre of Commons' work is the legal hearing. It is here that the meanings of 'property', 'liberty', 'person', and 'due process' are given new life. In *Institutional Economics*, he describes the hearing as an institution in which people use, and in using transform, an inherited language to talk to one another about conflicting interests:

> The hearing and decision are merely listening to pleadings and arguments and giving meaning to words; and it is by the changing of meaning of words that rights, liberties, duties, and exposures are changed in the changing economic conditions. For the court proceeds . . . by the judicial process of weighing practices, customs, precedents, statutes, and constitutions in the light of changing conditions . . . . This process has required changing the definitions of all the words of the Fifth and Fourteenth Amendments to fit the economic and ethical changes of the

> past sixty years. The process is still going on. Further changes cannot be predicted, but the more important in the past, for the science of economics, have been the changes in the meaning of the words: person, liberty, property, due process, and equal protection.
>
> For the meaning of all these terms arise out of the practices, customs, and habitual assumptions of the people and judges; and the changes that occur in these practices, customs, and assumptions bring with them changes in the meaning of words. Then, when conflicts arise between citizens and officials, the court itself must change the meanings of the terms as found in precedents, statutes, and constitutions in order to arrive at their application to the new disputes arising out of the change in conditions and assumptions. The court does so, not by trying to formulate academic or scientific definitions that shall be good for all time, but by the experimental process of 'exclusion and inclusion,' which is the universal process of the human mind by which language itself changes. By 'exclusion' a former meaning of these terms is deemed not to be applicable to the present dispute. By 'inclusion' the issue within a present dispute is brought within a former meaning which had not hitherto been deemed to include it. Thus constitutions, statutes, and even precedents change in process of time through the gradual but universal process of human speech which excludes old meanings and includes new meanings in order to fit the language to the changing practices and customs which require language to reach agreements.
>
> (Commons 1934a/1959: 690–91)

For Commons, a judicial opinion is part of a continuing process of discussion, one that joins together the past and the future in the process of making 'changes in the meanings of words' – a process that is not unique to the law but part of the 'universal process of human speech'. He thought economists could productively take language and culture seriously in order to serve an ever-transforming constitution. We can be sure that he hoped to contribute to the advancement of self-awareness (or attention*) by economists, especially concerning their own acts of 'exclusion and inclusion'.

Commons' work gives notice to what White calls the 'central moment' of 'the law', in which 'one version of its language' is placed 'against another' at a hearing, followed by 'a self-conscious choice between them' (White 1990: 24). Only a minority of economists seem to be interested in that kind of choice, the central concern of which is doing justice* to the parties involved. Most economists seem to do what the courts do not do, namely, 'trying to formulate academic or scientific definitions that shall be good for all time'. These economists are out of touch with a world that is in constant motion, with linguistic 'process' that 'is still going on'. They are preoccupied with 'the mathematical image of the person', as White has put it (1990: 64). In being 'most eager' to have their form of economics 'universalized as a mode of thought' (51), these economists are engaged in the activity 'imperialism' (31). This may be more visible when we place their work side by side with Commons' lawyerly economics.

'The Legal-Economic Nexus': Warren J. Samuels

In 1954, Samuels began graduate studies at the University of Wisconsin, having been attracted to the influence of Commons there. In the spirit of Commons, Samuels sought 'to generate greater and, to the extent possible, non-ideological clarity in understanding the economic role of government in the history of economic thought, in economic theory and in the real world' (Samuels 1992: 479). Such clarity called for a turn toward language and the identification of problems in the use of various key words in economics, including 'economy', 'law', and 'government'. Our inherited language, Samuels claims, is clumsy. Consider what he says in the introduction to his essay 'The Legal-Economic Nexus':

> One of the deepest conceptual structures of the modern mind and discourse . . . is the distinction between the 'economy' and the 'polity.' It is a distinction that roughly parallels that between 'private' and 'public.' . . . Political economic thought of Western civilization is imbued with the concepts, 'economy' and 'polity,' and 'private' and 'public.' . . . The predominant perception is that the concepts constituting each pair are fundamentally separate and distinct, self-subsistent *vis-à-vis* each other, and in conflict. In ordinary life, we share the fundamental belief that government and the economy are separate and mutually exclusive, a belief reinforced by language and ideology.
>
> The distinction between a self-subsistent economy and a self-subsistent polity is both reflected in and reinforced by the intellectual division of labor manifest in the coexisting disciplines of economics, political science, and law and jurisprudence. The distinction has actually been exacerbated by efforts (including my own) to trace the 'interrelations' between legal-political and economic-market processes. . . .
>
> This Essay . . . argues that the perceived spheres of polity and economy, of law and market, are not self-subsistent, and that it is helpful to understand what transpires by identifying the existence of a legal-economic nexus in which both seemingly distinct spheres commonly originate. . . . It will not go unnoticed from the very beginning that if the idea of a legal-economic nexus is correct, our understanding of economy and polity will have to change in fundamental ways. The great problem, however, is to escape from the hold of the conventional wisdom and ordinary language, and of the paradigm ensconced therein, a paradigm that posits the separate and self-subsistent existence of the two spheres. A difficult problem of writing as well as reading this essay is that there is no readily available terminology that avoids the use of the terms

'polity' and 'economy' (or the usual synonyms, such as 'law' and 'market'). The prevailing political-economic language carries and reinforces the nuance of separate and self-subsistent existence, which abetted by language, we then perceive in the world around us.

(Samuels 1989: 1556–8)

Samuels is acutely aware of the ways in which our 'language' for talking about the 'economy' can mislead us in regard to a 'fundamental belief'. This awareness is the source of a 'problem' for him: our clumsy 'ordinary language' is associated with a problematic 'predominant perception'. Samuels seeks to complicate a basic 'distinction' that we take for granted. A Brecht reader may well sense that he is asking questions that offer the experience of an alienation* from the commonplaces by which we live, an alienation that could mean that 'our understanding of economy and polity will have to change in fundamental ways.' If the word 'and' in the phrase 'economy and polity' becomes widely perceived as inaptly disjunctive, the discipline that we call 'economics' may once again become 'political economy'.

Samuels' term 'the legal-economic nexus' is the product of his efforts to 'transcend particular professional ideologies . . . , with their respective definitions of the world of economy and polity' (1572). He is resisting 'ideologues' who 'tend to reify certain specifications of polity and/or economy . . . , treating them as something exogenously or independently given' (1573). We might say that he seeks to 'transcend' that which Felix Cohen called 'transcendental nonsense' – the 'thingification' of non-things, such as 'property' and 'value' (Cohen 1935/1960: 40–43).

I owe the acquaintance of White to Samuels' essay. If my memory serves me well, the following passage initially connected me to White's work:

The belief or pretense that law is given independent of the economy, or that the economy pre-exists the state in any practical sense, gives effect to selective perception of government, economy, and their origins and continuing development. James Boyd White, commenting on the falseness of the distinction between the market and government, has stated that to 'talk about "government intervention"' implicitly assumes 'that there is a pre-governmental state of nature called the market into which the government intrudes. But this is obviously silly.' The belief treats both law and economy as given, antecedent, and preeminent to man, as existing to be discovered. In fact, law and economy are jointly created through complex human social decisionmaking processes. Both are not discovered, but created simultaneously in the legal-economic nexus.

(1568)

Samuels' efforts to complicate 'the distinction between the market and government' with his term 'the legal-economic nexus' threaten to expose as 'obviously silly' a vast amount of discourse. We might wonder what will become of the idea of the legal-economic nexus in the marketplace of ideas. Even better, we might wonder what might become the marketplace metaphor*.

In the above passage, Samuels quoted an essay titled 'Economics and Law: Two Cultures in Tension'. In the essay, White makes some general remarks about the nature and significance of language. Here is one passage:

> I start from the position . . . that the languages we speak, and the cultural practices they at once reflect and make possible, shape our minds by habituating them to certain forms of attention, certain ways of seeing and conceiving of oneself and of the world. This is in fact why we learn them. . . . For me . . . the major art of intellectual life is . . . to discover, and try to control, the ways in which our languages capture and drive our minds, so that we may recognize what they leave out or distort, both in ourselves and in others, and subject them to the discipline of other forms of thought and expression. Control of such a kind is most difficult, for it is at heart a species of self-control: when we speak our languages we cannot help believing them, we cannot help participating, emotionally and ethically and politically, in the worlds they create and in the structures of perception and feeling they offer us. In time the soldier wants to go to war.
>
> (White 1986: 166)

That passage may be of help for appreciating what Samuels is doing in 'The Legal-Economic Nexus'. Samuels is resisting the claims and suggestions that words such as 'economy', 'government', and 'intervention' are neutral and precise tools for pointing to an objective reality but, rather, fluid cultural artefacts for talking about a shifting realm of our lives, a realm that shifts with our talk about it. These words, he suggests, 'control' our minds – they direct our 'attention'*, 'perception', and 'feeling'. Samuels' term 'the legal-economic nexus' can serve to help us exercise a form of 'self-control'. For this, we need to populate it with our own intentions, our own accents, and so on. We also need to attend to what the term leaves out, lest we fail to do justice* to ourselves and to others.

In *Law and Literature: A Misunderstood Relation*, Richard Posner, who is well known for 'pro-market' writings in 'law and economics', claims that 'it is only since the publication in 1973 of James Boyd White's *The Legal Imagination* . . . that a distinct, self-conscious field of law and literature can be said to have merged' (1988: 12). In a review of Posner's book, White offers a response that will sound familiar to a Samuels reader:

> In framing his title as he does, Judge Posner assumes that two distinct entities named 'law' and 'literature' exist in the world, that they can be observed from the outside, as rain and sun might be, and that they have

> a preexisting relation between law and literature which can be 'understood,' or 'misunderstood.' But the relation between law and literature is not 'out there' in the world to be observed; it is constructed by each of us in our writing.
>
> (White 1989: 2026)

Posner would have done well to engage in acts of literature with the aim of complicating the distinction between 'law' and 'literature', perhaps by inventing a new term such as the legal-literary nexus.

Listening

'Am I Understanding You Well?': Harville Hendrix
'Listening Modes': Mark Weisberg and Jean Koh Peters

René Descartes proposed a basic 'truth', commonly known in philosophy as the *cogito*: 'I think, therefore I am' (1637/1968: 53). To whom was the 'I think' addressed? Was the audience listening? In *The Listening Self*, David Levin seeks to give the activity* of listening its due place in philosophy. He takes seriously the 'echo', which might trouble a self who wants a determinate order in life: 'the echo . . . sets in motion uncountable vibrations of uncertainty; . . . it cannot be possessed; . . . it decentres the ego' (1989: 237). Addressing the topic of justice*, Levin suggests that sound can dissolve the line between self and other:

> I can hear myself when I listen to the other: I can hear myself *in* the other, or in the position of the other. But the reverse is also true. I can hear the other when I listen to myself; I can hear the other . . . *in* myself. Between myself and the other, there are echoes and resonances: extremely deep reverberations . . . that will mix, blend, even reverse our role identifications. . . . The primary *sense* of justice is not seeing, but hearing. The sense of justice is channeled through the most communicative, most sensitively attuned of senses: our capacity for listening.
>
> (182–4)

How might we go about 'hearing' Levin? What will we need to say for him to hear himself *in* us? Might it be that Levin offers a resource that can help us continue trying to become 'attuned' to the activity of attunement*? His claim that the 'primary *sense* of justice is . . . hearing' may prod us to imagine that the heart of the law is not a set of rules but the hearing. The justice-loving judge may pursue 'echoes and resonances' in order to attempt to create a harmony between 'self' and 'other'.

'Am I Understanding You Well?': Harville Hendrix

Some years ago, a friend was having difficulties with her parents. I suggested that she and they get counselling. They all agreed to this, and I participated in it. 'Mirroring' was one of the first exercises that the counsellor, Jim, asked us to do. (The auditory metaphor* 'echoing' is perhaps better than the ocular 'mirroring'.) When one of us spoke to someone else, this someone else would then paraphrase what had been communicated and then ask for confirmation with this question: 'Am I understanding you well?' Jim directed us to Hendrix's *Getting the Love You Want* for a sense of how difficult mirroring can be. A fragment in it involves a conversation* that took place at one of Hendrix's workshops. He asked a couple to join him at the front of the group and talk about a sensitive issue, just as they would at home. Greg and Sheila, a young couple who had been living together for a few months, volunteered:

Greg: Sheila, I'm really bothered by your smoking, and I'd like you to be more considerate when you smoke around me.

Sheila: You knew that I smoked when you asked me to live with you. You accepted that fact in the beginning. Why are you always so critical of me? You should accept me as I am. You know that I am trying to cut down.

Greg: I acknowledge your efforts to smoke less. But I find it interesting that, when we come here and the sign in the dining room says 'No Smoking,' you follow it. Yet I feel invaded at home with the smell of tobacco smoke all over the place.

Sheila: Well, this is not my home. And I feel I have a right to smoke in my own home!

(in Hendrix 1988: 144–5)

At this point of assertive rights talk, 'there was a smattering of applause from the crowd.' Into what was the talk turning? 'The score was love-fifteen' (145). Perhaps because it seemed that an important kind of 'love' was missing, Hendrix spoke up, inviting a shift from 'confrontation' to 'communication'.

Greg started again, and then Hendrix spoke:

Hendrix: Good. Now, Sheila, I want you to paraphrase Greg, trying to mirror his feelings and thoughts without criticizing him or defending yourself. Then I want you to ask Greg if you have heard him correctly.

Sheila: I'm truly sorry that my smoking interferes –

Hendrix: No, I'm not asking you to apologize. Just mirror back to Greg what he was saying, and show your understanding and acceptance of his feelings.

Sheila: Could he possibly repeat himself?

Greg: Your smoking bothers me. I didn't think it would at first, but it does.

Hendrix: Now, try to feed that back to him with receptive warmth.

Sheila: I think I'd rather stop smoking! (Group laughter.)

Hendrix: Take a deep breath and be aware that he is experiencing some discomfort at one of your behaviors. Rather than hearing it as a criticism of your behavior, hear it with concern for his well-being.

Whether it's justified or not, he is feeling uncomfortable, and you care about him. I know this is hard to do in front of a lot of people, and I know that this is an issue you feel strongly about.

Sheila: What could be done –

Hendrix: No, don't try to solve it. You just want to paraphrase his message and the emotional content behind it, so that he knows that you understand what he is feeling.

Sheila: (Takes a deep breath.) OK. I think I get it now. I understand that it *really* bothers you that I smoke. You didn't realize how much it would bother you until we actually started living together. Now you are very troubled by it. Is that what you are saying?

Hendrix: Excellent. I could hear Greg's concern reflected in your voice. Did that check out with you, Greg? Is she hearing what you have to say?

Greg: Yes! That's just how I feel. What a relief! . . .

(145–6)

After reading Levin, we might say that Greg could hear himself when he listened to Sheila: he could hear himself *in* Sheila. For Hendrix, 'there is a tremendous satisfaction in simply being heard' (146). He believes that being heard in this way 'is a rare phenomenon in most marriages' (146–7). After demonstrating the exercise, he sends each couple to a room so that they can practise it. 'Invariably', he says, 'they return to the group reporting that it was a novel, exhilarating experience' – it is 'an unexpected luxury to have your partner's full attention' (147). We will do well to attend to our economies of attention*!

The exercise, for all of us, was an exhilarating experience*. For me, it was the first step in learning a new language*, the heart of which is 'agape' (169), a Greek word for love. Agape is 'one of the forms of love on a continuum with eros and philia' (289). It is 'a special way in which love is expressed' (290). Hendrix uses the word to refer to 'the act of directing eros, the life energy, away from oneself and toward the welfare of the other'. In a sense 'it is sacrificial, but what is sacrificed is not the self but preoccupation with the self' (290). He also says:

> Although it is used as a noun, and thus denotes an attitude, it is also used as a verb, and thus denotes the way one acts toward another. The merger of these two senses means that agape can be understood as an attitude that is expressed in behaviors. On this basis, I call it the 'power of transformation' that directs eros to the other, thus creating a new quality in relationships, called 'philia.'
>
> (289–90)

After reading that passage, the title of Hendrix's book may well have a different ring to it – I initially thought it was a corny title and then heard it quite differently.

What can a White critic learn from Hendrix?

Let us turn to an important introductory remark in White's *The Legal Imagination*:

> As you look at the readings, you will notice that in selecting them I have drawn heavily from my own reading of literature. Of course I hope that others will find this material and the lines of thought to which it gives rise of interest, but my purpose is not to claim that a literary education is the only one for a lawyer or for this course: it is to establish a way of looking at the law from the outside, a way of comparing it with other forms of literary and intellectual activity, a way of defining the legal imagination by comparing it with others. The non-legal readings are meant to give us a common sense (if an incomplete one) of what legal literature leaves out, of what others do that the law does not, and to define a context out of which judgments can begin to be drawn and against which they can be tested. In the notes and questions I bring to both sorts of literature some of the concerns of the literary critic, but I hope I do so in a way that the general reader can easily follow.
>
> (White 1973: xx)

In the spirit of Hendrix: Jim, your purpose is to create a place (one perhaps cavorting with the inside/'outside' distinction) from which to imagine 'the law', an 'activity'* that we might call, after doing some 'comparing' and making some 'judgments', 'literary'. (We might come to make the judgment* that unliterary law, which 'leaves out' too much, is no law at all.) Am I understanding* you well?

If we are understanding White well, we should hesitate to accept the name 'law and literature' for his line of inquiry in *The Legal Imagination* (and in his later books) as there is an important sense in which it is unfitting. Consider, for example, these words from the opening of Richard Posner's *Law and Literature*:

> The field of law and literature . . . is not completely new. . . . But it is only since the publication in 1973 of James Boyd White's *The Legal Imagination*, a book that audaciously claims that a study of literature should be a part of legal education, that a distinct, self-conscious field of law and literature can be said to have emerged.
>
> (Posner 1988: 12)

Posner should redirect his use of the word 'audaciously'. He has simply failed to read *The Legal Imagination* with any care, for White made no such 'claims'. Posner's inapt territorial 'field' metaphor* can readily deafen us to White's claim that law *is* a 'literary' 'activity' (*Imagination). Posner's clumsy language may do an injustice if it gets in the way of giving White a fair hearing.

OK. Dick, let's start this all over again and see if we can turn it into an exercise in communication, not win-rhetoric* in the service of promoting a selectively imagined 'field', namely 'law and economics'.[1]

'Listening Modes': Mark Weisberg and Jean Koh Peters

In 'Experiments in Listening', Weisberg and Peters invite their readers to reflect on their 'experiences of listening' and to think about how they might use those experiences 'to improve' their listening practices (Weisberg and Peters 2007: 428). To assist here, they draw from their own experiences in making a claim that 'a skillful listener will . . . have available a variety of listening modes and will carefully choose which mode is appropriate for the setting' (428). How are we to listen to Weisberg and Peters?

In one section of the paper, they ask their reader to 'play'* the 'believing game' and the 'doubting game' (437–8). Loosely, the believing game is listening 'with the grain'; 'doubting' is listening 'against the grain'.[2] When we listen 'with the grain', we are trying to believe what the speaker is saying – to accept unquestioningly. When we listen 'against the grain', we are trying to doubt what the speaker is saying – asking what has been left out, what problematic assumptions may have been made, and so on. We can catch a sense of the 'games' when they turn to 'a clinical legal context':

> [P]laying the believing game allows a new lawyer to establish rapport, to take her client's felt and presented views, and before asking critical or clarifying questions to hear and understand as a whole a client's story and his perspective as he has seen fit to present it. . . . [A]s their relationship progresses, it would be inappropriate for a lawyer to maintain a purely believing mode in her listening. As she begins to amass extrinsic evidence, which may contradict or make her skeptical about her client's position, the lawyer and her client must collaborate, and the client must be confronted with concerns about his case. In addition, the client must be prepared for skeptical adversaries, skeptical fact-finders and decision makers, and the range of doubt they will encounter throughout. In fact, we would expect that a lawyer who failed to make her client aware of the doubting to come would have neglected an important dimension of her job.
>
> [We suggest to students that,] as they listen to their client and prepare for the presentation of her case, they regularly think about the balance between doubting and believing that they have exercised in their interactions with that client and, at any point in any interview, decide consciously where they want to situate themselves on the doubting and believing spectrum. If a student or lawyer also has looked at critical incidents from his past, he may conclude that as a default, he feels more comfortable when he has situated his listening at particular places on the doubting and believing spectrum. This will remind him to make sure

> that he spends time with the client on the parts of the spectrum that do not necessarily come naturally to him.
>
> (438)

Might it be fitting to initially approach Weisberg and Peters in a believing mode, to accept what they say about the value of believing and of doubting? Might we then approach them in a doubting mode? The two 'games' involve asking different 'questions' (*Questioning), which channel our attention*. They suggest that we will benefit from paying attention to our attention with the aim of learning to 'consciously' shift it. This can build our capacity for *both* sympathetic understanding* and detachment and for moving between the two at appropriate times, a capacity that is vital for making a judgment* of 'fit' – the material of justice* talk.

What might Weisberg and Peters say if they addressed the task of a judge in hearing two rival lawyers who both play doubting and believing with their clients? They could profit from engaging with this passage in White's *When Words Lose Their Meaning*:

> If a judge is to respond to the demands and possibilities presented by a legal case . . . , he or she will have to speak in an extraordinarily rich and complex way, not in a voice that is merely bureaucratic and official. To be true to the actual difficulties of a real legal case, an opinion must be full of the kind of life that comes from a set of acknowledged tensions: between the two versions of the story before the court; between the stories so told and the language of legal conclusion; between the demand that like cases be treated alike and the recognition that cases never are 'alike'; between the fidelities owed to the past and the future and those owed to the present; . . . and so on. . . .
>
> Honesty requires the judge to acknowledge that his own act of choosing cannot be wholly explained or justified. The good judge thus speaks in a double voice, as one who has brought to bear as well as he can the sources of authority external to himself, and as one who makes a choice for which he is responsible. An opinion is not merely an organized defense of his decision, the 'best case' for the result reached, but an articulation of what he really thinks the case should mean, including an expression of his doubts. The best judge, like Socrates, exposes himself to refutation. The most important achievement of judicial writing, indeed, is ethical and intellectual: the manifestation in performance of a serious, responsible, and open mind, faithful to the sources of authority external to the self even while contributing to their transformation. . . .
>
> From a lawyer's point of view, the future offered by *McCulloch* and similar cases is a life of argument in which he puts together cases out of the materials of the world, addressing the tensions between ordinary language and legal language and among various strains within legal

> discourse, and then offers to the judge, or to the jury, an ideal version of the case for their consideration and persuasion. The task for the lawyer is not simply to persuade, using whatever cultural devices lie at hand, but to persuade a judge or jury that one result or another is the best way to act in the cultural situation defined by these facts or this evidence and by this set of statutes and opinions and understandings. . . . The . . . lawyer . . . speaks to the judge or jury not as they are defined by their individual interests, passions, and biases but as they are defined by their role, which is to do justice.
>
> (White 1984: 269–70)

Is not the concept of 'justice' in the last sentence so ill-defined that much room is left for appeals to 'individual interests, passions, and biases'?

That question, we might say, comes from someone playing the doubting game. It draws (almost word for word) from Posner's response, in *Law and Literature* (1988: 316), to the last six lines of the above passage. The doubter Posner leaves out the rest of the passage – the part that offers a 'performance'*-centred image of law that coalesces with an image of justice*. In leaving it out, Posner makes no place for his reader to engage in the activity* of attunement* to White's meaning of 'justice', a meaning that is concerned with a way of being, which cannot without great injustice be reduced to a mere 'concept'.

What would Posner have to do to play the believing game? Might he have to speak in a different voice*, 'in an extraordinarily rich and complex way' – 'in a double voice', one that has no hesitation in 'including an expression of his doubts'? Might he do well to expand the passage that he quotes, if only to become 'faithful to the sources of authority external to the self'? In doing so, might he then be in a position to do justice to White's use of the word 'justice'?

Metaphor

'Is all language metaphorical in all its uses, or does it make sense to isolate a certain activity or event and call that metaphor?' That question comes from White's *The Legal Imagination* (1973: 956). This chapter may be taken as a response to it.

'The Whole of Thinking': Composition and Literary Criticism at Amherst

White's interest in metaphor can be traced to Amherst College, where his composition teacher, Theodore Baird, centred a course on it. In an article on the naturalist Charles Darwin, an article that connects him to the essayist and historian Thomas Carlyle, Baird attends to the nature and significance of metaphor:

> Plainly Carlyle belongs to literature. Darwin's position is obscure. A popular textbook places him at the opposite pole, remarking that his work 'cannot be said to belong to literature, if in the definition of literary work is presupposed an effort towards artistic expression.' Yet Darwin, who certainly never thought of himself as a writer like Carlyle, was deeply concerned with literary composition . . . . Darwin's subject – the face of the earth, the processes of nature – had long been within the scope of literature . . . . When in the *Origin* Darwin came to express how Nature as a whole seemed to him, he . . . used a metaphor. Nature, he said, is like something else, a struggle for existence, in which the fittest survive. . . . He took pains to say that the struggle for existence is not a fact but only a figure of speech.
>
> The figure of speech . . . points to a complicated event. A blow by blow account . . . is impossible in the struggle of any organism's existence. How little he knew in detail Darwin is constantly reminding the reader . . . For him exists a language problem . . . .
>
> Galton's praise of Darwin, that he had 'studied veracity as the highest of arts,' belongs to him both as an observer and as a writer. Actually it is hard to see how these two processes can be separated and distinguished.

> It is easier to conclude that in 1859, at one of the great moments in modern thought, literature and science were united.
>
> (Baird 1946/1999: 163–71)

Plainly Baird belongs to composition, alongside Carlyle and Darwin. Baird's great talent was his ability to place students into the position of experiencing 'a language problem'. Baird's subject, the struggle of imagination* in the activity* of composing with language*, is a complicated event, aided with a talent for metaphor. For Baird, a metaphorical phrase is much more than what some people call 'mere ornament'. In a world not of stable ground but of constant 'evolution', metaphors are the medium in which a composer – beginner, intermediate, and advanced – can set sail.

Baird's imaginings on metaphor did not emerge in a vacuum. His colleague Robert Frost had a long teaching career at Amherst. Frost claimed that metaphor pervades our lives with language:

> Poetry begins in trivial metaphors, pretty metaphors, 'grace' metaphors, and goes on to the profoundest things that we have. Poetry provides the one permissible way of saying one thing and meaning another.
>
> I have wanted in late years to go further and further in making metaphor the whole of thinking . . . . We . . . ask boys in college to think . . . but we seldom tell them it is just putting this and that together; it is just saying one thing in terms of another.
>
> (Frost 1931/1966: 38 and 41)

Those claims are deeply at odds with ocularcentric Enlightenment thinkers who claimed that language can be made to function as a 'perspicuous' tool for objective inquiry, that it can be literal and thus devoid of metaphor.

Frost thought we would do well to attend to the metaphors we inescapably use, not the least because they 'will break down at some point' (38–9). When 'metaphor breaks down', as the hero in Austen's *Persuasion* learned at Lyme (*Character), we have an opportunity for becoming self-conscious composers of meaning. The experience* of 'breakdown' may be uncomfortable, especially when a metaphor frames our image of the world. The experience might prod one to take experience seriously in a method* for 'know'-ing.

Let us return to *The Legal Imagination*. In a section titled 'Is the Judge Really a Poet?', after reproducing material from Frost on poetry and metaphor, White asks: 'Can it be said of the judicial opinion (as Frost says of the poem) that it is metaphor, "saying one thing and meaning another, saying one thing in terms of another"? Is it "simply made of metaphor"?' To assist with that question, he says:

> What is to the parties a barroom fight, a dreadful auto accident, or an unsuccessful deal, is spoken of by the lawyers and the courts in terms of

> other things: cases, statutes, familiar arguments, and so on . . . . This is a way of talking of one thing in terms of another, of life in terms of law, and it could be seen as the central judicial activity. The events . . . are converted into a legal matter, and this conversion or metamorphosis is an act of the imagination. There are necessarily at least two languages here, two ways of talking; and in the judge's opinion, as in the poet's metaphor, the life of the expression comes in part from an initial tension, an incompatibility, between them. This tension creates a need that the conversion meets and fulfills. . . . It might indeed be said that every opinion is a 'new metaphor inside or it is nothing.'
>
> (773)

White here offers to transform the 'ordinary', an event that leads to a legal case, into the extraordinary, an image of law as a system of 'conversion or metamorphosis'. He performs an act of the imagination* about 'an act of the imagination'. His image of law attends to an 'activity'* that calls for creativity on the part of those who participate. Judges, and hopefully the parties to whom they speak, are to some degree noticeably metamorphosed.

'The Negotiation of Meaning': George Lakoff and Mark Johnson

Claims about metaphor pervading our lives have become commonplace in academic circles today. A landmark in the turn to metaphor is Lakoff and Johnson's *Metaphors We Live By*. Here they criticize 'objectivism', an influential tradition that has made 'metaphors objects of belittlement and scorn' (1980: 186). Members of this tradition, they claim, use metaphors without attending to them as metaphors. In doing so, the tradition has contributed to the development of a defective 'language about language' (10).

A central part of *Metaphors We Live By* criticizes the 'conduit metaphor', which 'masks aspects of the communicative process' (11). Integral to this metaphor are defective assumptions about 'meaning'. One assumption is 'MEANINGS ARE OBJECTS' – 'that meanings have an existence independent of people and contexts' (11). Another is that 'LINGUISTIC EXPRESSIONS ARE CONTAINERS FOR MEANINGS' – 'that words and sentences have meanings in themselves, independent of any context or speaker' (11). Those two assumptions link to another: 'COMMUNICATION IS SENDING', or 'The speaker puts meanings (objects) into words (containers) and sends them (along a conduit) to a hearer who takes the meaning/objects out of the word/containers' (10).[1] In short, communication is merely the transfer of information from one person to another. The 'person', however, is not a real person but some kind of machine.

For one who lives by the conduit metaphor, 'understanding'* is merely 'seeing' an objective meaning (103). Lakoff and Johnson offer a different image, three interdependent components of which are 'culture'*, 'experience'*, and 'imagination'*:

> When people who are talking don't share the same culture, knowledge, values, and assumptions, mutual understanding can be especially difficult. Such understanding *is* possible through the negotiation of meaning. To negotiate meaning with someone, you have to become aware of and respect both differences in your backgrounds and when these differences are important. You need enough diversity of cultural and personal experience to be aware that divergent world views exist and what they might be like. You also need patience, a certain flexibility in world view, and a generous tolerance for mistakes, as well as a talent for finding the right metaphor to communicate the relevant parts of unshared experiences or to highlight the shared experiences while deemphasizing others. Metaphorical imagination is a crucial skill in creating rapport and in communicating the nature of unshared experience. This skill consists, in large measure, of the ability to bend your world view and adjust the way you categorize your experience. Problems of mutual understanding are not exotic; they arise in all extended conversations where understanding is important.
>
> (231)

For Lakoff and Johnson, 'metaphor' is, to use what they call 'orientational metaphors' (14), not *peripheral* but *central* to the complex process of *under*standing. Acts of metaphor create a 'world view'. Further acts enable us to 'bend' it.

What Lakoff and Johnson say about the 'negotiation of meaning' is readily *transportable* to law. To exercise my 'metaphorical imagination', the case method* in law is a version of what they call 'extended conversations': lawyers make sense of a new case in terms of 'right' similarities with an analogous case, or 'metaphor'. For a person who lives by an image of the law as a system of rules, that exercise of my metaphorical imagination could lead to a 'bend' in her or his 'world view'. It could also lead to a 'conversation*' that 'bends' mine.

Let us continue to negotiate the meaning of that which Lakoff and Johnson call the 'negotiation of meaning'. Here we will connect their passage to a passage from White's *The Edge of Meaning* that concerns his engagement with Herbert and Frost:

> I read these two poets together here not only because there are interesting and important comparisons to be drawn between the ways in which they work, but also in order to exemplify a process deep in the heart of intellectual life, . . . namely, the process of reading one work, or set of works, in light of another. . . . Reading one work in light of another is the reader's equivalent of metaphor, which Frost once defined as saying one

> thing and meaning another, saying one thing in terms of another. Our experiences of reading naturally shape each other, for every text derives much of its meaning—in a sense all of it—from its context, and we cannot help placing what we read in contexts partly of our own making, defined by our educations. . . . What I say, then, has an irreducibly autobiographical element; this is not a mistake or embarrassment, for it is in fact part of my point that all of our readings have much the same elements, and that it might be good to make them more explicit than we usually do.
>
> (White 2001: 191)

White is concerned with the negotiation of meaning in the activity* of 'reading'*: that which we call 'meaning' is not in the text to be found like coal in the ground but created in part through 'the reader's equivalent of metaphor'. We may hope that in reading the passage from White 'in light of' the passage from Lakoff and Johnson that both passages acquire new meaning. We may also hope that the experience of reading both passages together helps us come to a fuller understanding of the vital 'place' of 'context' in the 'meaning' of a text.

The activity of translation is an extreme version of the 'negotiation of meaning'. In *Justice as Translation*, drawing from Ortega y Gasset, White describes every translation as involving two kinds of modifications: 'deficiencies' and 'exuberances' (1990: 235). Deficiencies are 'aspects of the original that are not replicated in the translations'; exuberances are 'aspects of meaning that appear in the translation but are not part of the original'. Exuberances and deficiencies have various 'sources': 'from the fact that the words we use have different histories in the two cultures, hence necessarily different and unreproducible meanings; from the very structures of the two languages, each of which will require that we specify something—gender, tense, aspect, number—as to which the other is silent; and from the differing social, cultural, and physical contexts into which utterance is an intrusion'. Interested in how we might conceive of and talk about the processes of translation, White develops the metaphor of the dance:

> We can think of an expression . . . not as a way of conveying a message or idea, as a 'vehicle' with a 'content,' but as a gesture the meaning of which is indissolubly tied to its immediate and unique context: to . . . the prior texts that its author and audience use to establish and understand its terms, to its location in a particular place in the physical world, and so on. Our responses to such expressions, whether interpretations or translations, are not to be thought of as replicating the originals or conveying their 'content' but as gestures themselves; as if the first expression were a piece of a dance, an invitation to make a dance together, and as if our response to it were answering movements. There is to such a gesture no single right response but an infinitude number of possible

> responses, many of them good ones, many not so good; in evaluating them we should not speak of accuracy so much as appropriateness.
>
> (236)

The metaphor of 'conveying' will be associated with questions that differ from the metaphor of the dance. A question such as 'Might there be more appropriate possibilities and contexts?' can replace one such as 'Have I got the right answer?' This will redirect the translator's attention* away from delusive objective meaning to the reality of different experiential meanings and the task of fittingly bridging them.

Failure in the effort to 'convey' meaning can be instructive to the extent that 'it brings one to a sense of self and language that is different from, and erosive of those that guide our initial expectations.' White continues:

> To attempt to translate puts you in a place between texts, between languages, where you must respect both; to attempt to interpret puts you between the text and the present, where again you must respect both. In either case the more fully you inhabit the original—the more familiar you make it—the stranger and more unsatisfactory your own language (or your own version of the text you are reading) becomes. . . . The effect is to render your own language problematic: opaque, awkward, restrictive. You open a chamber of the mind that before was closed and bring under scrutiny that which had theretofore seemed invisible, natural, beyond any imagined contemplation, your language itself.
>
> (255)

Translation offers an experience resembling travel, a movement* from 'place' to 'place', from 'the more familiar' to 'the stranger'. To 'inhabit' what is Other is to displace one's existing habit-at. White's language offers a resource for revisiting the possible virtues of alienation*: there is valuable kind of transcendence that involves a transformative experience* of coming to imagine oneself and others differently.

'The Economy of Intellect': D. N. McCloskey

Many economists stress the importance of what they call exchange. Exchange in markets, they claim or suggest, is vital for 'understanding' the process of resource allocation. There is an important sense, however, in which such understanding is shallow, for they commonly neglect the factors and forces – legal, moral, political, among others – that enable and structure exchange. In 'Economics and Law', White offers these critical remarks:

> The enormous matrix of productive human life and meaningful activity that lies outside the practices of exchange, like the matrix of the natural world, is simply excluded from the exchange mentality. Economics of the

> kind that I have been discussing is thus defective even as an economics, for it in principle abstracts from a larger context a set of activities that depend upon, and interact with, that context. A proper economics—in its Greek root meaning household management—would respect and reflect the conditions, natural and cultural, upon which the exchange itself depends and would seek to value properly what that system . . . radically undervalues.
>
> (White 1986: 191)

Is there a defective allocation of intellectual resources in economics? If there is, how might this change? Might White's words have weight and contribute to change? We might wonder about how his ideas will fare in the market-place of ideas.

A resource for thought and expression about 'the economy of intellect' resides in McCloskey's *The Rhetoric of Economics*. Here is a key passage:

> The notion of a conversation gives an answer to the demand for standards of persuasiveness. One recognizes with ease when a conversation in one's own field is working well. Most economists would agree, for instance, that at present the conversation about the real side of international trade is not working well, after a long period of excellence in the late 1950s and 1960s. . . . On the other hand, no economist familiar with the situation in economic history improved radically from the 1960s, and continues at this higher level.
>
> The conversations overlap enough to make one almost as sure about neighboring fields: examining the overlap is what editors, referees, and members of research panels do. The overlaps of the overlaps . . . keep all honest if some try to be. Q.E.D.: the overlapping conversations provide the standards. It's a market argument. There is no need for philosophical lawmaking or methodological regulation to keep the economy of intellect running just fine.
>
> It is best to cite philosophers against methodological philosophizing. . . . [I]n answering how serious philosophers are themselves to be distinguished from system-making lunatics[,] Amelie Oksenberg Rorty writes that what is crucial is 'our ability to engage in continuous conversation, testing one another, discovering our hidden presuppositions, changing our minds because we have listened to the voices of our fellows. Lunatics also change their minds, but their minds change with the tides of the moon and not because they have listened, really listened, to their friends' questions and objections.'
>
> (McCloskey 1985: 28)

What is it that McCloskey has in mind when he uses the metaphors 'market' and 'economy'? A metaphor can be an 'economical' way of avoiding an explanation. Some dissenting economists might well complain that McCloskey has been too economical with his words and that he has failed to listen to questions and objections relating to his metaphors. Might McCloskey have done well to set out to find the right metaphor for giving more life to the market metaphor? How might dissenters engage in the negotiation of meaning?

In his dissent in *Abrams v. United States*, a case involving a Russian immigrant and an anarchist and their leaflets criticizing President Wilson for sending American soldiers to Russia, Justice Holmes said: '[M]en . . . may come to believe . . . that the ultimate good desired is better reached by free trade in ideas—that the best test of truth is the power of the thought to get itself accepted in the competition of the market' (*Abrams* 1919: 630). In 'Legal Knowledge', White offers a close reading* of those words, and claims that Holmes engages in a constructive 'act of imagination', one that 'is not ideological or mechanical in character' (2002: 1421–2). After quoting the paragraph that contains the market metaphor, White does point out that what Holmes says 'can be criticized':

> The exchange of ideas, or their competition, is not really a market, in which people are paying more or less for what they value; what he has in mind is closer to what may be his deepest image of human life, the process of evolution by the survival of the fittest. But survival is a test of power, not of truth, and we all know that false, despicable, and dangerous ideologies or ideas can thrive for a long time. Particularly in the field of ethics and justice, there is no reason to think that we always move progressively toward a better world. And Holmes's view that significant speech consists of 'ideas' or 'thoughts' is highly limiting, for it tends to find the value of speech in its reified products, when one might think that its value is in fact processual, subtle, and far too protean to be reduced to something called 'ideas.' It is in fact one of the great merits of this very paragraph that it cannot be boiled down to a single idea, or concept, which can be simply carried away by the reader; it is itself too complex, too tension-filled, too alive, to permit such treatment.
>
> (1421–2)

How are we to read that passage? While there may be a side of us that wants to have it 'boiled down to a single idea, or concept, which can be simply carried away by the reader', there may be another side that 'might think that its value is in fact processual, subtle, and far too protean to be reduced to something called "ideas"'. We might say that the latter side is concerned with the activity* that we are calling attunement*. White is performing this activity in his engagement with Holmes' use of the market metaphor, trying to catch what 'he has in mind'. He is seeking to do justice* to Justice Holmes. In doing so, White offers the beginnings of a new story of the marketplace of ideas, a story that lends itself to productively transforming the way we imagine 'the economy of intellect'.

Method

The Case Method of Law: Anthony T. Kronman
'A New Horizon': Bernard Lonergan's 'Transcendental Method'

'A method is a way of bringing together what we think we are doing and how we are doing it: *meta* + *hodos* = about the way; the way about the way' (Berthoff 1981: 4). This chapter brings together materials relating to the 'what' and 'how' of our 'doing'.

The Case Method of Law: Anthony T. Kronman

What is involved in 'thinking like a lawyer'? An early lesson at law school is this: there are at least two sides to a case. In *The Lost Lawyer*, Kronman outlines the significance of the lesson as it concerns the intellectual and ethical demands placed on law students. Here is one passage:

> The case method of law teaching presents students with a series of concrete disputes and compels them to reenact these disputes by playing the roles of the original contestants or their lawyers. It thus forces them to see things from a range of different points of view and to entertain the claims associated with each, broadening their capacity for sympathy by taxing it in unexpected ways. But it also works in the opposite direction. For the student who has been assigned a partisan position and required to defend it is likely to be asked . . . for his views regarding the judge's decision in the case. To answer, he must disengage himself from the sympathetic attachments he may have formed as a committed, if imaginary, participant and reexamine the case from a disinterested judicial point of view. The case method thus works simultaneously to strengthen both the student's powers of sympathetic understanding and his ability to suppress all sympathies in favor of a judge's scrupulous neutrality. Most important, it increases his tolerance for the disorientation that movement back and forth between these different attitudes occasions. In this way the case method serves as a forcing ground for the moral imagination by cultivating . . . bifocality . . . .
>
> One aim of this . . . is the cultivation of those perceptual habits that lawyers need in practice. Forcing students to defend positions they do not believe in or that they consider morally offensive may seem arbitrary and

> insensitive, but it serves an important goal. The student who is put in this position must strain to see the claim he has been given to defend in the most attractive light. He must work to discover its strengths and to articulate them, and this he cannot do unless he temporarily puts his earlier convictions to one side. In this way students get used to looking with a friendly eye even at those positions they personally reject . . . . Gradually, much of this becomes habitual. . . . The gradual acceptance of this scheme marks a change in perception, in the way one sees legal conflict as well as thinks about it. . . . This perceptual adjustment forms the core of the student's nascent professional persona, and is reflected in the habits and reflexes that increasingly distinguish his approach to legal problems from that of a layperson uneducated in the law.
>
> (Kronman 1993: 113–14)

How are we to go about reading* that passage? Might we first play the 'believing game' and then the 'doubting game' (Weisberg and Peters – *Listening)? Doing so could define by performance* a version of the 'bifocality' that Kronman applauds.

For Kronman, the roots of 'understanding'* perhaps begin in 'movement'*. His remark about the 'movement back and forth between . . . different attitudes' brings to mind the capacity of the poetic imagination* for effecting a 'reconciliation of opposite or discordant qualities' (Coleridge 1817/1905: 150).[1] The law is an enterprise of the 'moral imagination', one that can transform 'uneducated' 'habits' into educated ones. Kronman does not oppose habit and reason but seeks to integrate them (*Integration). Uneducated habits provide a point of view that is unaware that it is a point of view. Educated habits can enable us to 'see things from a range of different points of view'. (These can equip us to make a judgment* in the direction of justice*.) In short, Kronman believes that good character* can be cultivated and that law is a culture* (collective 'habits and reflexes') in which the 'cultivation' can be done. This is not to say that such cultivation will actually happen, but rather to attend to the possibilities of law, possibilities that are frequently neglected and for which we can strive.

In 1996, White gave a talk in response to a talk by Kronman on the decline of civility in modern life. In his response, White joins Kronman in re-imagining the case method:

> [L]aw should be taught as a discipline of thought and argument with its own structure, . . . at the center of which is the activity of claiming meaning for human experience, . . . and doing so in a language that is at once a source of authority and itself subject to perpetual revision. It can best be taught I think through a revived case method; one in which the case is seen . . . as a kind of prospective apprenticeship, in which the student learns by doing. What the lawyer will face in her professional life

> is a series of cases, after all; a legal education can be conceived of as training her how to deal with cases, which . . . almost invariably have a quality of freshness or newness, testing the adequacy of prior formulations and calling for present invention. They involve her directly in the process . . . of claiming meaning for experience in an authoritative language that is made by others but open to transformation at her hands. What she can learn is the kind of complex thought and argument, at once general and particular, at once interpretative and creative, at once respectful of the past and responsive to the present, that characterizes the law at its best.
>
> (White 1996: 767)

The law is not an object but a dynamic 'activity'*, in which lawyers are active, 'doing': 'claiming meaning', 'testing the adequacy of prior formulations', and contributing to 'perpetual revision'. For White, 'the law at its best' involves more than winning an argument. What is important is that which happens all 'at once'. This is when, to use Kronman's language, there is simultaneous 'sympathetic attachment' (or feeling) and 'scrupulous neutrality' (or intellect). This is the material of integration*, which makes a place for the constructive 'transformation' of 'language'* and community.

'A New Horizon': Bernard Lonergan's 'Transcendental Method'

'Thoroughly understand what it is to understand, and not only will you understand the broad lines of all there is to be understood but also you will possess a fixed base, an invariant pattern, opening upon all further developments of understanding.' That is Lonergan's thesis in *Insight* (1957/1973: xxviii). At the base of his inquiry is the activity* of questioning*:

> Why is the wheel round? . . . Where does the 'Why?' come from? What does it reveal or represent? . . . It is that tension, that drive, that desire to understand, that constitutes the primordial 'Why?' Name it what you please, alertness of mind, intellectual curiosity, the spirit of inquiry, active intelligence, the drive to know. Under any name, it remains the same and is, I trust, very familiar to you.
>
> (9)

If 'the drive to know' may be *so* 'very familiar to you', an experience* of alienation* may be needed. This calls for the play* of question-and-answer.

For Lonergan, 'knowing is an organically integrated activity' (415–16) that consists of three interdependent parts: 'experience'*, 'understanding'*, and 'judgment'*. As a reader reads his work, she will do well to: (a) attend to the 'experience' of Lonergan addressing her; (b) ask questions about our experience, questions associated with her 'understanding' of it; (c) ask questions about the validity of Lonergan's claims, questions that call for a 'judgment' (273).

As she does this, she will be on the way to achieving what he calls 'self-appropriation' (xxii), which 'is first and foremost a process of taking possession of oneself as a knower and a doer' (Morelli and Morelli 2002: 18).[2]

The task of 'self-appropriation', being 'painstaking and slow' (xxiii), calls for a certain kind of character*. Lonergan emphasizes the character strength 'genuineness':

> Genuineness . . . does not brush questions aside, smother doubts, . . . It confronts issues, . . . studies their many aspects, . . . contemplates their concrete consequences in one's own life and in the lives of others. . . . Though it fears the cold plunge into becoming other than one is, it does not dodge the issue . . . . It is capable of assurance and confidence, not only in what has been tried and found successful, but also in what has yet to be tried. . . . Such genuineness is ideal. It goes far beyond the native endowment of detachment and disinterestedness that we possess in the pure desire to know. For it presupposes the accumulations of direct, introspective, and reflective insights that are needed to discriminate between issues. . . . Without due perspective and discrimination, the exercise of genuineness . . . results only in the earnest person with a remarkable flair for concentrating on the wrong questions. Nor can perspective and discrimination be acquired without asking the significant questions. There is, then, a vicious circle to be broken, for we cannot become wise and discriminating without concentrating on the right questions, and we cannot select those questions unless we are already wise and discriminating.
>
> (477–8)

That passage, which could serve as a valuable resource for thought and expression about Lonergan himself, brings to mind Gunnar Myrdal's work on social dynamics, especially the 'principle of cumulation' (Myrdal 1944/1996: App. 3). He described a process in which parts of a whole social system respond to or impact on other parts, and changes in the system can accumulate, causing changes in one or many directions through the whole system. There can be a 'vicious circle', with the dynamic process moving in a harmful direction, and a 'virtuous circle', with a movement in a positive direction. Lonergan's account of knowing has a place for both circles.

At the level of a person's accumulation of insights, moving from a vicious to a virtuous circle may require the help of a teacher. A genuine teacher is not a person who deposits information in a student but one who is able to connect to the questioner within us. Lonergan writes:

> [T]eaching . . . throws out the clues . . . that lead to insight. It cajoles attention to drive away the distracting images that stand in insight's way. It puts the further questions that reveal the need of further insights to modify and complement the acquired store. It has grasped the strategy

> of developing intelligence, and so begins from the simple to advance to the more complex. . . . [A]ll this is done by professional teachers that know their job.
>
> (174)

A good teacher will have learned how to learn, learned how to ask the right questions, and will invite a student to ask questions and to judge them for herself.

For Lonergan, learning through the activity of questioning is a movement that he associates with the word 'transcendence': 'despite the imposing name, transcendence is the elementary matter of raising further questions' (635). A less imposing word is 'beyond': 'inquiry, insight, and formulation do not merely reproduce the content of sensible experience but go beyond it' (635).

The regular asking of questions centring on experience, understanding, and judgment is the material of 'method' (602–4). 'Method', Lonergan says in *Method in Theology*, 'offers not rules to be followed blindly but a framework for creativity' (1972: xii). He goes on to say:

> A method is a normative pattern of recurrent and related operations yielding cumulative and progressive results. There is a method, then, where there are distinct operations, where each operation is related to the others, where the set of relations forms a pattern, where the pattern is described as the right way of doing the job, where operations in accord with the pattern may be repeated indefinitely, and where the fruits of such repetition are, not repetitious, but cumulative and progressive.
>
> (4)

We can call a method that is 'not confined categorically to some particular field or subject' a 'transcendental method' (14). Lonergan identifies these 'transcendental precepts' that animate his method: 'Be attentive, Be intelligent, Be reasonable, Be responsible' (20). His 'transcendental method' is nothing esoteric:

> Now in a sense everyone knows and observes transcendental method. Everyone does so, precisely in the measure that he is attentive, intelligent, reasonable, responsible. But in another sense it is quite difficult to be at home in transcendental method, for that is not to be achieved by reading books or listening to lectures or analyzing language. It is a matter of heightening one's consciousness by objectifying it, and that is something that each one, ultimately, has to do in himself and for himself.
>
> (14)

Lonergan invites his reader to attend to a cognitive process that is at work in 'everyone'. While turning 'in' might sound subjective, and thus beyond 'objectifying', we will do well to 'transcend' the objective–subjective opposition.[3]

Lonergan's approach to 'method' emerged out of his encounter with the work of Aquinas. Speaking generally of the process of 'encounter': 'it is the one way in which self-understanding and horizon can be put to the test' (247). Lonergan's 'horizon' is 'the limit of one's field of vision' (235). (He would not have us think of him as ocularcentric.) His 'horizon' is tied up with the questioning: beyond a person's horizon are questions that are without meaning or significance to her or him.

Lonergan's prime concern is with 'the movement into a new horizon', including one that 'involves an about-face': 'a conversion' (237–8).[4] He identifies three kinds: 'intellectual', 'moral', and 'religious' (238). All of them have to do with 'self-transcendence' (241). Intellectual conversion is a radical change in 'habits of thought' (239), a transformation in one's image of the world, as produced in the processes of experiencing, understanding, and judging. Moral conversion 'changes the criterion of one's decisions and choices from satisfactions to values'. One's basic questions change, from, say, 'What can I get?' to 'Is this becoming of me?' Religious conversion is 'being grasped by ultimate concern. It is other-worldly falling in love' (240). One's questions are a defining feature: 'Questions for intelligence, for reflection, for deliberation reveal the eros of the human spirit, its capacity and its desire for self-transcendence' (242).

Lonergan offers to unsettle conventional disciplinary boundaries, in part by expanding the conventional domain of philosophy. '[T]he task of philosophy', he claims, 'is to foster the emergence of authentic human beings' (1985: 246). That sentence could serve as a valuable starting point for responding to this question in White's *The Legal Imagination* (1973: 631): 'Can you find a way to bring together the lawyer and philosopher in your own life, or are they . . . hopelessly incompatible identities?'

After reading Lonergan, a law student might ask this: What do we 'know' when we know the law? White offers some suggestive remarks for a response:

> I once argued very strenuously that a certain administrative practice violated the constitution, and a friend kept asking me how I knew it was unconstitutional. I kept avoiding the question, feeling that the question put the issue wrongly but not knowing how to say so. It has since occurred to me that you never 'know' that a practice is unconstitutional or that a right has been violated the way you know that the Dodgers won or that your bike is stolen; instead you decide that the practice is unconstitutional or that the right is violated and explain why, or you urge upon another the rightness of your proposed decision. The question 'How do you know?' is a move from another game, a response to statements of description, not to statements of argument or decision. The question that should come next is 'How do you reach that conclusion?' or 'Why do you say so?'
>
> (231)

White and his friend, especially if she or he was a self-identified 'black letter' lawyer, may not have been seeing the same 'constitution'. A simplistic use of a visual metaphor* ('seeing') for the activities involved in 'knowing' can lead us to pursue a problematic line of questioning. White would have us get into the right 'game' – the justification ('rightness') game. We might wonder what questions White asked himself in coming to a judgment* on what questions to ask. What was his method*?

The Latin root of the word conversion means to 'turn around' or 'transform'. White's image of law explicitly has a 'conversion' process at its heart:

> The law is transformative. It acts upon certain material—the problem or dispute or trouble brought by the client to the lawyer—which has one principle of organization and intelligibility, and converts it into something that has to be understood in very different ways. In a case like *Cohen v. California*, for example, it converts a dispute about a vulgar motto on a jacket into a consideration of the fundamental nature of political speech in our society. In converting its material, the law converts us as well, both speakers and listeners, as we come to inhabit the world this language and culture define. Conversion of this kind is a radical form of human activity, for which our word is art: we convert earth and oil into paintings that may change the imagination; pleasing sounds into music, not always pleasing, but sometimes of incredible power and beauty; human actors and costumes and words into another dimension of reality, on the stage, with another claim on our attention altogether. So too, in the law: we convert immediate experience into the subject of thought of a particular kind, which has at its center the question of meaning: what this event means, and should mean, in the language of the law; and what that language itself means, as a way in which we articulate our deepest values and attain collective being. The life that gives meaning in such a way is itself a life of meaning.
>
> (White 1996: 770)

What White says about 'the law' is 'transformative'. He connects material from a legal case with materials from outside the law and converts them into a consideration of the fundamental nature of our 'collective being'. In converting these materials, he converts us as we come to inhabit the world that his language defines. White's image of the 'activity' of knowing resembles Lonergan's, for it begins with 'immediate experience' and then turns to 'the question of meaning', or what Lonergan would talk about in terms of 'understanding' and 'judgment'. This image has a dynamic structure, one that has a place for self-knowledge: 'the question of meaning' can be addressed not only in 'the language of the law', for we can know 'what that language itself means, as a way in which we articulate our deepest values and attain collective being'. Whilst materials in the law (the problem or dispute or trouble brought by the client to the lawyer) can be 'understood in very different ways', so too can 'the law' itself: different analogies about the law 'may change the imagination', may make 'another claim on our attention altogether'. In transforming the law, we transform humankind. What is to become of us? One achievement of 'transcendental method' is to make a place for that question, one that we can ask, as White suggests, in and out of 'the law'.

It may be tempting to say that Lonergan developed a 'theory' of knowledge, but we need to use the word 'theory' with care. It can be traced to the Greek *theoria*, which originally meant participation in the delegation sent to a festival for the sake of honouring the gods. *Theoria*, in this sense, involves 'a genuine sharing in an event', and this offers a 'way in which a human heightening of awareness penetrates and discovers itself' (Gadamer 1981: 18). Given that 'theory' has come to commonly mean a detached reflection, we might consider rehabilitating it. We might begin by engaging with White's 'way of reading' (White 1984: 3–23). In later work, he offers this image of reading*:

> Think of the way one engages with a literary text . . . . The central question one asks is about its meaning . . . . One might say that when we talk about our experience of the original we engage in a form of translation . . . . Reading of this kind thus works by a kind of constant dialogue between the original text and what we can say about it, which is also a dialogue between the other and the self. As we read, the strange becomes familiar, the familiar strange; in the process our own preexisting commitments, our ways of thinking about the world, are exposed to thought and criticism, and we become, for the moment at least, different from what we were. . . .
>
> There is an internal version of this dialogue, too, between different parts of the self, the part that experiences and the part that talks . . . . [E]ach part acts on the other to change it: the experience of reading (or responding) leads to words about that experience, which in turn lead to a different experience of the text, which leads to still more words about it, and so on until one can go no farther. The very process of engagement with a literary text is in this sense transformative in kind: it teaches not only by offering 'insights' translatable into other terms – new propositions of fact or logic or value – but transforming the self, as we become our own version of what the reader has to be to understand and respond to it. . . .
>
> Of course not all texts offer to transform us in ways in which we want to be transformed – think for example of the racist joke or the piece of political propaganda or pornography. This means that the dialogue I describe above is even more complex than I have yet suggested, for during our reading we are constantly testing the person that the text is inviting us to become against the other things we are, or wish we were, and we must try to remain open simultaneously to the possibility that the shift is corrective of our own deficiencies and that it is not, that we

> are right to resist it. . . . The process of reading a literary text is thus one of perpetual attunement and judgment . . . .
>
> (White 1989: 2018–20)

How are we to 'engage' with that text? Let us connect White's image of reading with Lonergan's image of knowing. Both images have the components of 'experience'* and 'judgment'*, which come to life with a 'question'. The movement* in which 'the strange becomes familiar, the familiar strange' is, in Lonergan's terms, a shift in a person's 'horizon' (the 'limit' of one's image of the world). The experience of horizon-shift permits one to get in touch with the limits of one's self-understanding*. The movement in which 'we become, for the moment at least, different from what we were' is the material of the 'transcendental' aspect in Lonergan's 'method'. From their respective moving standpoints, both White and Lonergan suggest that the line between the external and 'internal' as it concerns the 'self' may be impossible to draw.[5]

Where is this activity of making connections getting us? Why do we try to make connections? We might say that the connections that we have made are part of our struggle to attune to the language of transcendental method in Lonergan's work and the language of 'attunement'* in White's work. Are we not productively familiarizing the strange and estranging the familiar? Is not this activity of 'translation' a necessity to do justice* to White?

Movement

In order to write from a place that is neither a 'view from everywhere' nor a 'view from nowhere', Kristie Fleckenstein urges writers to 'make a contradictory but complementary commitment to immersion and emergence' (1999: 281 and 295). This will involve the 'blurring of boundaries between inside and outside' (296). The preface to a book may be a relatively easy place to begin such blurring. The critic Hillis Miller suggests as much in the Preface to *The Linguistic Moment*:

> Prefaces are like thresholds, frontiers, gates, or doorways to the infolded text within. Marginal, . . . they are neither quite inside the work they introduce nor quite outside it. . . . A preface can only be written after the book, and it can only be written by someone with full knowledge of where the book leads the reader, the goal it reaches. On the other hand, a preface is almost the first thing the reader encounters. It is the first step in the journey that will lead her or him to the goal of finishing the book. A preface is both a foretaste and aftertaste. Insofar as one must have read the book through in order to understand it, to take that panoramic view of it the preface claims to have, the preface will by definition be incomprehensible or at least partially opaque to the reader who encounters it first, at least until she or he has read the book, at which point she or he will not need the preface.
>
> (Miller 1985: xiii–xiv)

That passage prompted me to question whether such a preface could be possible in this book, for there is an important sense in which I cannot know 'where the book leads the reader'. This situation exists because there cannot be a 'panoramic view' worthy of the name – a situation in harmony with a commitment to immersion. That is not to say we cannot have *a* 'view'. I would simply stress its brokenness – it would perhaps be unusually 'opaque'. A spirit of candidness would connect this brokenness to an expression of hope about the reader 'getting lost' (Frost – *Play) on our 'journey'.

What kind of journey does this book offer? Where is the 'end'? What metaphors of movement might be fitting?

'Transcending Our Own Competitive Particularity': C. S. Lewis

'As you look at the readings, you will notice that in selecting them I have drawn heavily upon my own reading of literature.' So says White in the Preface to *The Legal Imagination* (1973; xx). After joining him in reading* Homer, Plato, Shakespeare, Austen, Dickinson, Twain, Frost, among others, White asks 'why' we read literature (1973: 764). We will do well to 'transcend . . . cliché' (728) in our responses.

Lewis asks a similar 'why' question in *An Experiment in Criticism*. Here is part of his response:

> The nearest I have yet got to an answer is that we seek an enlargement of our being. We want to be more than ourselves. Each of us by nature sees the whole world from one point of view with a perspective and a selectiveness peculiar to himself. . . . But we want to see . . . with other eyes, to imagine with other imaginations . . . . One of the things we feel after reading a great work is 'I have got out'. Or from another point of view, 'I have got in'; pierced the shell of some other monad and discovered what it is like inside.
>
> Good reading, therefore, though it is not essentially an affectional or moral or intellectual activity, has something in common with all three. In love we escape from our self into one another. In the moral sphere, every act of justice or charity involves putting ourselves in the other person's place and thus transcending our own competitive particularity. In coming to understand anything we are rejecting the facts as they are for us in favour of the facts as they are. . . . Obviously this process can be described either as an enlargement or as a temporary annihilation of the self. But that is an old paradox; 'he that loseth his life shall save it'.
>
> (Lewis 1961: 137–8)

After reading that passage, we will have a resource for responding to a doubter who wonders about the value of the introduction to literary criticism in *The Legal Imagination*. ('Literary criticism has no serious place in the law.') Like literature, literary criticism can help us 'seek an enlargement of our being'. Both sorts of writing can offer a ground from which to judge legal writing, not least to ensure that any 'competitive particularity' is kept in its due place.

Speaking of competition, the passage from Lewis lends itself to thought and expression about this remark in the Preface to *The Legal Imagination*: 'I do not think this course lends itself to teaching by competitive methods' (xxii). Such methods, to the extent that they promote 'win-rhetoric' (Booth – *Rhetoric), could be an obstacle to free and friendly exchange of criticism, which is a vital resource for transcending our own competitive particularity.

At the outset of *The Legal Imagination*, White expresses the hope that his reader 'will come to some new awareness of his place in the world, of his powers and obligations' (1973: xxi). (We might say that White hopes his reader will feel 'I have got out.') Coming to such an 'awareness' is the material of 'transcending our own competitive particularity', a movement at the heart of 'every act of justice'. Every time we communicate, in and out of the law, the justice question arises. Acts of literature are called for in order to perform well. We can be sure that White wrote *The Legal Imagination* with the hope of helping his reader become equipped to do so.

'Stuck': Mark Twain's *Huckleberry Finn*

Here we continue with Twain's novel and White's engagement with it (*Language). To recall: Huck's creative rule, 'do whichever come handiest at the time', enables him to resist the cultural pressure to turn 'nigger' Jim over to the authorities without becoming a 'low down Abolitionist'. This is an impressive achievement. White points to the possibility of an even greater achievement:

> What was called for in Huck's situation was nothing less than a new way of imagining human relationships and a new way of expressing one's imagination. Huck achieves the first – the experience of the boy and the slave on the raft is a genuine discovery – but he fails to do the second and retreats into silence: at the end of the book he 'lights out for the territories.' In this passage, Twain does achieve a new way of expressing a newly imagined relationship, but even he has difficulties. . . . Twain's crisis of imagination might become clearer if you pretend you are Twain, having written the passage you have just read. What will the rest of your novel be like: what will Huck and Jim do and say next, whom will they meet and on what terms? . . . Can you imagine a friendship between these two people expressed in their actual lives in the world? . . . You may be interested to know that Twain in fact stopped writing this book at this point for several years, apparently stuck, not knowing how to go on. Many critics think that the rest of the novel fails to live up to what was achieved here, that at this point the imagination collapses. . . . Are there matters as to which we are situated somewhat like Huck or Twain?
>
> (26)

White's questioning* here calls for a close reading* of *Huckleberry Finn*, one that involves putting ourselves in Twain's place. In efforts to respond to White's questions, I repeatedly had the experience that Twain 'apparently' had, namely that of 'not knowing how to go on', being 'stuck'. The experience was an uncomfortable one. At certain stages, various questions came up, such as 'What do I say?' and 'Who is this "I"?' This was a 'crisis' of decision and identity, with words having a kind of hollowness, and feeling as if I am at the edge of that which we call 'understanding'*. (Two questions that arose were: 'How am I to imagine this "edge"?' and 'With what language?') To draw from the language of David Tracy (*Experience), this is one of those 'genuine limit-situations', in which a person encounters 'a certain limit or horizon to his or her existence'. In the present case, to come back to White's language, this is the 'point' at which my 'imagination collapses'). I later learned that this is a state of perplexity (or confusion) of the kind that gadflies such as Socrates seem to consider productive for opening up new possibilities for thought and expression, ultimately for doing justice*.[1]

'Constitutional Transformation' in South Africa: A. J. van der Walt

As suggested above (*Justice), Bram Fischer found himself in a genuine limit-situation, playing the role of lawyer and revolutionary at the same time: supporting the armed struggle by Umkhonto whilst defending its members – including Mandela – in the Rivonia Trial. (We can be sure Fischer could have enriched Huck's rule, 'do whichever come handiest at the time'.) In 1966, he was alone in the dock constructed for the Rivonia Trial. In his speech, he said:

> My conscience, my Lord, does not permit me to afford these laws such recognition as an even plea of guilty would involve. Hence, though I shall be convicted by this Court, I cannot plead guilty. I believe that the future may well say that I acted correctly.
>
> . . . All the conduct, my Lord, with which I have been charged, has been directed towards maintaining contact and understanding between the races of this country. If one day it may help to establish a bridge across which white leaders and the real leaders of the non-whites can meet to settle the destinies of all of us by negotiation, and not by force of arms, I shall be able to bear with fortitude any sentence which this Court may impose on me.
>
> (quoted in Clingman 1998: 415)

The metaphor* of his conduct as a 'bridge' is an act of hope in the direction of justice*. This bridge could help transform South Africa from a culture* of destructive authoritarianism to a culture that is democratic and egalitarian.

The 1993 'interim' Constitution is a landmark in the early efforts to break away from apartheid. The opening of its epilogue, 'National Unity and Reconciliation', places the document within the larger cultural and political context in which it was written:

> This Constitution provides a historic bridge between the past of a deeply divided society characterized by strife, conflict, untold suffering and injustice, and a future founded on the recognition of human rights, democracy and peaceful co-existence and development opportunities for all South Africans, irrespective of colour, race, class, belief or sex.
>
> (Constitution of the Republic of South Africa Act 200 of 1993)

That fragment was not included in the 1996 final Constitution, but the figure of the 'bridge' has been influential in expression about it.

Some of this expression draws from Etienne Mureinik's article 'A Bridge to Where?' For Mureinik, the 'from'/'to' movement is this: from 'a culture of . . . apartheid . . . coercion' to 'a culture of justification . . . built on persuasion' (1994: 32). Whilst the figure of the 'bridge' aptly suggests a departure from the apartheid regime, caution with it may well be of value. Augmenting talk about 'constitutional transformation', André van der Walt warns against a simple reading in which there is a 'linear progression, a journey from one place to another' (2001: 259). Let him explain:

> The value of the move from A(partheid) across the B(ridge) to C(onstitutionalism) is . . . in the perception that being in one place is better than being in another. The assumption is that apartheid is a place, a position, and that constitutional democracy is another place, a different position, the two being separated by the divide of transition from the one to the other. This places a static . . . view on the notion of transformation, in that it privileges certain value choices. More or less uncontroversially, it privileges one *place or position* over another (constitutional democracy over authoritarianism), and one *transformation process* over another (peaceful and constitutional transition over violent revolutionary change), but it also privileges other, less obvious and more controversial value choices: a preference for eventual stability over continuous change (position is more important than movement); a linear vision over a more complex vision of the history of the transition from apartheid to constitutional democracy (transition is a linear movement from A across B to C, and will end once we reach C); . . . and a spatial, position-orientated and thus strictly past/present, outside/inside, absent/present vision over a more complex vision of the relationship between pre-1994 and post 1994 law and jurisprudence in the transition.
>
> (294–5)

Van der Walt here attends to different ways of imagining processes of 'transformation'. One is 'linear movement', which is built on the assumption that there can be a choice between 'eventual stability' and 'continuous change' and that there exists a bright line between 'past' and 'present', and between 'outside' and 'inside'. Another way is a 'more complex' movement that renders problematic that assumption.

In offering a 'more complex' image, Van der Walt draws from Robert Cover's work, which has bridge imagery at its heart.[2] Cover's metaphoric bridges are concerned with connecting not so much positions across space but moments in time. For Cover, our individual and collective pasts and futures are intertwined in a manner that negates any sense of a sharp distinction among them. Put in the context of modern South Africa, it is a 'fallacy . . . to think that we can rid ourselves of the legacy of the past as easily as crossing a bridge, leaving our accepted version of the past (and the possibility of other versions) behind us decisively' (296). In particular:

> The legacy of apartheid land law remains with us even after the transformation to constitutional democracy. For one thing, the . . . inequities of the past, the unequal distribution of land and housing and other resources, will continue to affect social and legal relations as long as the balance of social and political power remains unequal. . . . Secondly, . . . the ghost of apartheid land law will also stay with us as long as the dominant Roman-Dutch common-law vision of private property as a superior, exclusive and absolute right continues to influence the nature and balance of property holdings. Moreover, we cannot leave the legacy of struggle jurisprudence behind us either: the ghost of apartheid land law will also stay with us as long as transformation jurisprudence remains locked in the confrontational mode of demanding justice from the apartheid structures and hence feeding off its continued presence. . . . In all of these ways the codes of apartheid law still haunt us and restrict the futures we can imagine.
>
> (296–7)

South Africans have inherited not only property arrangements but also ways of imagining these arrangements that support the institutionalized in-equality* of the past. To imagine the bridge metaphor as a simple tool for one-way movement is to direct attention away from this inheritance. The inattention may be attractive for some people, but we can be sure that 'the ghost of apartheid law' will continue to dwell.

Van der Walt's critique of the image of 'linear movement from A across B to C' readily connects to White's reading of Burke's *Reflections on the French Revolution*. For White, part of Burke's 'remarkable achievement' in the *Reflections* is its 'form':

> The form of the text is literary . . . . It does not have the linear structure appropriate to abstract intellectual argument. Instead, it is circular or spiraling in shape. The reader finds himself returning again and again to the same questions, but on each new encounter he finds them transformed by the text that defines them. This text moves not . . . from proposition to proposition, but through a process of repetition and transformation, and the language thus made becomes more complete and more familiar. This means that the reader is not asked to move from one general proposition to another . . . ; instead, he is immersed in a world like the real world, in which judgments of fact and reason and value are continuous and where the questions that are asked are not merely general and not merely particular but both at once, as questions of statesmanship and citizenship always are. Burke starts where life starts, with the world as

> it is, and he speaks a language of criticism and feeling and judgment, a language for movement and life within the world he creates. To make one's way in the world this text creates, one must learn its language. . . . In such ways as these Burke in this text offers his reader a 'British Constitution' that is at once a version of the world that is England and a way of maintaining and improving it, since for him 'constitution' has the force not only of a noun but of a verb: it is a structure of relations that includes the method of its own change, an activity in which we all engage.
>
> (White 1984: 218)

A reader who is familiar with White's work will know that what he says about Burke's form can be applied to his own. (White's spiralling shape helps his reader to immerse herself in the world in which Burke is immersed.) Written out of questions that integrate the general and the particular, (*Integration) his books have a literary quality. He starts where Burke starts, not isolated with blank paper but with inherited language and with decisions to make with regard to what kind of community to 'constitute'. Not one to separate 'fact' and 'value', White speaks not a language of 'abstract intellectual argument' but 'a language of criticism and feeling and judgment'. In the process of learning this language, we can expect to experience the sort of 'transformation' about which he talks.

Performance

'Performances in Language': Composition and Literary Criticism at Amherst
Authority and Communication: Charles Bingham

'I look upon a poem as a performance.' That sentence from Robert Frost appears in Richard Poirier's *The Performing Self* (1971/1992: 89). Poirier suggests that there is much to a poetic performance: 'pacing, economies, juxtapositions, aggregations of tone, the whole conduct of the shaping presence' (86–7). Shall we compare a poem to . . . ?

'Performances in Language': Composition and Literary Criticism at Amherst

Poirier described Theodore Baird's freshman composition course at Amherst as a 'radical immersion in the waywardness of language' (1992: 180). When Poirier was a freshman, Walker Gibson contributed to the teaching of Baird's course. Gibson went on to write *Seeing and Writing*, a composition course book, dedicated to Baird. Like Baird, he had a will to connect disciplines. In 1961, connecting law and literature, he published an article in the *New York University Law Review* titled 'Literary Minds and Judicial Style'. At the outset of his article, he makes the claim 'that certain terms and attitudes familiar to modern students of literature and language can be of direct and practical use to writers of legal compositions' (Gibson 1961: 915). His questions – 'questions familiar to . . . the teacher of composition' (921) – include: 'To whom am I talking – who is my reader?'; 'Who am "I" – that is, what sort of speaking voice shall I project by the manner in which I compose my language?'; and, 'What relation should I express between this 'I' and my reader . . . ?' When talking about the 'voice'*-related 'who' questions, Gibson uses words that we apply to relations in our social lives – words such as 'equal', 'patronized', and 'respect' – to judge judges. In doing so, Gibson suggests that there is an unavoidable ethical element in writing:

> The problem of composing good judicial writing cannot finally be so very different from the problem of composing any kind of good writing. The issues to be faced . . . come down pretty simply to a recognition of the virtues of one's reader. If I can *recognize* my reader, if I can see in him a person of discretion and taste, one who shares with me a sense of the world's

> multiplicity and a sense of the tenuous relation between language and experience, then I am all right. By recognizing him, I define him, and we may hope to communicate across the guarded boundaries that divide us.
>
> The writer of legal documents . . . may be doing himself an injustice if he fails to accept such an ambitious and high-minded notion of his art, choosing instead to think of himself as a relatively mechanical and lowly worker in words. Not so. There is no reason why almost any piece of legal writing – and certainly judicial writing – may not move us with its sensitive and wise and gracious handling of language. It is true that the legal writer operates within limiting situations, and he must attend painstakingly to the minutiae of facts that confront him. Yet it is also true that he is engaged in expressing in words the chaos of life, and no poet can say more. Judicial opinions and poetry are obviously not identical forms of expression; yet, in Frost's memorable phrase about poets, the legal writer too is attempting 'a momentary stay against confusion.' It is hard to think of a finer thing to do.
>
> A curious humility, or an equally curious arrogance, is apparent in the attitude that legal writers sometimes express toward their performances in language. One hears a lawyer or a judge remark, 'Oh, I'm no stylist – I just write down the facts in plain words.' This is both humble and arrogant – humble in surrendering elegance to the 'creative artists,' arrogant in suggesting that only 'the facts' really matter. But the situation is surely quite otherwise. The poet or novelist, the historian, the physicist, the appellate judge are all deeply involved in one essential responsibility: the expression of life's complexities in mere man-made words.
>
> (930)

What sort of speaking voice do we hear? We hear shifts between formal and colloquial 'language'*, shifts that help him avoid the 'arrogant' voice that he faults. We also hear a conversational rhythm (one with short sentences combined with longer sentences) that helps establish him as an equal with his reader (*Equality). We certainly do *not* have all affirmation, in the sense of a voice telling his readers about the way the world *is*, one without 'multiplicity'. Gibson qualifies the affirmation that there is (such as 'This is both humble and arrogant . . .') with a sense of limitation, which we hear, for example, in his expression of 'hope'. Nothing but affirmation would present itself, for example, in a propositional form flowing from first principles, all in a single formal tone, leading to what *is* logical and correct. The passage may be read as one of Gibson's multi-vocal 'performances in language' that pursues 'a momentary stay against confusion'. We can connect this pursuit, the core of which involves the 'sensitive and wise and gracious handling of language', with talk about 'virtues', including 'justice'*.

In *The Legal Imagination*, a writing course book dedicated to Baird, White mentions Gibson in 'a rather small body of literature dealing with the lawyer's use of language that might be directly useful to you in this course' (1973: 968). A Gibson reader will readily make sense of this passage 'to the student' at the start of *The Legal Imagination*:

> I want you to begin this course . . . by trying to imagine as fully as possible how it might be said that law is not a science – at least not the 'social science' some would call it – but an art. And this course is directed to you as an artist. There is no body of rules expressing the art of the lawyer and more than that of the sculptor or painter. You are as free as they, and as responsible for what you do. It is true that one of the mediums of the lawyer's art is rules, and the lawyer must know rules, and the other materials of the law, as the sculptor must know clay and the painter paint and canvas. You must know what they are and how they work, before you can work with them. But what you must ultimately learn is what to do with rules and judicial opinions and all the other forms of expression that are the working stuff of a lawyer's life, just as the sculptor must learn what to do with clay and marble. You may feel that you are constrained by your material, as indeed you are. But compare the pianist, who is told what notes to play, in what order, how long and how loud; yet art is surely possible there. In asking you to define for the moment the lawyer as writer, to regard yourself in that way, I am asking you not to follow direction and example but to trust and follow your own curiosity; to work out in your imagination various future possibilities for yourself, defined by the real and imagined performances of your mind at its best; and to subject what you discover to criticism and speculation.
>
> (xxxiv–xxxv)

How does White imagine himself, his reader, and the relation between them? In responding to that question, imagine different ways of defining 'law' and 'art'. Some people would define them in propositional form: 'by law I mean . . .'; by art I mean . . .' They might then compare and contrast the two definitions, and in doing so continue their monologue. Such a method and manner will be familiar to one who has studied social science – at least a dry version of it. This is a version in which a teacher mechanically defines concepts and fills the student up with information about the world. White, by contrast, imaginatively exercises his analogical imagination*. He defines 'art' not with a sterile proposition but with what we might call an artistic performance, a dialogical one that invites the student, one with 'curiosity' and a capacity to 'trust' it, to self-consciously activate her 'imagination' in order to begin an attunement* to his image of it. Here 'the student' is not an empty vessel to be filled with information, but rather a fellow 'performer'.

White has fellow performers in his horizons in *When Words Lose Their Meaning*, in which he engages with Marshall's opinion in *McCulloch v. Maryland*. As we hear above (*Constitution), this case concerned the meaning of 'the people' in the Preamble to the Constitution. White has this to say about Marshall's contribution to a performing art:

> In . . . claiming the authority to 'expound' the instrument of national constitution, Marshall makes the largest of claims for himself and for the judiciary. But the way he discharges this authority he is careful to define and to respect sources of authority external to his own will, especially those that approximate as closely as possible the views of 'the People.' . . . The law that Marshall makes is . . . constitutive much in the manner of the common law, which determines what the law should be in large measure by what it is, i.e., by the customs and expectations that in fact mark the community and the culture: what we are is our law. This means that even when Marshall speaks in his most magisterial tones there is still a sense in which he speaks with the voice of 'the People.'
>
> In all of this, Marshall's opinion has a double voice rather like that of the Constitution itself: on some matters it declares itself with authority; on others it is silent, for these are of necessity left to others. . . . Marshall's opinion . . . is written in a similar combination of voices and is in this way continuous with the original text. Like the Constitution itself, Marshall performs the separation of powers that is essential to his official existence. At the end, despite its magisterial tone, this opinion turns to the reader it has instructed in its methods and says to him: it is now time for you to remake our language, to constitute and reconstitute our community and culture anew, as I have done; you must build on what I have made.
>
> (White 1984: 262–3)

Doing justice* to Marshall's *McCulloch* opinion requires the disciplined use of the auditory imagination, which, given the elusive nature of sound, might have difficulty in distinguishing internal from 'external authorities'. That Marshall does not speak in a single 'voice' is not merely a matter of style, for if he were to speak in such a voice, handing down supposedly 'plain' commands, he would constitute himself as an authoritarian conversation*-stopper and his reader as a passive receiver of The Law. His multi-vocal opinion may be heard as an invitational conversation-facilitator, continuing the work that the framers began.

Authority and Communication: Charles Bingham

The educationalist John Dewey criticized the Age of Reason for setting 'authority and freedom . . . in opposition to one another', for the two are in 'intimate and organic union' (Dewey 1936: 604). (For some people, a 'union' of the two will be as unimaginable as a union of 'law' and 'literature'.) In *Authority is Relational*, Bingham echoes Dewey's claim. In doing so, he takes a 'performative' turn and contributes to 'rethinking educational empowerment' (the subtitle of his book – 2008). Attending to his performative turn can help us in the activity of attunement* to White's performance-centred work.

At the outset of his book, Bingham attends to deficiencies in the way people talk about authority. He detects a tendency to reify 'authority':

> [C]urrent educational conceptions of authority assume that authority is primarily a thing that people have, a thing that is wielded by individuals who are in positions of power. . . . Thus it is common to hear statements such as, 'That person has a lot of authority because she is a teacher,' or, 'Unfortunately I do not have much authority since I am only a student.' Authority is usually construed as a possession to which one who lacks power either succumbs or does not succumb.
>
> (2–3)

After reading Brecht (*Alienation), we might readily imagine that 'common' authority-talk is a good place for putting to use the 'alienation effect'. A Brecht reader might begin a line of questioning* with this question: 'Have you really looked closely at that which you call "authority"?' The experience* of alienation could productively diminish the reification, especially if some valuable lines of questioning open up.

Why might we imagine 'authority' as a 'thing'? Addressing that question, Bingham turns to the way we imagine the activity of communication:

> [C]ommon presumptions about authority are actually based on even more fundamental presumptions about what it means to speak and listen. . . . Communication itself is much more of an interpretive event than is commonly realized. Therefore, when authority is construed as a substance rather than an interpretative relation, this misunderstanding is itself guided by a misunderstanding of language where language is said to be the transfer of a *substance* between autonomous human actors, that substance being *meaning*. . . . Once we understand that communication is not solely about the transfer of meaning, but is rather a matter of authoritative staging and interpretation, then we can see that the relation of authority is . . . literary from the ground up, from the very basic acts of listening and speaking all the way up to the more refined enactments of educational authority that take place between student and teacher.
>
> (53)

Bingham here echoes criticism of the conduit metaphor*, which contributes to the reification of 'meaning' and, as such, to a defective image of communication. (It might be helpful to remind ourselves that one purpose of our engagement with Bingham is that of 'staging and interpretation' for the activity of attunement to and from White.) He insists that 'language' is not a tool which we use to 'transfer' thoughts to one another but a medium in which we can establish a 'relation' with each other.

As an alternative to the sender–receiver model of communication, Bingham presents and points to the significance of a 'performative' model. Here are some fragments:

> [A] performative model construes that *the saying itself* is just as important as *what is said.* . . . The performative model helps us to remember that when a teacher addresses her class, she establishes a role by her very speaking.
>
> (58–9)

> [W]orks of literature can bring human beings to new levels of awareness . . . in a performative way. . . . Educational authority calls to us in ways that bring new levels of awareness.
>
> (61)

> Authority is a relation that acts performatively. Therefore, authority gets enacted through interpretation rather than through clear communication. It is not that someone 'has' authority and then communicates her ideas clearly by virtue of that authority. Instead, authority gets enacted through communication itself.
>
> (62)

> [A]uthority can neither be insisted on nor given up. Both stances will lead to domination and submission. . . . The way out of domination and submission is built on balance. . . . The teacher must be in a position to recognize the student as a separate center of self, one that is out of her own control. However, for such recognition to count, the student cannot be so far out of the teacher's control that she becomes a threat. There must be an oscillation, on the part of the teacher, between being in control and letting loose. And there must be such an oscillation on the side of the student, too.
>
> (142–3)

> [A]uthority must be seen as a dynamic and intersubjective process. . . . [A]uthority . . . enhances freedom when states of domination and submission are merely fleeting, fleeting to such an extent that they constitute momentary experiences of threat, vulnerability, omnipotence, and excess. . . . Authority must . . . be used, as Freire notes, so that 'through dialogue, the teacher-of-the-students and the students-of-the-teacher cease to exist and a new term emerges: teacher-student with students-teachers.'
>
> (144–5)

Those fragments could serve as a helpful resource for a reader of *The Legal Imagination* who is struggling to make sense of what kind of book she is reading and who she ('the student') and the 'teacher' are to each other. Let me begin to suggest how.

In the preface to *The Legal Imagination*, White says this: 'The student is addressed and asked to speak not as a student but as an independent mind' (1973: xxi). One becomes an 'independent mind', we might say, when she leaves behind a 'student-of-the-teacher' by speaking in a different voice*. Such a mind, paradoxically, is dependent upon the presence of another 'independent mind' for her existence. The two or more independent minds mutually create each other in 'dialogue'. The word 'dialogue' here is not just 'talk' but a genuine 'conversation'*, involving 'threat, vulnerability, . . .', that is built upon a deep trust.

Just after making the 'student'/'independent mind' distinction, White says that it is his larger 'hope' that 'the student will come to some new awareness of his place in the world, of his powers and obligations' (xxi). Drawing from Bingham, we might imagine *The Legal Imagination* as a 'work of literature' that seeks to bring us 'to new levels of awareness in a performative way'. In this regard, we may now better sense why White says that he is 'reluctant to call' his book 'a jurisprudence book' (xxi).

Later in his preface, White says that 'each student is charged with the responsibility of making his own course out of these materials' (xxi). Here we may hear White working his 'way out of domination' and showing a will to 'recognize the student as a separate center of self, one that is out of his own control'. What might become of his reader with such freedom? How is she to imagine 'it'?

In *Acts of Hope*, White directs us to Matthew Hale's essay 'Considerations Touching the Amendment or Alteration of Lawes', written about 1665. Hale belongs to a conservative tradition that reveres tradition – a literary tradition that pays no respect to the mechanistic image of law as commands from a sovereign to subjects bound by them. The words 'conservative' and 'tradition' are frequently used in a simplistic way, such as to label someone as for the 'status quo' rather than changing it. But 'it' is not a fixed entity. On defining Hale with regard to 'tradition', White says: 'He thinks of tradition as containing principles of change as well as constancy, thus capturing in one image the whole habit of his mind to think in terms of contrary tensions' (1994a: 145). 'Reforming' tradition, we might say, is a method of continuing with tradition. For Hale, we can never step entirely outside of tradition. Reforming law involves movement within tradition. In a passage that concerns the inside/outside distinction and that connects 'authority' and performative communication, White writes:

> It is an apparent premise of most of our talk about law, perhaps built into the nominalizing and labeling tendencies of our language, that law exists outside of us, as the speaker and hearer, in the world, as a social phenomenon. And of course in some sense it does, but only insofar as we define

> ourselves as external to the community and discourse it defines. Once we recognize that this is our law, either because we are lawyers or because it speaks to us, things change. Law has its meanings in the readings we give it; I believe it has its continued life and authority, indeed its continued shape, through our understanding and acquiescence, and through the texts we make as well. For what is granted authority is not only the set of prior texts themselves but the processes by which they are both interpreted and rewritten (or 'reformed'), and our participation is essential to both. . . . Hale in his context makes plain . . . that the authority of the laws he discusses is secondary to the authority of the discussion itself, and not merely to its intellectual aspect: to the community he establishes in his text, with the past and its texts, with his inherited languages, and with his readers, actual and potential. Here is the performance of the text, is where its claim to authority rests; and this performance works as a definition of the 'law' it speaks about . . . .
>
> (147)

We will do well to alienate ourselves from habitual modes of thought and expression about language*, from the conduit metaphor* that is associated with 'the nominalizing and labeling tendencies of our language'. These 'tendencies' can mislead us into imagining that language merely points to *things* 'outside' of itself in The Real World, such as The Law and The Church, and that knowledge worthy of the name is propositional in form, with matters of voice* *utterly* irrelevant. White imagines acts with language as a 'performance', which can and should by judged according to the kind of 'community' that is created through voice. White, we can be sure, would hope that his reader attends to his own 'performance' in composing Hale. Just as there is no 'the law itself', there is not any 'Hale himself'. White unavoidably gives Hale's essay some of the meaning he claims for it. If White's reader can tune in to his performance, then she will be well placed to tune in to her own performance in composing White.

Play

A 'True Question': Hans-Georg Gadamer
'Your Getting Lost': Robert Frost

How are we to imagine *Homo sapiens*? In *Homo Ludens*, Johan Huizinga plays with 'our way of thinking' that commonly sets 'play' as 'the direct opposite of seriousness' (1949: 5). In identifying a 'play-element' in a wide range of activities (including law and poetry), Huizinga connects aspects of our lives that may seem unconnected. In this regard, we can readily connect *Homo Ludens* to *The Legal Imagination*. In the preface to his course book, White writes:

> The student . . . is asked to speak out of an awareness of four sorts of material: the literature of the law, the introduction to literary criticism this book is meant to afford, his intellectual activity outside the law, and his ordinary experience of life. The premise upon which we operate is that the activity called the law can be seen as an activity of the imagination, an activity that creates and uses a literature which we are interested in assessing . . . and to which the student is asked to contribute, feeling free to bring into play anything that he knows or is. The questions and assignments in this book, therefore, do not ask for answers of the sort that the questions in a property book might be said to call for, but rather are meant as occasions for the play of the individual mind and imagination, as invitations to talk. The student is addressed and asked to speak not as a student but as an independent mind.
>
> (White 1973: xx–xxi)

White's 'questions' may unsettle a student who seeks not to become an 'independent mind' but to work towards determinate 'answers'. His book may unsettle a teacher who wants to be addressed as a teacher and who imagines the law not as an elusive 'activity'* but as a field with distinct boundaries. The boundaries, however, are not distinct but malleable cultural artefacts that we can reconstitute with 'the play of the . . . imagination'. This 'play' will include developing the capacity to distinguish voices (*Voice): How does a student know when she is speaking 'as a student' rather than 'as an independent mind'? Might she be impelling the teacher to speak as a teacher rather than as an independent mind? Much is at stake, including character* formation.

A 'True Question': Hans-Georg Gadamer

'What are the conditions that make good talk on a particular subject possible?' That question resides in the opening chapter of *The Legal Imagination* (27). Let us seek help.

'Conversation'* is a central theme in Gadamer's *Truth and Method*, which, as discussed below (*Understanding), addresses 'the problem of hermeneutics' (1975: xi). In providing an image of understanding as 'conversation', he gives 'questioning'* a central place:

> To conduct a conversation requires first of all that partners to it do not talk at cross purposes. Hence its necessary structure is that of question and answer.
>
> Dialectic, as the art of asking questions, proves itself only because the person who knows how to ask questions is able to persist in his questioning, which involves being able to preserve his orientation towards openness. The art of questioning is that of being able to go on asking questions, ie the art of thinking. It is called 'dialectic', for it is the art of conducting a real conversation. . . . A person who possesses the 'art' of questioning is a person who is able to prevent the suppression of questions by the dominant opinion.
>
> (330)

That passage offers a resource for thought and expression about various character* strengths, including wisdom and creativity (one 'who knows how to ask questions'), perseverance ('is able to persist in his questioning'), 'open'-mindedness, and courage ('is able to prevent the suppression of questions by the dominant opinion'). We might readily associate those strengths with someone who 'justices' (Hopkins – Justice*).

That which Gadamer calls 'a real conversation' has a life of its own. Drawing from Huizinga, Gadamer gives 'play' a key place in conversation. On the dynamics of play, he writes:

> Play fulfills its purpose only if the player loses himself in his play. . . . One who doesn't take the game seriously is a spoilsport. The mode of being of play does not allow the player to behave towards play as if it were an object.
>
> (92)

> If we examine how the word 'play' is used and concentrate on its so-called transferred meanings we find talk of the play of light, the play of the waves, . . . the play of forces, the play of gnats, even a play on words. In each case what is intended is the to-and-fro movement which is not tied to any goal which would bring it to an end. This accords with the original meaning of the word spiel as 'dance' . . . .
>
> (93)

If 'the player loses himself in his play', there will be a 'movement' in his patterns of attention*, as was the case with Austen's Frederick Wentworth when he was caught up in 'the power of conversation' and dropped the pen (*Conversation). When we 'lose' ourselves, we create 'I–Thou' rather than 'I–It' relations. These are of great political and ethical significance, creating a basic equality*, 'I–Thou relations create an encounter with the Other that is characterized by mutual respect (i.e. treating the Other like a human being who has something meaningful to say, rather than an object to be dominated' (Vilhauer 2010: xvi). Acts of justice*, we might say, begin in play (Sammons 2010).

The epigraph to *Truth and Method* draws from a poem by Rainer Maria Rilke. It suggests much about the significance of play:

> Catch only what you've thrown yourself. All is
> mere skill and little gain;
> but when you're suddenly the catcher of a ball
> thrown by an eternal partner
> with accurate and measured swing
> towards you, to your center, in an arch
> from the great bridgebuilding of God:
> why catching then becomes a power –
> not yours, a world's.

With that passage, we might imagine that Gadamer is discarding the famous principle 'I think, therefore I am'. What might be a fitting replacement? Perhaps something like this: 'We are questioning (or throwing and catching), we are bridgebuilding.' This 'bridgebuilding' is the material of what Gadamer calls 'the fusion of horizons'.[1]

We might ask whether real 'play' can happen in the classroom between teachers and students. Gadamer invites the question:

> To ask a [true] question means to bring into the open. The openness of what is in question consists in the fact that the answer is not settled. . . . Every true question achieves this openness. If it lacks this, then it is basically no more than an apparent question. We are familiar with this from the pedagogical question, the curious difficulty and paradox of which consists in the fact that it is a question without a questioner.
>
> (326–7)

When a teacher asks a student a question with a certain 'answer' in mind, it is an 'apparent' one. Given that this does not involve the teacher in any risk of losing herself, we might say that she is not in 'play'. What might this suggest about the nature of teacher–student relations?

At the outset of *The Legal Imagination*, White offers some words about the questions in it and their significance for classroom relations:

> One warning: to build a class around the writing of students is to subject their egos and emotions to considerable strain, especially when the recurring questions are perplexing and important ones – what sort of life can I make myself as a lawyer? how do I define myself and my future in what I write? – and a class taught this way can work only if it its members trust each other, if there is a sense of shared interest and concern. Partly for this reason I encourage the students to talk matters over outside of class and to feel free to read and criticize each other's papers while they are in a process of composition. . . . But most of all, it may help create the sense that we are all colleagues here. I do not think this course lends itself to teaching by competitive methods.
>
> (xxii)

That passage could be attractive to a dissenting economics teacher, one who resists reducing all motives to 'self-interest' and who suspects that 'competitive methods' may sometimes undermine meaningful community, which shapes both the 'self' and its 'interest'. In response to the passage, some curious students might ask questions such as these: Why the 'perplexing' questions? How does White define himself in what he writes? Can we 'trust' him with our fears? What does he mean by 'trust'? Might 'competitive methods' undermine 'trust'?

White hopes to contribute to good 'conversation'*, as he suggests in an assignment titled 'What Is a Good Conversation?' White gives his reader some 'questions' that 'may be of interest to you as you work out this assignment':

> To ask what makes a good question is to address a real complexity. For one thing, as you know from your law classes, there is a matter of seriousness: is the question really meant as a question, to elicit a response in which the questioner has an interest? Or is it a fake question, a kind of manipulation or patronization? There is also the matter of its substance: is it cast in a way that invites genuine discussion, is it . . . a serious question or a fake one?
>
> (952–3)

To ask who asks a good question is to address a real complexity. For one thing, there is a matter of playfulness, which is hard to define. (Might we 'know' it when we see it?) There is also the matter of our response: who are we becoming in our response to the questioner?

'Your Getting Lost': Robert Frost

One of Frost's words for poetry was 'play'. We can be sure that he did not set 'play' in opposition to 'seriousness': 'Play no matter how deep has got to be so playful that the audience are left in doubt whether it is deep or shallow' (in Pritchard 1984: xvi). Frost's 'Directive', which White brings into play in *The Legal Imagination*, may be the material of this kind of play. Here is the beginning:

> Back out of all this now too much for us,
> Back in a time made simple by the loss
> Of detail, burned, dissolved, and broken off
> Like graveyard marble sculpture in the weather,
> There is a house that is no more a house
> Upon a farm that is no more a farm
> And in a town that is no more a town.
> The road there, if you'll let a guide direct you
> Who only has at heart your getting lost, . . .
>
> (Frost 1946/1947: 7)

These lines may strike a chord with one who finds *The Legal Imagination* 'too much', especially in regard to 'detail'. What's a Frost poem doing in a law course book? Is White a 'guide . . . Who only has at heart your getting lost'?

'Directive' is a multi-level journey, including across space and time. Soon after the middle of the poem we come to these lines:

> The height of the adventure is the height
> Of country where two village cultures faded
> Into each other. Both of them are lost.
> And if you're lost enough to find yourself
> By now, pull in your ladder road behind you
> And put a sign up CLOSED to all but me.
> Then make yourself at home. . . .
>
> (8)

What might be said about '[t]he height of the adventure' in *The Legal Imagination*? Here we may find that two communities of discourse – law and literature, among others – have 'faded Into each other' – 'lost'. In losing them, White's reader may hope to 'find [her-]self'. She can then 'make [her-]self at home.' In exile? The in-between? Where?

Let us rejoin the journey:

> First there's the children's house of make-believe,
> . . .
> This was no playhouse but a house in earnest.
> Your destination and your destiny's
> A brook that was the water of the house,
> . . .

> I have kept hidden in the instep arch
> Of an old cedar at the waterside
> A broken drinking goblet like the Grail
> Under a spell so the wrong ones can't find it,
> So can't get saved, as Saint Mark says they mustn't.
> (I stole the goblet from the children's playhouse.)
> Here are your waters and your watering place.
> Drink and be whole again beyond confusion.
>
> (8)

Frost here combines the 'earnest' (especially the biblical references) and the world of 'play' (including the confession about stealing the goblet). Might Frost hope that his reader will be able to comfortably live with confusion in relation to what it might mean to be 'beyond confusion'?

After reproducing Frost's poem in *The Legal Imagination*, White asks a series of questions, including these:

> What is the message of 'Directive'? What more is there in this poem than its message? Is 'Directive' an expression of what a legal education should involve? (Do you ever hear a judge talk as if he is, or ever has been, 'lost enough to find himself'? A law student?)
>
> (782)

Let us turn White's questioning* in the direction of his own book. What is the message of *The Legal Imagination*? What more is there in this course book than its message? Is it an expression of what a legal education should involve?

Concerning that last of White's questions above, we might do well to ask: What should we listen out for in a judge or a law student that is, or ever has been, 'lost enough to find himself'? How might such a person talk? With what voices? How will she define her listener?

Questioning

'The Edge of an Abyss': Composition and Literary Criticism at Amherst
'The Socrates within Us': R. G. Collingwood

In the Introduction to this book, I said that there is no single road for reading it. There is an important sense, however, in which this chapter lends itself as an opening one for framing the book as a whole. It presents questions that are at the foundation of the activity* that I am calling attunement and that in one way or another flow through the other chapters.

'The Edge of an Abyss': Composition and Literary Criticism at Amherst

White's *The Legal Imagination* is full of questions, many of which are arranged in distinct patterns and sequences. One place to begin making sense of them is this acknowledgment: 'Theodore Baird of Amherst College . . . taught me . . . how to ask a question . . .' (1973: xvii). As I mentioned in the Introduction to this book, Baird directed a freshman composition course, English 1–2. As suggested in the following fragment from a course description, Baird resisted pedagogy that imaged teachers as sending information to students:

> English 1–2 can become, at its best, a dramatic dialogue, where you and your teacher exchange remarks, you and your fellow students converse, with a certain amount of common understanding.
>
> As for your teacher, he does not exist to give you the answers. His function is to ask questions, and if by inadvertence he should ever chance to tell you something, you should immediately turn the questioning on him.
>
> (quoted in Varnum 1996: 251)

Baird lived by the Socratic midwife metaphor*, in the sense of serving as a midwife to students' learning. This metaphor, unlike the transmission metaphor, suggests that the learning process is a collaborative enterprise, the core of which is 'questioning'. Baird's ideal of 'a dramatic dialogue', which is a form of equality*, could serve as a model for what other professions 'can become at [their] best'.

Baird developed a custom of preparing a set of new assignments each semester. In an article addressed to alumni, he said this about the function of the assignments:

> We begin our thinking by saying that writing is an action, it is something the student does, and the teacher aims at putting the student in a position where he can do it. The assignments are our means of locating that situation in which the student knows what he is talking about, in which he feels the desire to express what he knows. When we make an assignment we do not say 'Discuss—' or 'Write a paper about—,' but give explicit directions that once they are followed the student will find himself saying something he did not know he could say. . . . For the teacher the assignments are his means of controlling conversation, of saying over and over again and always more particularly, tell me what you know. They are stimuli spring boards, invitations to stand on the edge of an abyss . . . .
>
> (Baird 1952/1999: 201)

Etymologically, to express is a pressing forth. What comes forth may surprise: 'the student will find himself saying something he did not know he could say.' With 'the student in a position where he can do' the activity of 'writing', he is also in the position to engage in 'conversation'*, a risky activity 'on the edge of an abyss'. Here at 'the edge', we may take it, is a place that can be productive for composition. There may be method in this madness – Lonergan-style transcendental method*.

After Baird's general remarks about the assignments, there is an example from ordinary life, an action in tennis:

> A student who is a good tennis player sets out to write a paper on what he does when he serves a tennis ball. He knows he knows what he is writing about, yet as he begins to address himself to his subject he immediately encounters the inescapable fact that his consciousness of his own action contains a large area of experience quite beyond his powers of expression. The muscular tensions, the rhythm of his body as he shifts his weight, above all the feel of the action by which he knows a stroke is good or bad almost before the ball leaves the racket, all this and much more lies beyond his command of language, and rendered almost speechless he produces a mess. He knows in the sense that he can perform the action, but he does not know in the sense that he can communicate this action to a reader. At this point the teacher tries to get him to distinguish between these two levels of experience, to become aware of them, to generalize about them.
>
> (202–3)

We will do well to begin composing by engaging with the familiar – with an activity* that we do (tennis, reading, . . .). The destination is an engagement with the unfamiliar (the 'beyond') – with talking about what we do. The initial effect of the assignment is to disturb the student's relationship with language*. One aim, it would seem, is to reduce the 'area of experience . . . beyond his powers of expression'.

The Legal Imagination is full of Baird-like 'spring boards'. For example, White invites his reader to respond on behalf of Abraham Lincoln to Stephen Douglas's 'Springfield' speech, which is a reply to Lincoln's 'House Divided' speech addressing the slavery question. In framing a position from which to respond to Douglas, White says:

> It would be remarkably instructive for you to draft a complete, argumentative answer. . . . It is important, in drafting a response, to write as if you were a person seeking to become senator from Illinois in 1858. There is no difficulty in scribbling down self-righteously the language of equality which, thanks in no small measure to Lincoln's responses to Douglas, is widely accepted today – so widely accepted, in fact, that it is a cliché, a dead language. What was the world like when that language was being made?
>
> It will require the greatest exercise of the imagination to put yourself in such a world. . . . Your feelings may be such that such a compromise of principle for expediency is unthinkable; no concession could be made for a moment to the institution of slavery, and nothing said on the subject except that it should be abolished instantly at absolutely any cost.
>
> It is easy to assume the position of moral superiority that such feelings imply, because the battle against the law of slavery (if not against its consequences) has been won. But let me ask you this: do you favor immediate, unilateral destruction of the government of the Union of South Africa by American arms? . . . Whatever your private views, what would you say if you were now running for the United States Senate: would you demand the end of South African apartheid instantly and at any price? Would you have any chance at election?
>
> (842)

White's exercise of his analogical 'imagination'* in the direction of the apartheid regime can help his reader in the activity of attunement* to a different 'world'. If we begin 'scribbling down self-righteously the language of equality' we will fail to do justice* to either Lincoln or Douglas. White means his analogizing to help his reader imagine what it was like when the language of equality was being fashioned. In visiting this other world, White offers his reader the experience of an alienation* from this 'dead language', one that will enable her to see a 'cliché' as a cliché.

The to-and-fro movement* between Lincoln and Douglas is of particular interest to White, for it offers the experience* of legal argument at its best. White says:

> In the Lincoln-Douglas arguments, one side answers another, and is answered itself. The listener or reader asks, at the end of one statement, 'How on earth can the other man respond?' yet when the answer comes, he feels that it is complete and carries the day – only to have his mind changed again. Only the most painful thought can enable the reader to resist such pressures and define his own position. The literary question is, 'What can he say now?' and the literary experience is surprise and wonder at what he does say. I mean by this to lead you to recognize your feelings at the end of Douglas's speech: do you not ask yourself 'What can Lincoln possibly say now?' and at the same time expect that his response will satisfy you?
>
> (842)

Here is a resource for thought and expression on the principle of 'hear the other side'. If we take the principle seriously in law, we will do well to attend to 'the literary experience'. We might do well to wonder about the status of law as law if there is no such experience. In doing so, we might hear in a new way White's claim that 'the art of the lawyer is . . . a literary art' (758). What can doubters (especially those who are extending without limit mechanistic economic thought) say now?

White's analogizing in the direction of the apartheid regime lends itself as a resource for our analogical imaginations in the direction of White himself. Might *The Legal Imagination* resemble Lincoln's responses to Douglas in that it is a self-conscious effort to create a radically new 'world'? Might it require the greatest exercise of the imagination to put yourself in White's world? How might you do this?

Engaging with White's questions on the Lincoln–Douglas arguments has stimulated various reflections. A fragment from them is as follows. Our world today is one in which apartheid-like atrocities can be done by otherwise reasonable people if they do not make a point of exercising their imaginations in the way White invites. The injustices of the apartheid regime, as with the injustice of slavery in America, were at their root failures of the imagination. If we fail to imagine such injustices as failures of the imagination, we may well be destined to repeat dehumanizing histories. White offers a resource for avoiding them.

'The Socrates within Us': R. G. Collingwood

Lines of questioning do not emerge out of nothing. White's questions, for example, drew from Baird's. Who was behind Baird? Baird left behind this remark: 'The great thing I learned from Collingwood was that you had to learn how to ask a question' (quoted in Varnum 1996: 121).

Soon after the outbreak of the First World War, Collingwood took up residence in London and worked with a section of the Admiralty Intelligence Division. He regularly walked across Kensington Gardens and past the Albert Memorial. In *An Autobiography*, he mentions some questions that arose:

> The Albert Memorial began by degrees to obsess me. . . . Everything about it was visibly mis-shapen, corrupt, . . . ; for a time I could not bear to look at it . . . ; recovering from this weakness, I forced myself to look, and to face day by day the question: a thing so obviously, so incontrovertibly, so indefensibly bad, why had Scott done it? To say that Scott was a bad architect was to burke the problem with a tautology; to say that there was no accounting for tastes was to evade it by *suggestio falsi*. What relation was there, I began to ask myself, between what he had done and what he had tried to do? . . . If I found the monument merely loathsome, was that perhaps my fault? Was I looking in it for qualities it did not possess, and either ignoring or despising those it did?
> (Collingwood 1939/1951: 29–30)

That passage lends itself to thought and expression about the plural 'I'. Who is the 'I' who 'could not bear to look' at the Albert Memorial? Who is the 'I' who 'forced myself to look'? Who asked 'the question'? Who responded to it? (Might the responder be someone concerned with doing justice* – in this case to Scott?) There are others, including the 'I' who composed the story, putting together the plural 'I'.

Collingwood went on to make connections between his work in archaeology and some landmark works in philosophy:

> My work in archaeology . . . impressed upon me the importance of the 'questioning activity' in knowledge . . . The *Novum Organum* and the *Discours de la Méthode* began to have a new significance for me. They were the classical expressions of a principle in logic which I found it necessary to restate: the principle that a body of knowledge consists not of 'propositions' . . . or whatever name logicians use in order to designate assertive acts of thought . . . , but of these together with the questions they are meant to answer. . . . There have always been people who saw that the true 'unit of thought' was not the proposition but something more complex in which the proposition served as an answer to a question. Not only Bacon and Descartes, but Plato and Kant, come to mind as examples. When Plato described thinking as a 'dialogue of the soul with itself', he meant (as we know from his own dialogues) that it was a process of question and answer, and that of these two elements the primacy belongs to the questioning activity, the Socrates within us. When Kant said that it takes a wise man to know what questions he can

> reasonably ask, he was in effect repudiating a merely propositional logic and demanding a logic of question and answer.
>
> (30–5)

Like Lonergan (*Method), Collingwood would put 'questioning' at the base of a method of knowing. How are we to make a judgment about such a placement? Might we reach for 'the Socrates within us'? Who is Socrates?

I have heard it said that we can perhaps best get to know who a person is by attending to the questions that they ask. What kind of questions did Socrates ask and why? In *When Words Lose Their Meaning*, White talks about Socratic questioning during his reading of Plato's *Gorgias*. Here is an introductory fragment:

> Plato's *Gorgias* is a dialogue, not a treatise . . . . [T]he dialogue itself is meant to exemplify the kind of life that Socrates calls 'dialectic'. The form of the dialogue is not a primitive or bizarre method for setting forth a doctrine that Plato is too perverse or incompetent to say straight out; what it offers is an engagement in an activity, and this activity is its true subject. . . . Socrates does occasionally say something to describe dialectic, but its clearest and truest definition is to be found not in what he says but in what he does. . . . It is worth observing . . . [that] in the *Apology* . . . we are told that Socrates would typically seek out a person who claimed to know how to do something—here the teaching of rhetoric, elsewhere generalship or mathematics or teaching virtue—and ask his interlocutor his central questions: Who are you? What do you do? and what do you know? Since we all know how to do things that we cannot explain, things we have never thought about beyond saying 'I am a banker' or 'I am a surgeon,' this line of questioning has the result of making conscious what before was not, the relation between the self and culture. I am a football coach or a law professor, I say, and only then begin to realize, when for Socrates that is not a sufficient answer, that this identity is a cultural one, not necessary but chosen, and chosen by me without my wholly knowing or understanding it.
>
> (White 1984: 94–5)

This passage will be familiar to anyone who knows Baird. In the echo of what Baird said about his assignments: 'I am a tennis player, and I'll happily write an assignment on how to serve a tennis ball.' In the process, the student has a potentially productive experience* of alienation* from her culture*, and she may come to doubt whether she wholly understands what 'understanding'* is.

White introduces the discussion form of questioning for purposes of 'refutation', which 'results in mortification' relating to one's selves: 'One part of the self is appealed to against another part, and in the process a previously unknown self-contradiction is revealed' (95). This refutation is part of 'dialectic'. Of particular significance, the reader is not a detached observer. Concerning the textual community, White writes:

> What the text really seeks to teach its reader is not how to speak this language but how to remake a language of his own. It does not teach a particular set of questions and dialectical responses, to be repeated on other occasions, but . . . how to ask questions of one's own. To do this, the reader must be a center of independent intellectual energy, a remaker of language and a composer of texts, and it is with helping him to become these things that this text is ultimately concerned.
>
> How does the text seek to do this? It treats the reader rather as Socrates treats his interlocutors. It works on him in large part by isolating and disorientating him, by creating a conscious gap between self and language that makes the nature of both problematic in new ways. Like the interlocutor, the reader is broken out of his culture, out of the language and activities that define him; he is thus prevented from defining himself by simply repeating established forms of speech or conduct. He is forced to function on his own: to take and define positions of his own creation and to respond to those . . . asserted by Socrates. . . .
>
> Dialectic . . . proceeds not by making lengthy statements or exhibitions but by questioning and answering, one to one. Its object is to engage each person at the deepest level, and for this it requires utter frankness of speech on each side, a kind of shamelessness in saying what one really thinks. One's concern is not with what people generally think . . . but only with what one thinks oneself and what the other thinks. This is not a competition to see who can reduce the other to his will; it is a process of mutual discovery and mutual refutation. One accepts refutation gladly, for it reduces the divisions and disharmonies within the self, which Socrates tells Callicles are so much worse than those in an orchestra or those between oneself and others. The object of it all is truth, and its method is friendship, the full recognition of the value of self and other in a universe of two.
>
> (109–10)

That passage brings to mind the dedication in *The Legal Imagination* – 'To My Friend and Teacher Theodore Baird'. It certainly seems fitting to say that Baird sought to teach his students 'how to ask questions of one's own' and that the structure of his assignments 'work on' his students 'in large part by isolating and disorientating' them. Also, their aim is 'to engage each person at the deepest level'. This is the material of 'friendship' worthy of the name. It cannot be emphasized enough that one's experience of the interchange will be influenced by one's sense of its purpose. If one adopts the mindset that there is a 'competition' in which the object is to defeat one's opponent, then 'refutation' is not a movement* that '[o]ne accepts . . . gladly'. Refutation can be embraced, however, when the object is deeper self- and mutual understanding, a productive alienation* from the commonplaces by which one lives. The process by which one 'reduces the divisions and disharmonies within the self' might be fittingly called an attunement*.

Reading

'Ear Training': Composition and Literary Criticism at Amherst
'Good Reading': J. Hillis Miller

The word 'reading' is commonly used today to suggest a passive taking in of a text. According to the *Oxford English Dictionary*, the word originally implied a more active process: 'The original senses . . . are those of . . . having or exercising control over something, etc.' The kind of reading with which we are concerned readily connects with the older usage. The active/passive opposition, however, is too simple to do justice* to the activity*. In *Legal Writing and Analysis*, Linda Edwards suggests as much:

> It is easy to assume that writing is a one-way street . . . . We tend to think that we, as writers, are the only speakers. We think this because we cannot hear anyone else talking. In reality, the most important party to the conversation, the reader, *is* talking, but we cannot hear her. Each of us has a voice in his or her mind—an opinionated . . . and talkative 'Commentator.' . . . The reader has such a Commentator too . . . . The Commentator will be saying things like 'No, that's not right, because . . .' or 'What in the world do you mean by that?' or 'But wait, where is the discussion about . . . ?' Think of yourself as a reader. Haven't you been reading this chapter listening to both the written word and to your own Commentator?
>
> . . . [E]ach time the Commentator speaks, the reader must listen to two voices at once: the writer must compete with the Commentator for the reader's attention. . . . As a writer you must anticipate the Commentator's chatter before the conversation occurs and try to preempt that chatter.
>
> (Edwards 2003: 72)

What does Edwards' reader need to do to read that passage well? Does he need to guide his Commentator on what lines of questioning* to pursue? Does the Commentator need to adopt different modes of 'listening'* in order to contribute to a 'conversation'* worthy of the name? In order to 'listen to two voices at once' (the Commentator and the writer), might there be value in developing an economics of 'attention'*? Might such an economics help a reader to pursue a harmony among his various selves?

How might we learn to 'anticipate the Commentator's chatter'? Might an ability 'to preempt that chatter' be vital for facilitating the activity of attunement* to a writer's way of imagining the world?

'Ear Training': Composition and Literary Criticism at Amherst

In the early 1950s, William Pritchard studied English at Amherst, where he encountered a voice*-centred tradition of inquiry, one heavily influenced by Robert Frost. When he began teaching there in 1958, he sought to maintain the tradition. His contribution to *Teaching What We Do* has much to say about 'ear training':

> [W]hat I remember most about my Amherst English teachers is the way they took words off the page and brought them to life through the speaking voice. . . . This . . . insistence on getting the tone right—of (in Frost's own words) seizing the special 'posture' needed to deliver it correctly—informed . . . my 'approach' to literature . . . . My education at Amherst . . . was essentially training in ear reading . . . . Do you want to sound like *that*? was the direct or implied question we were invited to put to our own prose. . . .
>
> (Pritchard 1991: 128–30)

The 'question we were invited to put' offers a long line of inquiry from the basic existential 'who' question – Who are you? The 'insistence on getting the tone right' is a basic relational question – Who are you and I to each other?

Echoes of Amherst ear training can be heard throughout White's work. For example, in *When Words Lose Their Meaning*, in an engagement with Swift's *A Tale of a Tub*, White engages with a forerunner in ear training:

> The way of reading it teaches consists largely in listening for a voice, then asking who speaks that way, then judging it. It thus constantly trains what could be called the ethical ear, for to be read at all one must constantly be assessing character as it is manifested in language. The defects that appear in the text as delusion, false questions, withdrawals from reality, unlimited ambitions, failures to connect, and the like are not merely intellectual or cognitive deficiencies but diseases of character, the only remedy for which is the kind of wholeness and health Swift seeks to stimulate in the reader. To read sensibly, to write sensibly, and to be sensible are, for Swift, intimately connected.
>
> (White 1984: 136)

Who speaks that way? Does White sound sensible? What kind of 'character'* does he create in 'language'*? How are we to go about making a judgment*?

Throughout *When Words Lose Their Meaning*, White develops 'a way of reading' (the title of his opening chapter), one that is 'a kind of writing', 'for the process is completed only in the organization and expression of our responses to what we have read' (5). The image of the 'reader as writer' is more fitting than a common one: 'Writing is never merely the transfer of information, . . . from one mind to another, . . . but is always a way of acting both upon the language, which the writer perpetually reconstitutes in his use of it, and upon the reader' (6). In elaboration, he develops the construct of an 'ideal reader':

> [A] writer always gives himself a character in what he writes; it shows in the tone of voice he adopts, . . . in the straightforwardness or trickiness with which he addresses his reader—his honesty or falseness—and in the way he treats the materials of his language and culture. The reader is also a character in the world created by the text. For in acting on the reader as he does, the writer calls on him to function out of what he knows and is . . . and to realize some of his possibilities for perception and response, for making judgments and taking positions. To engage with a text is to become different from what one was. There is a sense in which every text may be said to define an ideal reader, which it asks its audience to become, or to approximate, for the moment at least and perhaps forever.
>
> (15)

'Reading', for White, is thus an ethical activity*, a way of becoming someone in relation to another. Who, one might ask, is White's 'ideal reader'? Is she or he perhaps someone you want to 'become'? How will 'you' know? In a paradoxical sense, is a kind of detachment needed in order to really 'engage with a text'?

'Good Reading': J. Hillis Miller

In *The Legal Imagination*, White provides his reader with an 'introduction to literary criticism' (1973: xxi), and he invites her 'to become a critic as well as a writer' (50). In taking up White's invitation, and in trying to make sense of what it is that critics do and of how to judge them, I have found myself reading the critic Miller. Here are some suggestive fragments:

> [T]he end of literary study is . . . elucidation of the intrinsic meanings of poems, plays, and novels. In the effort toward such elucidation the proper model for the relation of critics to the work they study is not that of scientist to physical objects but that of one person to another in charity. . . . Love wants the other person to be as he is, in all his recalcitrant particularity.
>
> (Miller 1967/1991: 74–5)

> Good reading means noncanonical reading, that is, a willingness to recognize the unexpected . . . present in canonical works. . . . I do not mean . . . a freedom to make the work mean anything one likes, but just the reverse. I mean a response to the demand made by the words on the page, an ability, unfortunately not all that common, to respond to what the words on the page say rather than to what we wish they said or came to the book expecting them to say.
>
> (Miller 1987/1991: 338)

'Good reading' involves a disposition of openness – 'a willingness to recognize the unexpected'. This readily connects to 'charity', a word that deserves a significant place in this alphabetical lexicon.[1] 'Charity', says a Miller reader, 'is what allows the critic to read with the greatest degree of rigor because it insists on preserving difference, rather than assimilating and classifying' (Williams 2005: 65).

In *The Legal Imagination*, White offers some thought and expression about 'good writing' that overlaps the drift of what Miller says about 'good reading':

> You have probably noticed that neither the good opinion nor the good poem can be read through once only, that both require reading again and again in light of where they come out. Both must be addressed with the whole mind, both demand all the attention one can give; and one consequence of reading of this sort is not only an increased understanding of what lies outside of oneself, but a change in the reader himself, an expansion of sympathy or an opening of a new capacity to perceive.
>
> (White 1973: 803)

'Good writing' calls for good reading. As the reader changes as she reads, she can then re-read with the hope of 'understanding'* the person the text has helped her become. This will 'demand all the attention one can give'. We might say that such attention* is central to an act of justice*.

Rhetoric

Since at least the time of Socrates, the word 'rhetoric' has been part of a conversation about the way we humans talk. A turn in the conversation began in the 1950s, with a collection of efforts to rehabilitate the word. In *Ramus, Method, and the Decay of Dialogue*, Walter Ong provides a history on the devaluation of the word in his account of Ramus' preoccupation with 'method' (of an anti-humanistic kind). In the 1540s, based on a belief that the curriculum, especially the teaching of rhetoric, had many redundancies, Ramus set about reorganizing the arts. In doing so, he contributed to a shift from aural to visual figures for knowing the world. Ong tells us:

> Instead of carrying on a dialogue in the give-and-take Socratic form, the university don had largely reduced the oral component by converting it into a classroom monologue . . . . At the same time his interest both in logic and explicitness . . . had driven him further still toward the visile pole with its typical ideals of 'clarity,' 'precision,' 'distinctness,' and 'explanation' itself – all best conceivable in terms of some analogy with vision and a spatial field.
>
> In this economy where everything having to do with speech tends to be . . . metamorphosed in terms of . . . vision, the rhetorical approach to life—the way of Isocrates and Cicero and Quintilian and Erasmus, and of the Old and New Testaments—is sealed off into a cul-de-cac. The attitude toward speech has changed. Speech is no longer a medium in which the human mind and sensibility lives. It is resented, rather, as an accretion to thought, hereupon imagined as ranging noiseless concepts or 'ideas' in a silent field of mental space.
>
> There are difficulties . . . in the tendency to reduce . . . sensory knowledge to visual terms. An oscillograph of a sound gives everything about the sound – except the sound itself. . . . The description of a word (*verbum*, or *vox*) as a sign (*signum*) suffers from the same disability insofar as the notion of sign is based on a visual analogy. A word is more than a sign of some*thing*. . . . It is a cry, a voice, something which comes from

> the interior of a person, who as a *person* can never be 'explained,' and which somehow manifests this interior.
>
> (Ong 1958: 151, 291, and 109–10)

Ong identifies shifts in the meaning of the word 'rhetoric' as pivotal in the evolution of Western civilization. Efforts to rehabilitate the word could have great consequences, perhaps dramatically shifting the 'economy' of attention*, a shift that could silence* 'noiseless concepts'. A devaluation of such 'concepts' might help promote 'dialogue in the give-and-take Socratic form'. At the level of 'ideas', that kind of change in the classroom could promote not 'distinctness' but the principle of 'hear the other side', which places 'voice' against 'voice'*. This may help us to rehear the hearing.

To 'Rediscover Rhetorical Elements': Kenneth Burke

'Some theorists may choose to look upon the rhetorician as a very narrow specialist.' So says Burke in *A Rhetoric of Motives* (1950/1969: 51). Burke dissents and joins those who offer 'grounds for widening the scope of rhetoric to make it the center of an entire educational system' (51). At the outset of his book, he indicates this direction:

> [W]e seek to mark off the areas of rhetoric, by showing how a rhetorical motive is often present where it is not usually recognized, or thought to belong. In part, we would but rediscover rhetorical elements that had become obscured when rhetoric as a term fell into disuse, and other specialized disciplines such as esthetics, anthropology, psychoanalysis, and sociology came to the fore (so that esthetics sought to outlaw rhetoric, while the other sciences we have mentioned took over, each in its own terms, the rich rhetorical elements that esthetics would ban).
>
> (xiii)

For Burke, the will to 'outlaw rhetoric' led to an unnecessary and unhealthy fragmentation, with various 'specialized disciplines' becoming seemingly unconnected to each other. The rehabilitation of the R-word could be an act of integration*, in the sense of helping put together parts of life that are thought to have little or nothing in common.

Burke pursues novel and sensitive lines of questioning* relating to the nature and significance of ideology. His inquiry involves cavorting with the relation of rhetoric to science. Engaging with Marxism, he writes:

> Whatever may be the claims of Marxism as a 'science,' its terminology is not a neutral 'preparation for action' but 'inducement to action.' In this sense, it is unsleepingly rhetorical, though much of its persuasiveness has derived from insistence that it is purely a science, with 'rhetoric' confined to the deliberate or unconscious deceptions of non-Marxist apologetics.

> Thus, we once saw a Marxist (he has since left the Communist Party) get soundly rebuked by his comrades for the suggestion that leftist critics collaborate in a study of 'Red Rhetoric.' Despite their constant efforts to find the slogans, catchwords, and formulas that will most effectively influence action in given situations, and their friendliness to 'propaganda' or 'social significance' in art, they would not allow talk of a 'Red Rhetoric.' For them, 'Rhetoric' applied solely to the persuasiveness of capitalist, fascist, and other non-Marxist terminologies (or 'ideologies'). (101)

Alas for you, Marxists, hypocrites! How can a Marxist say to his brother, 'Let me take the rhetoric out of your mouth,' when . . . ??? With his suggestion of hypocrisy, Burke sets himself up for talking about a 'rhetorical' equality*. 'Marxists have a rhetoric, a persuasion' (101–2), just like every human speaker. We may momentarily transcend 'us versus them' talk when we sense that we are all rhetoricians.

'Rhetoric', Burke says, 'is concerned with the state of Babel after the Fall' (23). Making sense of this state requires a language*, the making of which is an act of the imagination*. The rehabilitation of 'rhetoric' goes hand-in-hand with 'imagination' (78–83). The association between the two words connects with the law, as Burke suggests in a critique of Jeremy Bentham:

> Bentham's great contributions to the study of persuasion were made almost in spite of himself. In trying to promote ways of discussion that could truly transcend the suggestiveness of imagery, he revealed how thoroughly imaginal our thinking is. Scrutinizing the most abstract of legalistic terms, asking himself just what it meant to plead and pass judgment in terms of 'legal fictions,' he proposed a methodic search for 'archetypes.' By 'archetypes' he meant the images that underly the use of abstractions. . . . Bentham here discovered a kind of poetry concealed beneath legal jargon usually considered the very opposite of poetry. It was *applied poetry*, or rhetoric, since it was the use of poetic resources to affect judgments, decisions, hence attitudes and actions. (90)

Whilst Bentham might have wanted to 'transcend' 'legal fictions' and get into the real world, Burke suggests a need to re-imagine the real. He provides material for re-imaging law as an enterprise of the 'poetic' imagination.

After reading Burke, titles of White's such as 'the rhetoric and poetics of the law' may not sound so strange. Here is what White says when introducing *Heracles' Bow*:

> The reader may at the outset be puzzled by the analogies suggested by the titles to many of the essays. Law is like, they seem to say, a language,

> but it is also like drama and poetry and rhetoric and narrative. . . . I do indeed mean each of these analogies, but I also mean to say something about analogic thinking more generally. Part of my object is to establish a way of thinking by drawing analogies, by making metaphors—by talking about one thing in terms of another—and these essays can be taken in that spirit: not as proposing comparisons between law and other things, . . . but as manifesting a bent of mind, a disposition and a method, that works by looking at law as one cultural and social activity among others. My emphasis is for the most part on the similarities rather than the differences, partly because . . . one of my aims is to get behind these activities to what they can be seen to share. The kind of analogy I draw is thus not a point-by-point comparison of features, but an attempt by looking at two things to make real and vivid the ground that they share, against which each is a somewhat different figure.
>
> I have no certain name for this ground (or activity, or discipline) and my best definition of it naturally enough lies in my performances in these pages. I would like to call it the art of constituting character, community, and culture in language; if I were to give it a name it would be 'constitutive rhetoric' . . . or perhaps 'the poetics of community.' But these would be only names, and I would not want to be bound by all their implications, nor by what they seem to omit, as a way of defining the arts of communal and cultural life with which I am concerned.
>
> (White 1985a: ix–x)

What's in a 'name'? Perhaps not much after a 'performance'* of 'figure'–'ground' reversals. After reading White's 'constitutive rhetoric', the meanings of commonly used 'thinking like . . .' phrases – such as 'thinking like a lawyer', 'thinking like an economist' – may well change. The ordinary kind of reasoning by analogy in the law may be closely analogous to 'thinking' in economics and elsewhere. In the process of comparing academic disciplines, we may come to sense the university as a unified place, in which various specialists 'share' some basic common ground.

'Probing for Common Ground': Wayne Booth's Rhetorology

In 1961, Booth contributed to the rehabilitation of 'rhetoric' with the publication of his first book, *The Rhetoric of Fiction*. For him, unlike many claims and suggestions to the contrary, an author 'cannot choose whether to use rhetorical heightening', for her or his 'only choice is of the kind of rhetoric' to be used (1961: 116). Booth here resists the image of rhetoric as 'mere ornament' and its associated image of the ignoble art of persuasion. For him, rhetoric can be noble or ignoble, or various mixtures of both.

Over many years, Booth developed a vocabulary of rhetoric. He made one effort in this direction in a contribution to a colloquium on general education. Here is one passage from it:

> Instead of referring to an art of persuasion about a case that is entirely known beforehand, rhetoric for Aristotle is the *faculty* or *capacity* . . . *of discovering* or *inventing* 'the possible means of persuasion in reference to any subject whatever.' . . . Rhetoric in this view is not a dressing added to the case to make it persuasive; the rhetorician discovers the case itself, using the art of rhetoric as an art of discovery. . . . This art . . . is a marvel and a wonder. A scholar-teacher might honorably spend a whole career mastering its subtleties. . . . [I]ts true home will be what we call 'value disputes': in the political arena at its best, when a Pericles or a Lincoln or a Churchill reminds a nation of its deepest commitments; . . . or in quarrels about the law or about constitutions. . . . There is nothing 'mere' about it. . . . [It] is . . . the art of the good lawyer . . . and it is not to be scoffed at or ignored. But it does not itself teach us what ends it should serve. . . . The world it builds, left on its own, is a world of a free market of atomized persons and ideas, each privately seeking victory and hoping that in the melee a public good will be produced by some invisible hand. Thus all thinkers, from Plato and Aristotle on, have felt the need to subordinate it to some higher discipline capable of revealing proper ends or goods.
>
> (Booth 1981/1988: 110–11)

A 'good lawyer' might marvel at Booth's performance in the ongoing dispute about the 'value' of rhetoric. Booth, to be sure, is not 'seeking victory' in the dispute, for he is trying to talk about a realm of talk – a 'higher discipline capable of revealing proper ends or goods' – that can connect diverse forms of talk. This may be disturbing to those who give privileged standing to 'a world of a free market of atomized persons and ideas'. Such people might imagine Booth to be advocating 'interference in the market'. That phrase, however, might well be little more than a clumsy tool for someone 'seeking victory' in the political arena at its worst. How are we to make a judgment*?

Let us be all ears for Booth's definition of the 'higher discipline':

> Is it not *the art of appraising the warrants for assent in any symbolic exchange?*
>
> The definition may seem anti-climactic until we think about the ground covered by its four terms:
>
> *Appraising*—the judging of the real validity or force, the power or weakness of something.
>
> *Warrants*—the reason or motives given by one human being to another as support for some belief or action or change of mind. . . .
>
> *Assent*—rather than dissent, because, though the two notions of saying 'yes' and saying 'no' are indissolubly linked in all human exchange, assent

> is really prior. Of the many reasons one might mention, the most obvious is that 'thinking together about warrants' cannot even be undertaken without a primal act of assent: 'I' must assent to 'your' equal right to a hearing in our mutual endeavors; note . . . the 'I' who assents or dissents was long since constituted in a series of incorporations of other selves. Hence:
>
> *Symbolic exchange*—like the other, inferior rhetorics, this one is indissolubly bound with the notion that it takes at least two to tango. But unlike the other definitions, this one rejects the very notion of the private individual 'self' thinking by 'itself.' We move, instead to a kind of thought possible only for a radically social self; the dichotomy between the individual and his past and present 'context' is unreal.
>
> (113–14)

Must you and I assent to Booth's definitions? Booth's way of imagining this 'rhetoric' directs attention to communal forces at work on a person. To whatever 'I' (and 'you') 'assent', 'I' come to assent through an interchange with another, including another 'I' within that which 'I' call 'myself'. A lawyer might wonder about the place of the legal language in Booth's 'higher discipline'. What can warrant having an 'equal right to a hearing'?

Booth boldly, if somewhat ungainly, named the 'higher discipline' rhetorology. Let him define the life of a rhetorologist:

> The rhetorologist will be interested not so much in whether Mr. A or Mr. B wins a particular debate as in the structures of assumption and proof that both share, and in how these structures might differ from the structures found in neighboring disciplines, or in the same discipline a decade before or a decade after. . . . [T]here are a lot of rhetorologists around, traveling under other names. Indeed in most disciplines these days one finds people who are reopening 'settled' questions about what constitutes good warrants for assent in that discipline—they are exploring the ways we think about the ways we think. . . . The work of the rhetorologist is . . . to pursue the comparative worth of different warrants in different persuasive enterprises, and to invent—or, if you prefer, discover—improved ways for minds to meet within disciplines and among seemingly different or conflicting disciplines.
>
> (125–6)

Booth is seeking to give a name to a 'comparativist of rhetorics', the person 'who probes how disparate rhetorical practices and theories compete and are finally, inescapably related' (Booth 1995: 116). For Booth, a fundamental question for those concerned with the rhetoric of rhetoric is this: How should we talk about our talk? We can ask that question in any community. If we are to reject his calls for a 'rhetorology' for any reason, how should we do so? Should we not make a place for the possibility that we have misunderstood him and that we might need a rhetorologist?

In *The Rhetoric of Rhetoric*, Booth offers a broad definition of rhetoric: 'the entire range of resources that human beings share for producing effects on one another: effects ethical (including everything about character), practical (including political), emotional (including aesthetic), and intellectual (including every academic field)' (2004: xi). Much of the 'bad' rhetoric that we encounter, suggests Booth, deserves to be called 'rhetrickery', or '[t]he whole range of shoddy, dishonest communicative arts producing misunderstanding – along with other harmful results' (11). He distinguishes 'rhetrickery' from what he calls 'listening-rhetoric', '[t]he whole range of communicative arts for reducing misunderstanding by paying full attention to opposing views'. He uses 'rhetorology' to refer to 'the deepest practice' of listening*-rhetoric: 'the systematic probing for "common ground"' (10).

In the year 2000, in the service of academic integration*, White initiated a conversation with a collection of scholars from various disciplines – anthropology, classics, economics, history, law, philosophy, theology, among others – addressing the question, 'How should we talk about religion?' In 2006, the conversation produced a volume, which White edited. Booth contributed a chapter, to which White gives these introductory remarks:

> In this essay Wayne Booth faces head-on one of the deepest and most difficult problems relating to religion—namely, how to imagine a connection between that side of life and what we call 'science,' which seems to many to be so deeply opposed to it. If one talks like a scientist, there seems to be no respectable and respectful way to talk about religion; yet if one talks as some religious people do—as though a particular narrative or set of sacred texts or ritual practices state or embody the only real truth—it is impossible to talk respectably and respectfully about science. Booth finds the beginning of an answer in what he calls a 'rhetorological' approach, one that tries to uncover the deepest commitments of contrasting ways of thinking and speaking, which in this case, he argues, demonstrates that true science and genuine religion share several deep and crucial understandings. On this basis it is possible to imagine a far more constructive conversation about the tensions and overlaps between science and religion than any we have yet enjoyed.
>
> (White 2006b: 144)

Shall we compare a rhetorologist to a judge – one committed to the principle 'hear the other "side"'? To a legal comparatist? Beginning with *The Legal Imagination*, White has sought, in the service of 'constructive conversation', to uncover the deepest commitments of contrasting ways of thinking and speaking – law versus poetry, and so on. As we engage in reading White, we join him in the activity* of being a rhetorologist. Aha, so this is what we have been doing from time to time!

Silence

Nelson Mandela's Speech from the Dock
'A Silent Professor': Mark Weisberg

Simone Weil defined 'justice'* as 'a certain kind of attention'* (1943/1977: 333).[1] This attention involves a capacity 'to listen to someone' (332), to really listen (*Listening).[2] Weil considered it important to 'learn to distinguish between two cries' (334): 'Why am I being hurt?' and 'Why has somebody got more than I have?' The first cry should have privileged status, for when it 'arises from the depth of a human heart . . . there is certainly injustice' (315). Weil goes on to talk about the place that this cry should have in public life:

> Apart from the intelligence, the only human faculty which has an interest in public freedom of expression is that point in the heart which cries out against evil. But as it cannot express itself, freedom is of little use to it. What is first needed is a system of public education capable of providing it, so far as possible, with means of expression; and next, a régime in which the public freedom of expression is characterized not so much by freedom as by attentive silence in which this faint and inept cry can make itself heard; and finally, institutions are needed of a sort which will, so far as possible, put power into the hands of men who are able and anxious to hear and understand it.
>
> (316)

Here is a resource for giving new life to the common phrase 'thinking like a lawyer'. We might say that real lawyering in the direction of justice begins in 'attentive silence'.

Nelson Mandela's Speech from the Dock

In the early 1960s, Mandela took up the leadership of Umkhonto we Sizwe, or 'Spear of the Nation', a new military organization that sought to end the brutal apartheid regime and to begin a worthy democracy in South Africa. When the regime failed to respond to invitations to talk, Umkhonto soon engaged in acts of sabotage, damaging government offices and infrastructure. The South African Parliament responded by empowering the courts to impose the death penalty on saboteurs. In 1962, the police found Mandela and arrested him. The following year, when in prison for other crimes, he and a number of his colleagues were charged with sabotage. At the trial, the prosecutor produced numerous documents found at Umkhonto's hideout. The defendants could reasonably expect the death sentence.

At the outset of their defence, Mandela made a statement from the dock, hoping to make the most of a momentary rhetorical equality*. In his autobiography, *Long Walk to Freedom*, he says about his final words:

> I had been reading my speech, and at this point I placed my papers on the defence table, and turned to face the judge. The courtroom became extremely quiet. I did not take my eyes off Justice de Wet as I spoke from memory the final words.
>
>> During my lifetime I have dedicated myself to this struggle of the African people. I have fought against white domination, and I have fought against black domination. I have cherished the ideal of a democratic and free society in which all persons live together in harmony and with equal opportunities. It is an ideal which I hope to live for and to achieve. But if needs be, it is an ideal for which I am prepared to die.
>
> The silence in the courtroom was now complete. At the end of the address, I simply sat down. I did not turn and face the gallery, though I felt all their eyes on me. The silence seemed to stretch for many minutes. But in fact it lasted probably no more than thirty seconds, and then from the gallery I heard what sounded like a great sigh, a deep collective 'ummmmm', followed by the cries of women.
>
> I had read for over four hours. It was a little after 4 in the afternoon, the time court normally adjourned. But Justice de Wet, as soon as there was order in the courtroom, asked for the next witness. He was determined to lessen the impact of my statement. . . . When I finished my address and sat down, it was the last time that Justice de Wet ever looked me in the eye.
>
> (Mandela 1994: 354)

Mandela's reading of the call for 'the next witness' may remind us that we can use the word 'silence' as a verb. Did Justice de Wet seek to use the next witness to silence either Mandela's words or the silence just after them? (If so, what might that say about the limits of the principle of justice 'hear the other side'?) A key question facing Mandela's various audiences concerned how to manage the 'impact' of his speech. We might wonder about the life of Justice de Wet's mind during the silence after Mandela's *cri de coeur*. Were Mandela's words echoing? If so, with what disposition (say, belief, doubt, or a bit of both) was he listening*? Was he working out how to justify a death sentence? Was he seeking to end the 'face'-to-face with Mandela as soon as possible?

In *Heracles' Bow*, which is a contribution to the rehabilitation of rhetoric*, White stresses that his 'attention is focused on the expressive and constitutive life that is the center of law—in this sense on the ethics of rhetoric'. Whilst elaborating, he provides a resource for thinking about what it means 'to think as lawyers':

> [A] conception of the law as an art of language and community may help explain why the object of law school is to teach students 'to think as lawyers' rather than merely to teach them 'the rules.' In their practical lives after graduation, what they will be asked to do by their clients, what they will be paid to do, is to act in the poetic and rhetorical way I describe: to bring to bear the materials of the past upon a present question, remaking those materials as they do so, with the idea of creating a new set of relations in the present and the future—relations between the lawyers themselves and the clients, relations between the clients, and so on. It is the moment of silence, when the lawyer must speak, and in speaking make something new out of his or her language and the world, to which our deepest attention should be directed, in the law school and after.
>
> (White 1985a: xiii–xiv)

Our deepest attention here perhaps should be directed to where White would have us direct 'our deepest attention': 'the moment of silence'. This moment should be one of 'attentive silence' (Weil), lest we miss the cry of someone being hurt, with an injustice possibly being done in the name of the law. The passage from White can remind us that 'the heart of law is . . . the open hearing' (1984: 273) and that the law is not an object ('the rules') but an activity, which people 'do'. Justice, in this spirit, is not an abstract concept that is 'out there' but a certain kind of performance* with words, including the language of silence.

'A Silent Professor': Mark Weisberg

In an essay, 'Discerning the Gift', Weisberg reflects on a legal writing course, Legal Imagination, using White's *The Legal Imagination*. (We hear from Weisberg above – *Listening.) In one part of the essay, which offers much for those who think that character* matters in the law, he talks about 'silence' as a teaching strategy:

> I have come to understand being silent in class as one way to help fulfill . . . every teacher's obligation: helping students become responsible for their own meanings. For me this also is a form of encouraging them to think for themselves as individually responsible for the shape of the law, not simply as fungible clerks at the bottom of the professional hierarchy.

> Usually as the classes progress throughout the term, people become more comfortable with my silence, and comfortable setting their own agenda for discussions. As people become more comfortable with each other, as they begin to trust themselves and each other, I occasionally intervene, usually with a question or a brief comment, occasionally offering a perspective I think might advance the discussion. Bolstered by the personal commitment and curiosity the writing assignments produce, as well as by the freedom to say what they want without fear of being corrected, in their discussions people achieve an unusual honesty and depth. And the curiosity also fosters an openness to differences, an ability to listen to and appreciate other people, and to entertain other points of view.
>
> (Weisberg 1999: 35–6)

That passage lends itself as a resource for thought and expression about the integration* of 'the personal' and the professional and of 'the law' and justice*. (It assumes that 'meanings' are not impersonal entities but experiential processes.) If a law teacher talked and talked and talked without stopping to listen to her students (or to herself), how could she possibly do justice* to the most basic principle of justice, hear the other side? Silence is a vital part of orientating oneself toward hearing others and of constituting a rhetorical equality* (*Rhetoric).

When people speak with the kind of 'honesty and depth' mentioned by Weisberg, we have ingredients for what White calls 'living speech'. Silence, of a certain quality, is a vital part of such speech:

> An essential feature of this kind of speech or writing is that its use of language is not automatic, but shaped or chosen. The speaker or writer tries to be aware of his language and its limits, and invites his audience to be so too; this requires of both of them an inner as well as outer silence. And this silence is not simply empty space or time, an absence of words; it is a state or condition that must be attained, by work and art and discipline, and it must be . . . used well. It is a crucial part of what we mean by an engagement of the whole mind.
>
> Much of what we say and hear is of course not like this—not shaped by inner and outer silences—but is simply a stitching together of locutions in predictable and uninteresting ways. . . . On these occasions we speak or write as if our words and phrases were simply stored in an antechamber to the mind, ready for immediate use upon demand. Lawyers are all too familiar with this sort of speaking and writing, of which a certain kind of brief can be taken as an example: one that pieces together rules and quotations, makes distinctions, argues to conclusions, but without ever making it the work of the individual mind . . . . His effort is . . . to sound like a lawyer, not to be one.
>
> (White 2006: 15)

When a person's language is 'shaped or chosen', she does not take meanings for granted but, rather, self-consciously makes meanings, in the process of 'making' herself and her audience. That passage could prompt an economist, one who wants to discard the conventional one-dimensional *Homo economicus* and make room for a multi-dimensional 'individual mind', to remove the word 'demand' (and its companion 'supply') from the antechamber of her mind, lest she merely sound like an economist. With a heightened 'aware'-ness of the costs of dead speech, she may contribute to an increase in the *desire* for living speech. With such an increase, White's ideas on silence could begin to soar in the marketplace of ideas.

How does one discern the dead metaphor*? What place might the various modes of silence have in doing so?

Understanding

'The Contents of this Treaty': Waitangi
'Fusion of Horizons': Hans-Georg Gadamer

As I said at the outset of this book, what I am calling 'attunement' is a way of orientating ourselves to meaning, which is not an object but an experiential process. The meaning of a text to a person will differ at least slightly from its meaning to another person. If the different meanings are a source of 'legal' conflict, they may find themselves turning to lawyers for help. All parties involved will do well to keep in mind that there can be more to a case than winning it. Felix Cohen suggests as much:

> The judge who understands how two lawyers can disagree on the elementary facts of a simple case, why each lawyer thinks the other's precedents are not in point, and how they can differ even in their causal judgments, may achieve a higher level of understanding than the most brilliant of advocates. (Cohen 1950: 269)

Lawyers and non-lawyers alike might do well to wonder how a judge could 'achieve a higher level of understanding than the most brilliant of advocates'. What role might the lawyers have in such an achievement?

When two 'understanding' judges disagree, we may find ourselves turning to a judicial critic for help. The critic who understands why they disagree may help us achieve a higher level of understanding of 'a higher level of understanding'. When two critics disagree, we may find ourselves working toward a transcendental method*.

'The Contents of This Treaty': Waitangi

On 6 February 1840, William Colenso asked Captain William Hobson a question relating to the Treaty of Waitangi's addendum, which states that the Maori 'Chiefs' had been made 'fully to understand the Provisions of the foregoing Treaty':

Colenso: May I ask your Excellency whether it is your opinion that these Natives understand the articles of the treaty which they are now called upon to sign?

Hobson: If the Native chiefs do not know the contents of this treaty it is no fault of mine. I wish them to fully understand it. I have done all that I could do to make them understand the same, and I really don't know how I shall be enabled to get them to do so. They have heard the treaty read by Mr. Williams.

Colenso: True, your Excellency; but the Natives are quite children in their ideas. It is no easy matter, I well know, to get them to understand – fully to comprehend a document of this kind; still, I think they ought to know somewhat of it to constitute its legality. I speak under correction, your Excellency. I have spoken to some chiefs concerning it, who had no idea whatever as to the purport of the treaty.

(Colenso 1890: 38)

The language here images the Treaty to be like a container, for it has 'contents'. These are words, which are implied to hold meanings or 'ideas' that are like objects that can be transported without change to another place. To 'understand' the text supposedly involves being able to grasp the meanings in the words. ('Comprehend' is from the Latin *com* + *prehendre*, 'to grasp together'.) Failure to achieve complete mutual understanding, for those who live by the metaphor* of *understanding is grasping*, arises from a communication blockage, the responsibility for which resides with either the sender or the receiver or both. Hobson seems certain that he himself is not responsible: 'If the Native chiefs do not know the contents of this treaty it is no fault of mine.' Colenso's claim that 'the Natives are quite children in their ideas' implies that the 'Natives' are the source of the blockage, perhaps lacking the minds with the capacity to unpack the meanings in the words. When translation is involved in situations of disagreement about meaning, it is common for accusations to be made about the competence and/or faithfulness of the translator (Williams).[1]

What might have happened at Waitangi had someone asked what it meant to 'understand' the Treaty? (We could put the question this way: Can we 'fully understand' what it means to 'fully understand'?) It might have become apparent, for example, that Colenso's image of the Treaty differed from Hobson's and from Williams' image, and that none of them could 'fully understand' the Treaty. (To draw from one of the epigraphs to this book, they might have come to 'feel the spectral sadness of the written word without a voice to fill it' – Ortega.) A conversation* among the three of them concerning how best to talk about 'understanding' might have started a cross-cultural conversation* (*Culture), in which all parties learn from each other, with each party engaging in the activity of attunement* to the language and reality of the other. (Starting such a conversation could have helped challenge the problematic prejudices associated with Colenso's claim that 'the Natives are quite children in their ideas'.) One result of a cross-cultural conversation could have been the recognition of a basic equality*, a common humanity. That result could have led to a collaborative enterprise in the process of expounding the Treaty in situations of conflict over its meaning.

The beginnings of such an enterprise did take place. Governor FitzRoy and a collection of chiefs agreed to amend the Preemption Clause[2] – FitzRoy was very constrained financially – and the chiefs acquired the power to sell land to whomever they pleased. FitzRoy's replacement, Grey, however, adopted a different line. For him, there was no better way of controlling chiefs than by refusing to buy land from those who opposed his views (Adams 1977: 197). He queried the 'legality' of the waiver of the Queen's 'right' of 'preemption'. Colonial officials created a court case, *The Queen v. Symonds* (1847). A Crown grant was issued to Symonds for land that had been conveyed with a certificate used during the FitzRoy era. The certificate was held by a Hunter McIntosh, who petitioned the Governor to have the grant set aside. The resemblance to the United States Supreme Court case *Johnson v. McIntosh* (1823) may be striking for some readers: 'a collusive case' (Robertson 2005: xi) directly involving only Europeans and indirectly involving indigenes, namely 'the power of Indians to give, and of private individuals to receive, a title which can be sustained in the courts of this country' (*Johnson* 1823: 572).[3] *Johnson*, as one critic put it, 'created . . . a set of legal rationalizations to justify the reduction of Indian rights without allowing any room for listening to the Indian voice' (Wilkins 1997: 30). We can readily apply those words to *Symonds*. We might say that in-justice* begins in non-'listening'*.

My account of *Symonds* differs markedly from conventional rule-centred accounts. Listen to McDowell and Webb's textbook *The New Zealand Legal System*:

> It is widely recognized that the first reported decision of the colonial Supreme Court, *{The Queen} v Symonds*, affirmed the obligations and rights of Maori laid down in the Treaty of Waitangi. . . . The Court upheld the . . . claimant's case, finding that the waiver of preemption was invalid and that, in accordance with established common law doctrine, the Crown was the only legal source for obtaining private title to land. . . . This common law principle existed independently of, and pre-dated the Treaty. . . . {T}he principle is reflected in Article II.
>
> (McDowell and Webb 2006: 181)

We will do well to resist reifying talk about 'rights' of 'Maori' being 'laid down in the Treaty'. The Treaty is not akin to a container that holds things, which can be 'affirmed' or not. Like Colenso and Hobson, McDowell and Webb live by inapt metaphors for imagining the Treaty – and thus for coming to a deeper 'understanding' of it. These metaphors fail to call for a voice to fill the written word, and for an ear to listen to such a voice and to judge it.

Efforts to enrich Waitangi talk today may benefit from turning to White. In *Justice as Translation*, he makes these suggestive remarks about communication:

> Thinking about translation . . . brings us to face the facts, present in all reading and writing and talking, that perfect communication is impossible, that we always write and talk across our languages, as well as within them, and that there is no such thing as 'understanding' in any simple sense of the word. Think, for example, of the definition of what we ordinarily mean by 'a language': when I say I will translate this text from 'French' to 'English,' the question can be asked, 'What French and whose English?' We speak as if all French-speakers spoke the same language, but obviously that is not true. No two people speak exactly the same French; their vocabularies overlap imperfectly, the prior texts that make up their reservoir of resources and allusions vary, their life experiences and range of associations differ, and so on. In the real world all language is idiolect . . . .
>
> (White 1990: 254)

Here, with the benefit of a productive question (*Questioning), the familiar words 'understanding' and 'language'* become less familiar – we experience, that is, an alienation* from the familiar. Are we under-standing White's text? We may do well to acknowledge incompleteness of 'understanding' and to strive toward a deeper understanding. If we talk as if we understand a text *completely* we will be talking as if we have nothing to learn, which could be a conversation-stopper and the beginning of in-justice*.

'Fusion of Horizons': Hans-Georg Gadamer

Gadamer's *Truth and Method* addresses 'the problem of hermeneutics' (1975: xi).[4] He is 'concerned with . . . the commitment involved in all understanding', with 'what happens to us over and above our wanting and doing' (xvi). (For him, the categories 'doer' and 'done to' are inadequate for talking about understanding.) At the heart of his concern, as suggested above (*Play), is 'the play of language' (446).

Gadamer stresses that language* is not a tool for pointing to objects that are out there in the world and for conveying thoughts from one person to another. For him, 'the nature of language is one of the most mysterious questions that exist for man to ponder on' (340). An inquiry can serve to create a constructive alienation*, for '[l]anguage is so uncannily near to our thinking and when it functions it is so little an object that it seems to conceal its own being from us' (340).

Gadamer resists 'the fundamental prejudice of the enlightenment', which is 'the prejudice against prejudice itself' (239–40). 'There are such things as préjugés légitimes', he says with a nod to Burke (*Character). (He is interested in how one 'distinguishes legitimate prejudices' from others.)

One's 'prejudices' constitute the 'standpoint' and a 'horizon' from which an interpreter works (269–72). 'The horizon is the range of vision that includes everything that can be seen from a particular vantage point.' His language here connects with ordinary language: 'we speak of narrowness of horizon, of the possible expansion of horizon, of the opening up of new horizons etc.' (269). Gadamer attends to movement*: 'The horizon is . . . something into which we move and that moves with us' (271). The 'understanding' that interests him involves a process in which an interpreter achieves a distance from some of her prejudices. (Here there is room for adopting Lonergan's language of transcendence – Method*.[5]) He images understanding as a 'conversation'*, in which there is a non-assimilative accommodation of standpoints, which he talks of as a 'fusion of horizons' (273). The 'fusing' of horizons, whilst building common ground through a common language, does not erase all differences – a sharpened shared sense of differences may emerge.[6] We might hope for a greater capacity to live with differences.

In genuine conversation, the participants change as 'prejudices' are challenged and modified. Such a conversation can be talked about in terms of an 'I'–'Thou' relation, about which Gadamer says:

> In human relations the important thing is . . . to experience the 'Thou' truly as a 'Thou', ie not to overlook his claim and to listen to what he has to say to us. To this end, openness is necessary. But this openness exists ultimately not only for the person to whom one listens, but rather anyone who listens is fundamentally open. Without this kind of openness to one another there is no genuine human relationship. Belonging together always also means being able to listen to one another. When two people understand each other, this does not mean that one person 'understands' the other, in the sense of surveying him. Similarly, to hear and obey someone does not mean simply that we do blindly what the other desires. We call such a person a slave.
>
> (324).

This use of the word 'openness' connects to a basic claim in Western ethical thought: the importance of treating another person not as an object (where 'there is no genuine human relationship') but as an end in herself, a 'Thou'. This 'openness' would include the character* strength of being willing and able to 'listen' to evidence against one's prejudices. This strength is essential to acts of justice*. (Waitangi comes to mind.)

In genuine conversation, the parties involved are in a situation of rhetorical equality* (*Rhetoric) in the sense that neither can be said to be in control of its direction and flow. Gadamer offers this imagery:

> We say that we 'conduct' a conversation, but the more fundamental a conversation is, the less its conduct lies within the will of either partner. Thus a fundamental conversation is never one that we want to conduct.

> Rather, it is generally more correct to say that we fall into conversation, or even that we become involved in it. The way in which one word follows another, with conversation taking its own turnings and reaching its own conclusion, may well be conducted in some way, but the people conversing are far less the leaders of it than the led. No one knows what will 'come out' in a conversation. Understanding or its failure is like a process which happens to us.
>
> (345)

'Understanding' is not the passive taking in of a fixed meaning by detached and stable minds but, rather, a collective and experiential process that changes the mind-ing of those involved. Mutual under-standing begins in a 'conversation' in which each participant has a respect for the claims of the other: 'Reaching an understanding in conversation presupposes that both partners are ready for it and are trying to recognise the full value of what is alien and opposed to them' (348). 'Understanding', says a Gadamer critic, 'requires love: not just interest in a person *in abstracto* but interest in and patient attention to what that person is saying' (Vanhoozer 2005: 34). It's all in the 'attention'*!

Shall we compare Gadamer's concerns to . . . ? In *The Legal Imagination*, in a section that explicitly addresses the topic of justice*, White and his reader 'attempt to find an occasion where . . . a legal speaker does justice to the complexity and profundity of the experience of another' (364). White offers a 'note' on how Austen's *Pride and Prejudice* 'might be read in such a way as to shed light on the problems of the sentencing judge' (401). Contemplating models of excellence in judgment* to whom we can turn:

> Darcy's judgment of Elizabeth is at first impeded by a stupid, if explicable, pride that leads him to a gross rudeness to Elizabeth; her judgment . . . is apparently discolored by a prejudice against Darcy that leads her to misinterpret his behavior and misjudge his qualities, and indeed blinds her usually acute critical sense with respect to Wickham. When Darcy finally does ask for her hand, it is in the most patronizing way; her rejection is sufficiently violent, one might imagine, to close off the future entirely. How is it that they come together at the end? What do they have that overcomes their own misjudgments . . . ? . . . An obvious part of the answer is this: each has the capacity to move to a new position from which the old self can be regarded and rejected. Judgments not only of others but of oneself can be discarded. . . . What do you call this process?
>
> (405)

The word 'critical' is significant here.[7] The word has roots in the Greek *krinein*, to judge. It readily connects to the word 'prejudice' – a key word for Austen and for Gadamer. Directly concerning the passage from White, the ability to identify 'prejudice' in 'oneself' is clearly one important ingredient in 'the capacity to move to a new position from which the old self can be regarded and rejected'. It would seem that one will need to be able to step into the shoes of another, who imagines the world from a different position, in order to identify such prejudice. This ability connects to a collection of character* strengths and virtues such as creativity, curiosity, integrity, open-mindedness, and wisdom. These will be vital for a person to transcend his or her reality into the reality of others. When two people who are in conflict can perform a significant movement* 'outside' and 'come together', we have a model 'fusion of horizons'.[8] We might call this process attunement*.

Voice

'Officialese': Hannah Arendt's *Eichmann in Jerusalem*
'At Once Serious and Conversational': Lani Guinier's Demosprudence

White's *The Legal Imagination* established 'a course in writing' (1973; xxi). His reader 'is asked to write as a lawyer, judge and legislator, and to . . . speak in his own voice about his experience of writing' (xix). White's concern with 'voice' has roots in his 'ear training' as a student in the Department of English at Amherst College (*Reading). In *When Words Lose Their Meaning*, he suggests that Swift's *A Tale of a Tub* is a forerunner in such training:

> The way of reading it teaches consists largely in listening for a voice, then asking who speaks that way, then judging it. It thus constantly trains what could be called the ethical ear, for to be read at all one must constantly be assessing character as it is manifested in language. The defects that appear in the text as delusion, false questions, withdrawals from reality, unlimited ambitions, failures to connect, and the like are not merely intellectual or cognitive deficiencies but diseases of character, the only remedy for which is the kind of wholeness and health Swift seeks to stimulate in the reader. To read sensibly, to write sensibly, and to be sensible are, for Swift, intimately connected.
>
> (White 1984: 136)

What questions might we ask of that passage in order to pursue a sensible way of reading/writing (*Questioning)? Concerning the activity* of 'listening'*, how are we to go about listening to White's 'voice'? How are we to go about assessing his 'character'* and 'language'*? In what way might we fail to 'connect'?

'Officialese': Hannah Arendt's *Eichmann in Jerusalem*

In 1960, Israeli agents abducted Adolf Eichmann in Argentina and took him to Jerusalem, where he was put on trial for his participation in the mass murder of Jews. Hannah Arendt attended the trial as a reporter for *The New Yorker*. Her reports became a book, carrying the striking subtitle *A Report on the Banality of Evil*. After some considerable close listening to Eichmann, she detected a certain hollowness in his voice. Here is one passage:

> Dimly aware of a defect that . . . amounted to a mild case of aphasia—he apologized, saying, 'Officialese . . . is my only language.' But the point here is that officialese became his language because he was genuinely incapable of uttering a single sentence that was not a cliché. . . . [T]he judges were right when they finally told the accused that all he had said was 'empty talk'—except that they had thought the emptiness was feigned, and that the accused wished to cover up other thoughts which . . . were not empty. This supposition seems refuted by the striking consistency with which Eichmann . . . repeated word for word the same stock phrases and self-invented clichés . . . each time he referred to an incident or event of importance to him. . . . The longer one listened to him, the more obvious it became that his inability to speak was closely connected with an inability to *think*, namely, to think from the standpoint of somebody else. No communication was possible with him, not because he lied but because he was surrounded by the most reliable safeguards against the words and presence of others, and hence against reality as such.
> (Arendt 1963: 43–4)

When a person speaks with a mass of clichés, there is a sense in which he or she is not a person worthy of the name, not a 'presence' with whom one can engage in meaningful 'communication'. 'Language'* for such a 'person' is not a vital resource for (re)creating a genuine community but a tool for supporting that which Arendt says is 'against reality'. The 'person' becomes a tool in the service of a dehumanizing force. In the case with which Arendt engaged, Eichmann became one of Hitler's bureaucrats.

Arendt's account of the trial suggests much about the ways in which language use and character* are connected – defective language use is associated with character flaws and weaknesses. Consider this fragment:

> Eichmann was not Iago and not Macbeth, and nothing would have been farther from his mind than to determine with Richard III 'to prove a villain.' Except for an extraordinary diligence in looking out for his personal advancement, he had no motives at all. And this diligence in itself was in no way criminal; he certainly would never have murdered his superior in order to inherit his post. He *merely*, to put the matter colloquially, *never realized what he was doing*. It was precisely this lack of imagination which enabled him to sit for months on end facing a German Jew who was conducting the police interrogation, . . . explaining again and again how it was that he reached only the rank of lieutenant colonel in the SS and that it had not been his fault that he was not promoted. . . . It was sheer thoughtlessness – something by no means identical with stupidity – that predisposed him to become one of the

> greatest criminals of that period. And if this is 'banal' and even funny, if with the best will in the world one cannot extract any diabolical or demonic profundity from Eichmann, that is still far from calling it commonplace. It surely cannot be so common that a man facing death, and, moreover, standing beneath the gallows, should be able to think of nothing but what he heard at funerals all his life, and that these 'lofty words' should completely becloud the reality of his own death.
>
> (in Hinton 2002: 102–3)

Had Eichmann exercised his 'imagination'* and self-consciously resisted the clichés, he may have *'realized what he was doing'*, at which time he could have made some authentic choices concerning who he was becoming. If he had been more in control of his language, he may have been capable of having an experience to which he could try to do justice* with language. If he could have done justice to his own experience, he might have been able to do justice to the experience of Others.

What might we say about Arendt's voice? The longer one listens to her, the more obvious it becomes that she is the opposite of Eichmann. She certainly does not turn her arresting phrase, 'the banality of evil', into a cliché. Her phrase is the product of a person with an ability to think from the standpoint of somebody else, in this case the 'thoughtless' Eichmann; it is an expression that comes from a person boldly asserting the worth and validity of her own experience*, understanding*, and judgment*.

Beginning with *The Legal Imagination*, 'cliché' is a central term in White's critical vocabulary (1973: 956). He talks about 'success' for the lawyer 'as a matter of one's relationship with language' (49). As a base for 'defining the relationship between self and language', White asks his reader to read Shakespeare's *Troilus and Cressida*:

> Read the speeches of Troilus with particular care. He has only the formal language of love with which to respond to the events of the play, and it is wholly inadequate even as a means of establishing and expressing a relationship with Cressida. For example, the decision to send Cressida to the Greeks is made without argument or dissent from him. When Cressida asks whether she must indeed go . . . Troilus does not answer her, but gives instead a Beautiful Farewell Speech . . . He then falls into a language of lover's cliché . . . What you see . . . is what it means to have only one resource for expression, and how impossible it proves in any situations both those few to which it (by its nature) is directed. . . . Do you see this as pathetic? Do you know any lawyers (or law teachers) who are defined by a single language in a similarly pathetic way? If one who talks only one way has lost control of his language, how do you plan to establish a different relationship, one of control, with the legal language that you will use all day every day?
>
> (53–4)

> . . . It seems fair to say that Troilus is wholly defined by the formal language of love, with no indication of any unexpressed or private life, while Cressida is defined as standing outside the language of love, which she treats as inadequate to express her private experience. . . . One might . . . draw an analogy to this course: our purpose is to define and take a position with respect to legal language like Cressida's with respect to love language: outside and skeptical of it.
>
> (54)

If we were to modify *The Legal Imagination* and replace Shakespeare's play with the Eichmann trial, we might say: 'Read the speeches of Eichmann with particular care. He has only the language of officialese with which to respond to the questions put to him, and it is wholly inadequate even as a means of establishing and expressing a relationship with. . . .' Also: 'When standing beneath the gallows, he falls into a language of lover's cliché, telling his audience that "we shall all meet again".'

How can one avoid being 'wholly defined' by a language (say, officialese, the language of law, or the language of economics)? How, that is, can one 'control' a language? White's questions can be taken as an invitation to develop a language, or rather a collection of languages, with which to talk about the ways people 'talk' and to make judgments about these ways. What is to become of us in our talk about talk?

Arendt's account of the Eichmann trial, including her judicial criticism, suggests much about the value of 'ear reading'. In the echo of White's reading of Swift's *Tale*, we might say: 'The way of reading Arendt's *Eichmann* consists largely in listening for a voice, then asking who speaks that way, then judging it. Such a way can help us hear Eichmann's delusion, false questions, withdrawals from reality. . . .'

'At Once Serious and Conversational': Lani Guinier's Demosprudence

In 2008, Lani Guinier wrote the Foreword to the *Harvard Law Review*'s yearly survey of the Supreme Court's work. She begins with a visit to the Court's decision in *Parents Involved in Community Schools v. Seattle School District No. 1* (2007), which concerned efforts by communities to integrate their public schools. She notes that in 'a matter of sentences . . . , Chief Justice Roberts', for the majority, 'declares Seattle's and Louisville's voluntary school integration plans unlawful because they consider race as a factor in student assignment' (2008: 7). She then turns to the dissent:

> Justice Breyer . . . forcefully challenges Chief Justice Roberts' view of 'the law' of the land. 'The majority is wrong' to conclude that consideration of race is per se unlawful. To the contrary, when used to include rather than exclude, taking race into account is constitutional. . . . The Supreme Court

> has routinely given 'significant practical leeway' to democratically elected school boards to make educational policy that 'tries to bring people together.' . . .
>
> Justice Breyer's oral dissent . . . used some of the authoritative texts and legal conventions that are Supreme Court Justices' standard fare. But he also summoned memories, values, and practices that might – were his oral dissent widely distributed – have resonated with a less educated audience, including those who never graduated from high school but had seen evidence in their own lives of what he described. Justice Breyer was at once serious and conversational. . . . [H]e appealed to shared and heartfelt values, not just compelling logic and clear reason. . . . [The] tone and . . . craft [of his oral dissent] contained the outlines of a different kind of social criticism. Although he did not speak to a youth culture steeped in the theatrical art of the 'spoken word,' his conversational style nonetheless equipped him with twenty-first-century tools to reach out to new listeners. The platform of Justice Breyer's oral dissent offered a novel and potentially interactive pedagogical space, one that . . . could spark a lively conversation among, and with, a decidedly non-professional and non-elite audience. In this sense, Justice Breyer's oral dissent hinted at the possibility of a larger phenomenon, a new forum for deliberative democracy being carved out of the formal authority and awe-inspired reverence associated with the Supreme Court of the United States.
>
> (8–12)

Guinier applauds Justice Breyer for speaking to a wide audience. He does this, she suggests, by combining talk about 'reason' and talk about 'values' (*Integration). For Guinier, 'tone' matters a great deal. A 'conversational style' can be imagined not as that which some people call 'mere style' but as a way of constituting a valuable social reality. Guinier's own voice resembles her description of Breyer's voice: 'at once serious and conversational', a 'tone and . . . craft contain[ing] the outlines of a different kind of social criticism', all of which combine into an artefact that could begin a constructive conversation among 'the people', broadly defined.

Let Guinier continue:

> [S]ome ordinary people were listening. The Roberts majority may have moved the law as if it were a mere chess piece, but Justice Breyer's critique had legs in directly affected communities like Louisville, Kentucky. Local civil servants, like Pat Todd, an educational administrator in Louisville . . . armed herself with Justice Breyer's dissent, which she read aloud at the beginning of all of her community forums. She and others in Louisville readied themselves to continue the struggle within the framework of our democratic system. Their goal was to elaborate ideas and practices of racial integration in ways that may eventually realign our constitutional law with the prevailing view of constitutional culture.

> Emboldened by the dissent, Todd and her cohorts are . . . pushing back on the majority's formulation because it is inconsistent with the values of the community they represent.
>
> To the extent Justice Breyer's dissent triggered an ongoing conversation with thought leaders . . . like Todd, he created a dynamic relationship of accountability. . . . When social and cultural intermediaries like Todd tune in, they can act as amplifiers and translators for the Court. Even if the conversational loop they join does not ultimately yield policy change, the outcome may still be democracy-enhancing. First, these intermediaries can make oppositional constitutional norms more salient based on the lived experience of ordinary people. Second, the interactive dialogue can engage more people in the decisionmaking process.
>
> (12–13)

Guinier may be read as offering an unconventional response to the conventional core question in jurisprudence courses, namely, What is the nature of law? With her use of aural/oral metaphors ('conversation'*, 'dialogue', 'listening'*, 'tune in', 'voice'), she invites her reader to attend not to an object but to discourse. Her aural turn invites a shift from imagining the legal subject (a person who attempts to understand the law) as that of a passive spectator to a citizen intent on full participation in 'deliberative democracy'. We might say that she invites her reader to ask not 'How do I abide by The Law?' but 'What and how can I contribute to the law's becoming?'

Guinier's Foreword gives life to the word 'demosprudence', which she and Gerald Torres coined (15). This is her name for the 'different kind of social criticism'. 'Demosprudence', she says, 'is a democracy-enhancing jurisprudence' (15). It is 'focused on enhancing the democratic potential of the work of lawyers, judges, and other legal elites' (16). For her, there is more to law than rules: it is an aspirational 'work' with a certain 'potential'.

Guinier's image of an authoritative democracy offers a challenge for those who utter the slogan 'law is politics'. She invites the re-imagining of the law/politics relationship:

> [O]ral dissents remind us that Supreme Court Justices have a choice of audience. . . . Deciding to expand the Supreme Court's audience has implications for the role of the Justices as teachers and curators of democracy, and may involve rethinking our understanding of the Court's ultimate authority and the law/politics distinction.
>
> (30–31)

> Demosprudence is not a call to ordinary politics, whether electoral or quasi-electoral. Its democratic faith rests on a more deliberative view of the relationship between lawmaking and democracy – that elections are valuable aggregation devices but that they are not the only way to legitimate lawmaking. Instead, demosprudence as a lawmaking or legal practice

> is animated by the intuition that citizen participation over time in the form of deliberation and iteration is vital to the legitimacy and justice function of lawmaking and to the sustainability of democracy itself.
>
> (48)

> To the extent that Justices . . . speak out in a demosprudential voice that is more prophetic than authoritative, that is more colloquial than technical, they are speaking to and empowering the people. They are inviting the public into the hallowed halls of the courtroom, transforming an elite stage into a democratic agora. In this tradition, Justices teach the public to identify with the constitutional values at stake and invite them to speak back in a voice that is all their own. They channel the energy of 'we the people' into a revitalized, robust democracy. They do this by speaking, not through the complex diction of authoritative experts, but directly to the people in a language they can understand.
>
> (137–8)

Demosprudence is a call to extra-ordinary politics, which can help in 'transforming' the 'ordinary', in part by destabilizing both the opposition of 'law versus politics' and the unifying slogan 'law is politics'. For Guinier, a fundamental question of law concerns how 'we' may do justice* to one another. With many different voices among us, we must somehow try to bring together a multiplicity of voices without falling apart, which is what happens when, for example, some voices go unheard or are not given any or due weight. This activity of bringing together is the material of a complex conversation, one to which she contributes with her article. We can be sure that the 'ultimate authority' with which Guinier is concerned is a way of talking, defined in terms of 'voice'.

The direction of Guinier's judicial criticism bears a striking resemblance to White's. Consider, for example, his reading, in *Justice as Translation*, of Justice Brandeis' dissent in *Olmstead v. United States*, in which he rejected the majority's 'unduly literal construction' of the Fourth Amendment' (*Olmstead* 1928: 476). After quoting a passage from Brandeis on the Constitution, White offers these words of endorsement:

> This is a translation not only into contemporary legal language but beyond it, into contemporary ordinary language, into the vernacular. It thus invites a conversation not only among lawyers but among citizens, a conversation that is in a sense democratic. But this language does not supplant the law—the last thing Brandeis would argue for is the elimination of our cultural past in favor of the uninformed view of the moment. It is in fact his work with the legal language preceding this passage that has both made possible and justified this return of the Constitution to the people.
>
> (White 1990: 154)

Like Guinier, White imagines 'the law' not as an entity distinct from 'democratic' politics but as a broad and inclusive 'conversation' that has potentially valuable consequences for 'the people'. This image is familiar from our engagement with his reading of *McCulloch* (*Constitution), *Prigg* (*Attention), and *Cohen* (*Alienation).

With 'demosprudence' in mind, we might ask: What's in a name? In attempting to compose an order on White's work, which defies simple placement with conventional categories, that famous question has come to have greater significance for me. While we might read some of his work as a contribution to jurisprudence, White distances his work from that name. Consider these prefatory remarks in *The Legal Imagination*:

> Although many of the issues with which this book deals – what it means to speak in a language of rules, how the judicial mind connects the particular and the general, and so on – are sufficiently familiar to lead one to the supposition that this is really a jurisprudence book in disguise, I trust you can see why I am reluctant to call it that. Such a name would make claims that I want to avoid – and which would indeed not be warranted – and in any event, the focus of this course is far from the center of usual philosophical discourse. The effort of the book is not to reach conclusions, even tentative ones, but to define responsibilities. The hope is not that a systematic view of life will be exposed, but that the student will come to some new awareness of his place in the world, of his powers and obligations. In every paper he defines himself as a mind, and you might say that this act of self-expression is our real subject. Not a legal writing course, then, but a course in writing.
>
> (White 1973: xxi)

While White has not written *The Legal Imagination* as a 'jurisprudence book', it does offer itself as a model for composing our lives together, a model we might name in order to 'place' it, and ourselves, in the world. What about 'demosprudence'? A 'demosprudence' book may well avoid claims that White would not want to make. Like Guinier, White seeks 'not to reach conclusions . . . but to define responsibilities'. Also, they are centrally concerned with the 'act of self expression'. In particular, they are both interested in enhancing our capacity to hear tones of voice, to judge the human relations constituted by them, and to do justice through one's own voice. It is this demosprudential aspect of White's work with which this book is concerned.

Notes

Activity

1 The word 'reification' comes from the Latin *res* ('thing') and *facere* ('to transform'). For a discussion of this activity in law and legal theory, see Litowitz (2000). 'Reification', Litowitz remarks, 'is a silent and subtle phenomenon, one that is best noticed in a comparative context where we recognize the reification within our own legal system by comparing it with other alternative arrangements, both real and imagined' (403).

Attention

1 For some suggestive remarks on Abraham's attentiveness, remarks that reside in a discussion on 'attunement', see Fishbane (2008: 19 and 109–10).

2 'To listen to someone is to put oneself in his place while he is speaking.' This is a difficult task when the 'someone' is suffering from 'affliction'. It requires one to 'annihilate oneself' (Weil 1943/1977: 332).

3 For background on the Fugitive Slave Act, see Eisgruber (1988). Some details are as follows. In 1793, Congress passed the Act, which identified procedures for the return of runaway slaves. The Act allowed masters to capture runaways and bring them to any magistrate, state or federal, to request a certificate of removal. Armed with a certificate, the claimant was then free to take the runaway slave out of the state where he or she was found and back to the claimant's state. There was tension between the Northern and Southern states over the process of working out relative rights of masters (or agents) and those claimed to be slaves. The Northern states enacted procedural restrictions on the recapture of slaves, restrictions embodying a presumption of freedom in an attempt to affirm through law the presumption that 'all men are free until proven otherwise by orderly procedures.' This went against the grain in the Southern states where there was a presumption that all blacks were slaves.

4 The word 'slave', said Roger Sherman in the Constitutional Convention of 1787, was 'not pleasing to some people' (quoted in Finkelman 1993: 613). 'The Framers', writes Finkelman, 'understood they were writing a Constitution which protected slavery . . . but realized that openly using the word slave might undermine chances of ratification' (613).

5 White talks about this question in a reading of Plato's *Crito* – see White 1994a: 34–5.

Character

1 Here I draw from Jeremy Bentham (1776/1988: vi).
2 Kronman (1993) has explored the character of the 'lawyer-statesman'.
3 An image that Burke used for the corrupting power of language is Babel. Here I draw from Blakemore (1988: 103).
4 Burke writes, for example: 'The beauty of women is considerably owing to their weakness, or delicacy, and is even enhanced by their timidity, a quality of mind analogous to it' (1757/1987: 116). Blakemore (1997: 26–7) offers a summary of Burke's usage of these terms.
5 For example: 'You may have convinced them [aristocratic women] that *littleness* and *weakness* are the very essence of beauty; and that the Supreme Being, in giving women beauty in the most supereminent degree, seemed to command them . . . not to cultivate the moral virtues that might chance to excite respect. . . . Thus confining truth, fortitude, and humanity, within the rigid pale of manly morals, they might justly argue, that to be loved . . . they should learn to lisp, to totter in their walk . . .' (Wollstonecraft 1790/1997: 80).
6 Blakemore (1997: 26–83) discusses Wollstonecraft's linguistic entanglements.
7 *Persuasion* opens with Sir Walter reading Debrett's *Baronetage*, which contains aristocratic family histories plainly told by men who have an interest in keeping women in their second-rate place. Sir Walter 'never took up any book but the Baronetage' (9). One literary-legal commentator senses that 'the *Baronetage* . . . operates as Sir Walter's book of statutes' (Phelps 1994: 379).
8 For a discussion of the role of propriety in the interrelations between Lady Russell, Anne, and Frederick, see Nardin (1973: 143–54).
9 Many commentators make some rather bold inferences. For example: 'Swayed by passion and unclear about reasons, Anne crumbles under Lady Russell's vehement resolve against Wentworth's addresses. Pulled between opposing voices, one cautious, the other headstrong, she consoles herself with a logic she never shared' (Swanson 1981: 6). We simply do not know very much at all about Anne's 'logic'. The unreliable narrator offers fragments of an evolving story. We don't know how much she 'shared' and what the quality of the listening was like.
10 For one persuasive claim, see Terry (1996). Concerning the making of a misjudgment on Anne's 'weakness and timidity', connections can be made to White's reading, in *Acts of Hope* (1994a), of Fanny's supposed meekness in *Mansfield Park*.
11 Gadamer's interest in the activity of catching is suggested in the epigraph to *Truth and Method* (1975), Rilke's poem on the play of the universe: 'Catch only what you've thrown yourself, all is / mere skill and little gain; / but when you're suddenly the catcher of a ball / thrown by an eternal partner / . . . from the great bridgebuilding of God: / why catching then becomes a power – / not yours, a world's'.
12 Gallop (1999) makes connections between Aristotle and Austen.
13 The key moment here is when Neoptolemus gives up some vital interests, including defeating Troy, and accepts Philoctetes' request to take him home. When Neoptolemus does this, he creates a real community of friendship. Heracles then appears and persuades Philoctetes to enter battle. See White (1985a: 7, 13 and 15).

Constitution

1 'WE THE PEOPLE OF THE UNITED STATES, in Order to form a more perfect Union, establish Justice, insure domestic Tranquility, provide for the common defence, promote the general Welfare, and secure the Blessings of Liberty to ourselves and our Posterity, do ordain and establish this Constitution for the United States of America.'

2 Words always come from someone, who is directing them to someone else (even in a soliloquy), and, as such, claims about 'the meaning' of the 'plain' or 'literal' words problematically erases this relational and contextual dimension of language. On *McCulloch*'s 'never forget' warning, Paul Kahn writes: it 'is a direct response to the critic who wants merely to look at the Constitution. Not sight but interpretive doctrine is required. Sight alone is inadequate, for with respect to most questions there is no text to be seen' (Kahn 1997: 226).

Conversation

1 For a helpful 'rhetorical' approach to *Persuasion*, see Kastley (1997).

2 As I mention elsewhere (*Play), Gadamer's interest in the activity of catching is suggested in the epigraph to *Truth and Method* (1975), Rilke's poem on the play of the universe.

3 *Attorney-General v. Ngati Apa* [2003] 3 NZLR 643.

4 Efforts to enrich and civilize sovereignty talk can be traced through influential common law lawyers, including Matthew Hale and Edmund Burke. I have connected Hale to Waitangi sovereignty talk in an *Otago Law Review* article (2008), and I have done the same with Burke in a *Canterbury Law Review* article (2009).

5 For a fuller discussion of Cullen's absolutist talk in a different context, see Dawson (2007a).

6 For an extended discussion of interchanges leading up to the *Foreshore and Seabed Act*, see Dawson (2006). In 2009, the Attorney-General established a Foreshore and Seabed Review Panel, which concluded that aspects of the 2004 Act were 'wrong'. The Act was replaced with the *Marine and Coastal Area (Takutai Moana) Act* 2011. Indigenes got more 'rights', but there was no 'longer conversation' worthy of the name.

7 For a discussion of similar 'lost moments' in early Waitangi talk, see my 'Treaty of Waitangi Sovereignty-Talk: Lost Moments' (2008).

8 For a fuller discussion of constructive and liberating aspects of Earl's work, see my article 'Judging Economics Teaching and Textbooks' (2007b).

Equality

1 In the *Wealth of Nations*, after mentioning the 'invisible hand', Smith writes: 'By pursuing his own interest he frequently promotes that of society more effectually than when he really intends to promote it' (1776/1937: 423). Notice that the pursuit of 'self-interest' does not *always* advance the public interest, only 'frequently'.

2 For a discussion of this language in Commons' work, see Dawson (1998).

3 The phrase 'laissez-faire constitutionalism' refers to an ideological disposition held by some justices of the Supreme Court at the time, a disposition that neglected

'degree' and that was particularly influential in the 1905 *Lochner* case. For a discussion of the legal-economic critique of 'laissez-faire constitutionalism', see Fried (1998).

Experience

1 For a valuable discussion of Baird's 'shock'-approach to teaching, see Pritchard (2003: 269–81).

Integration

1 For a comprehensive discussion of Fuller's 'integrative' jurisprudence, see Teachout (1986).
2 On Fuller's reader: 'the reader is treated to a decentering hermeneutical experience in which competing rhetorical claims all resonate with the reader's prejudices and aspirations to some degree, and none quite capture the reader's allegiance to a degree of absolute certitude' (Mootz 1999: 449–50).

Justice

1 See, for example, Brookfield (1999: 128–30).
2 A landmark case here is *Hoani Te Heuheu Tukino v. Aotea District Maori Land Board* (1941: 596).
3 In an effort to transcend the objective–subjective opposition, the economist McCloskey has coined the term 'conjective'. 'It is neither . . . the objective nor the subjective. It is what we know together, by virtue of a common life and language' (1993: 76).
4 In Mackenzie 1990: 141. For a guide to the poem see Mackenzie (1981: 149).
5 For a reading of Hopkins' use of the verb 'to justice', see Derrida (2005). Here is one passage:

> Hopkins . . . has the magnificent audacity of an unusual verbal form: to *justice*, *justicing*, the act of doing justice, of justi*fying* justice, of *putting* justice *to work*. . . . Justice shines forth, it radiates, and so does the just. . . . The just one has a gift. For Hopkins, it can only be a gift from God, who nevertheless leaves us free to be just in our own names and to say 'je,' 'I' at the moment of being just. The just has the gift, he has the grace and the power to see to it that justice comes about outside itself in itself. He succeeds in making it happen that justice be justice, that justice *justices* without this being a simple tautology. It is given to the just, and the just gives himself the power to see to it that justice be produced justly, precisely, *by justicing*, as the justice it is, that it must be, and that it will have been. In the beginning will have been the verb: *to justice*.
>
> (230)

We may hope that after reading Derrida's efforts at justicing on Hopkins' '*justicing*', we can never hear the word 'justice' in quite the same way again.
6 In 1994, Joe Slovo remarked on Fischer's relation to communism: 'he wasn't a communist in the sense that we used to understand the way a communist operated.

. . . In his personal relationships with people he had a sort of humanistic approach to the way people should operate in a political party' (quoted in Clingman 1998: 452).

7 On Aristotle and regret, I have drawn from Kronman (1993: 83).

8 The identity-defining choice expressed in Fischer's letter brings to mind an opening question in White's *The Legal Imagination*: 'Can you stand far enough back from your legal education to ask, "What am I becoming?"' (1973: 10).

9 Concerning Fischer's 'beliefs' as they relate to communism: Did he believe, following Marx, that certain socioeconomic transformations were inevitable? If so, how did this sit with his revolutionary practice? Those questions can lead to others. Did he believe that we become what we believe? If so, is that which we 'believe' beyond adequate expression, especially to a nonbeliever? If yes, how might Fischer have talked to the judge (Boshoff) about his 'beliefs'? With what hopes might he have talked? What about the hope that the judge would be persuaded that Fischer acted 'correctly'? What about the hope of a resignation (with the judge protesting against the statute under which he was prosecuted)?

Language

1 For a comprehensive account of the process of owning and disowning a language, see Kathleen Norris' *Amazing Grace* (1998).

2 The Eminent Domain Clause of the Fifth Amendment: 'No persons shall be . . . deprived of life, liberty or property, without due process of law; nor shall private property be taken for public use without just compensation.' The Due Process and Equal Protection Clauses of the Fourteenth Amendment: 'Nor shall any state deprive any person of life, liberty, or property, without due process of law; nor deny to any person within its jurisdiction the equal protection of the laws.'

Listening

1 At the outset of *Law and Literature*, Posner sets 'law and literature' against 'law and economics' (1). For helpful talk about 'law and economics', see the chapter above engaging with Samuels' term 'the legal-economic nexus' (*Language).

2 Here I am drawing from Elbow (2005: 394). Weisberg and Peters draw from Elbow's work.

Metaphor

1 I have modified the original, which uses the word 'ideas' instead of 'meanings'.

Method

1 In White's *The Legal Imagination*, Coleridge's remark is an epigraph to the section 'Is the Judge Really a Poet?' (1973: 762).

2 On 'self-appropriation' in a legal context, see Glendon (1994) and Brennan (2002).

3 'Genuine objectivity is the fruit of authentic subjectivity' (Lonergan 1972: 292). In this regard, 'Objectivity, then, is a matter not of running into something hard—but of answering the questions of experience and reflection' (Brennan 2002: 338).

4 For an extended treatment of Lonergan's 'horizon'-analysis, see Tracy (1970). Lonergan's horizon-analysis has an important place in Tracy's *Blessed Rage for Order*, with which we engage above, (*Experience).
5 My reading of White and Lonergan together has benefited from Kalscheur (1996) and Brennan (2003).

Movement

1 The word 'aporia' has a significant place in talk about Socratic perplexity. Concerning the etymology: the word 'poros' means a route or a way; 'a-poros' means being without a route. 'One speaks of a *poros* when it is a matter of blazing a trail where no trail exists, of crossing an impassable expanse of territory, an unknown . . . and boundless world . . .' (Kofman 1988: 10).
2 'Law may be viewed as a system of tension or a bridge linking a concept of a reality to an imagined alternative' (Cover 1983: 9).

Play

1 My reading of Rilke has benefited from Lawn (2006: 141–3).

Reading

1 White makes an important reference to charity in his criticism of 'the language and culture of economics'. He resists claims by econocrats that the motive of 'altruism' can be included in 'self-interest':

> It is a very reduced idea of 'altruism' to say that it is what apparently—but only apparently—serves someone else's interest rather than one's own. In such a language there can be neither the virtue nor the duty of charity.
>
> (White 1990: 55)

'Charity' comes from the Latin *caritas*. For a discussion of the word that could inspire a lexicon beginning with *agape*, see Tracy (1979).

Silence

1 For a helpful discussion of Weil's work on the topic of justice, see Bell (1998).
2 Weil writes: 'To listen to someone is to put oneself in his place while he is speaking.' This is a difficult task when the 'someone' is suffering from 'affliction'. It requires one to 'annihilate oneself' (332).

Understanding

1 For a response to many such accusations, see Dawson (2005).
2 This concerns the second part of Article II, which states: 'the Chiefs . . . yield to Her Majesty the exclusive right of Preemption over such lands as the proprietors thereof may be disposed to alienate at such process as may be agreed upon between

the respective Proprietors and persons appointed by Her Majesty to treat with them in that behalf.'

3 For more about *Johnson*, see Dawson (2001: 43–7).

4 'Hermeneutics' connects to Greek mythology, in particular to Hermes. 'On the one hand, he had to translate the wishes of the gods into terms that mortals could understand, and on the other he had to transpose the language of humans into an idiom that the immortals might grasp' (Davey 2006: 171).

5 For connections between Gadamer and Lonergan, see Lawrence (1972). 'Transcendence' is a key word in Davey's reading of Gadamer. 'The reappropriation of transcendence as the process of understanding is the philosophical move that initiates the central reflections of this essay' (Davey 2006: xiii).

6 'Philosophical hermeneutics contends that the vitality of understanding depends on difference' (Davey 2006: xii). 'Focusing on Gadamer's notion of understanding as "play" will allow us to see more clearly the way that understanding always remains a dynamic process in which difference is the lifeblood' (Vilhauer 2010: xiii).

7 One 'task' for White's reader is 'fashioning a language of criticism in which to define and express your perceptions of success and failure in yourself and others' (1973: 50).

8 For an extended engagement with Gadamer that connects to the concerns of the literary lawyer, see Warnke (1999). Warnke offers a reading of *Pride and Prejudice* that resembles White's. In particular, she is interested in 'how it is possible for Elizabeth Bennet to move as quickly as she does from her initial unproductive prejudices to a clearer understanding of herself and others' (1999: 162).

Bibliography

Articles and Books

Adams, P. (1977) *Fatal Necessity: British Intervention in New Zealand 1830–1847*, Auckland: Auckland University Press.

Amar, A.R. (1987) 'Of Sovereignty and Federalism', *Yale Law Journal*, 96: 1425–1520.

Arendt, H. (1958) *The Human Condition*, Chicago and London: University of Chicago Press.

Arendt, H. (1963) *Eichmann in Jerusalem: A Report on the Banality of Evil*, London: Faber.

Aristotle (*c*.350 BCE/1976) *Nicomachean Ethics*, Harmondsworth: Penguin.

Austen, J. (1814/2003) *Mansfield Park*, London: Penguin.

Austen, J. (1817/1998) *Persuasion*, Oxford: Oxford University Press.

Baird, T. (1931) *The First Years: Selections from Autobiography*, New York: Farrar & Rinehart.

—— (1946) 'Darwin and the Tangled Bank', *American Scholar* 15: 477–86; reprinted in T. Baird (1999) *The Most of It: Essays on Language and the Imagination*, 162–71, Amherst: Amherst College Press.

—— (1952) 'The Freshman English Course', *Amherst Alumni News*; reprinted in T. Baird (1999) *The Most of It: Essays on Language and the Imagination*, 199–205, Amherst: Amherst College Press.

Bakhtin, M. (1981) *The Dialogic Imagination: Four Essays*, ed. M. Holquist, Austin: University of Texas Press.

Balkin, J.M. (1996) 'Interdisciplinarity as Colonization', *Washington and Lee Law Review*, 53: 949–70.

Ball, M.S. (1975) 'The Play's the Thing: An Unscientific Reflection on Courts Under the Rubric of Theater', *Stanford Law Review*, 28: 81–115.

—— (1989) 'Confessions', *Cardozo Studies in Law & Literature*, 1: 185–98.

Ball, M.S. and White, J.B. (1996) 'A Conversation between Milner Ball and James Boyd White', *Yale Journal of Law & the Humanities*, 8: 465–94.

Becker, A.L. (1988) 'Attunement: An Essay on Philology and Logophilia', in P. Kroskrity (ed.), *On the Ethnography of Communication: The Legacy of Sapir*, 109–46, Los Angeles: UCLA Department of Anthropology; reprinted in A.L. Becker (1995) *Beyond Translation: Essays toward a Modern Philology*, 369–43, Ann Arbor: University of Michigan Press.

—— (1992) 'Silence Across Languages', in C. Kramsch and S. McConnel-Ginet (eds), *Text and Context: Cross-Disciplinary Perspectives on Language-Study*, 115–23; reprinted in A.L. Becker (1995), *Beyond Translation:* Essays toward a Modern Philology, 283–94, Ann Arbor: University of Michigan Press.

—— (1995) *Beyond Translation: Essays toward a Modern Philology*, Ann Arbor: University of Michigan Press.

Bell, C. (2002) 'The Big "OE": Young New Zealand Travellers as Secular Pilgrims', *Tourist Studies*, 2: 143–58.

Bell, R.H. (1998) *Simone Weil: The Way of Justice as Compassion*, Lanham, Maryland: Roman & Littlefield.

Bentham, J. (1776/1988) *A Fragment on Government*, Cambridge, UK: Cambridge University Press.

Berthoff, A.E. (1981) *The Making of Meaning: Metaphors, Models, and Maxims for Writing Teachers*, Boynton: Cook Publishers.

Bickford, S. (1996) *The Dissonance of Democracy: Listening, Conflict, and Citizenship*, Ithaca: Cornell University Press.

Bingham, C. (2008) *Authority Is Relational: Rethinking Educational Empowerment*, Albany: State University of New York.

Blair, W. (1960) *Mark Twain & Huck Finn*, Berkeley: University of California Press.

Blakemore, S. (1988) *Burke and the Fall of Language: The French Revolution as Linguistic Event*, Hanover, NH: University Press of New England.

—— (1997) *Intertextual War: Edmund Burke and the French Revolution in the Writings of Mary Wollstonecraft, Thomas Paine, and James Mackintosh*, London: Associated Presses.

Booth, W.C. (1961) *The Rhetoric of Fiction*, Chicago: University of Chicago Press.

—— (1981) 'Mere Rhetoric, Rhetorology, and the Search for Common Learning', in *Common Learning: A Carnegie Colloquium on General Education*, 23–55, Washington DC; reprinted in *The Vocation of a Teacher: Rhetorical Occasions 1967–1988* (1988), Chicago: University of Chicago Press.

—— (1995) 'Our Best Rhetorologist', *Philosophy and Literature*, 19: 116–26.

—— (1996) 'Reading Poetry as Immersion: George Herbert and James Boyd White', *Michigan Quarterly Review*, 35: 379–86.

—— (2004) *The Rhetoric of Rhetoric: The Quest for Effective Communication*, Malden, MA: Blackwell.

Boulding, K. (1956) *The Image: Knowledge in Life and Society*, Ann Arbor: University of Michigan Press.

Brecht, B. (1936) 'Alienation Effects in Chinese Acting'; reprinted in J. Willett (ed. and trans.) (1964/1978) *Brecht on Theatre: The Development of an Aesthetic*, 91–9, London: Methuen.

—— (1951) 'Short Description of a New Technique of Acting which Produces an Alienation Effect'; reprinted in J. Willett (ed. and trans.) (1964/1978) *Brecht on Theatre: The Development of an Aesthetic*, 136–47, London: Methuen.

Brennan, P.M. (2002) 'Realizing the Rule of Law in the Human Subject', *Boston College Law Review*, 43: 227–350.

—— (2003) 'Meaning's Edge, Love's Priority', *Michigan Law Review*, 101: 2060–83.

Broderick, J.H. (1958) 'A Study of the Freshman Composition Course at Amherst: Action, Order, and Language', *Harvard Educational Review*, 28: 44–57.

Brooker, P. (1988) *Bertolt Brecht: Dialectics, Poetry, Politics*, London: Croom Helm.

Brookfield, F.M. (1999) *Waitangi & Indigenous Rights: Revolution, Law & Legitimation*, Auckland: Auckland University Press.

Burke, E. (1757/1987) *A Philosophical Enquiry into the Origin of our Ideas of the Sublime and Beautiful*, ed. J.T. Boulton, Oxford: Basil Blackwell.

—— (1790) *Reflections on the French Revolution*; reprinted in E.J. Payne (ed.) (1898) *Burke: Select Works* (Vol. II), Oxford: Clarendon Press.

Burke, K. (1950/1969) *A Rhetoric of Motives*, Berkeley and Los Angeles: University of California Press.

Carleton, H. (1874) *The Life of Henry Williams, Archdeacon of Waimate*, Auckland: Upton.

Clingman, S. (1998) *Bram Fischer: Afrikaner Revolutionary*, Amherst: University of Massachusetts Press.

Cohen, F.S. (1935) 'Transcendental Nonsense and the Functional Approach', *Columbia Law Review*, 35: 809–49; reprinted in L.K. Cohen (ed.) (1960) *The Legal Conscience: Selected Papers of Felix S. Cohen*, 33–76, New Haven: Yale University Press.

—— (1950) 'Field Theory and Judicial Logic', *Yale Law Journal*, 59: 238–72.

Colenso, W. (1890) *The Authentic and Genuine History of the Signing of the Treaty of Waitangi*, Wellington: Government Printer.

Coleridge, S.T. (1817/1905) *Biographia Literaria*, London: Bell.

Collingwood, R.G. (1939/1951) *An Autobiography*, London: Oxford University Press.

Commons, J.R. (1924/1995) *Legal Foundations of Capitalism*, New Brunswick: Transaction.

—— (1934a/1959) *Institutional Economics: Its Place in Political Economy*, Madison: University of Wisconsin Press.

—— (1934b) *Myself*, New York: Macmillan.

Cover, R.M. (1983) 'The Supreme Court, 1982 Term – Foreword: *Nomos* and Narrative', *Harvard Law Review*, 97: 1–68.

Cullen, Hon. M. (2004) 'Waitangi Tribunal Report Disappointing', http://www.beehive.govt.nz/node/19091 (accessed 2 December 2011).

Cunningham, C.D. (1994) 'Learning From Law Students: A Socratic Approach to Law and Literature?', *University of Cincinnati Law Review*, 63: 195–220.

Dane, P. (1990) 'Maps of Sovereignty: A Meditation', *Cardozo Law Review*, 12: 951–1006.

Davey, N. (2006) *Unquiet Understanding: Gadamer's Philosophical Hermeneutics*, Albany: State University of New York Press.

Dawson, R. (1998) 'Sovereignty and Withholding in John Commons's Political Economy', in W.J. Samuels (ed.), *The Founding of Institutional Economics: The Leisure Class and Sovereignty*, London and New York: Routledge.

—— (2001) *The Treaty of Waitangi and the Control of Language*, Wellington: Institute of Policy Studies.

—— (2005) 'Waitangi, Translation, and Metaphor', *Sites: A Journal of Social Anthropology & Cultural Studies*, 2: 33–63.

—— (2006) 'Doing Justice in Property "Takings" Cases: From Coal to Sand', *Canterbury Law Review*, 12: 292–316.

—— (2007a) 'Distinguishing Elias CJ from Radical Maori', with Sophocles' *Antigone* as an Analogical Source', *Waikato Law Review*, 15: 190–211.

—— (2007b) 'Judging Economics Teaching and Textbooks', *Journal of Australian Political Economy*', 60: 73–97.

—— (2008) '*Treaty of Waitangi* Sovereignty-Talk: Lost Moments', *Otago Law Review*, 11: 683–702.

—— (2009) 'Connecting the Common-Law Mind and Sovereignty-Talk, with Shakespeare's *King Richard II* as an Analogical Resource', *Canterbury Law Review*, 15: 237–62.

Derrida, J. (1987) 'The Laws of Reflection: Nelson Mandela, In Admiration', in J. Derrida and M. Tlili (eds), *For Nelson Mandela*, New York: Seaver Books.

—— (2005) 'Justices', in B. Cohen and D. Kujundzic (eds), *Provocations to Reading: J. Hillis Miller and the Democracy to Come*, 228–61, New York: Fordham University Press.

Descartes, R. (1637/1968) *Discourse on Method: and Other Writings*, trans. F.E. Sutcliffe, Harmondsworth: Penguin.

Dewey, J. (1936) 'Authority and Freedom', *Survey Graphic*, 25: 603–13.

Earl, P. E. (1983) *The Economic Imagination: Towards a Behavioural Analysis of Choice*, Armonk, New York: M.E. Sharp.

—— (2000) 'Indeterminacy in the Economics Classroom', in P.E. Earl and S.F. Frowen (eds), *Economics as an Art of Thought: Essays in Memory of G. L. S. Shackle*, 25–55, London and New York: Routledge.

Eastman, H.A. (1995) 'Speaking Truth to Power: The Language of Civil Rights Litigators', *Yale Law Journal*, 104: 763–880.

Edwards, L.H. (2003) *Legal Writing and Analysis*, New York: Aspen Publishers.

Eisgruber, C.L.M. (1988) 'Justice Story, Slavery, and the Natural Law Foundations of American Constitutionalism', *University of Chicago Law Review*, 55: 273–327.

Elbow, P. (2005) 'Bringing the Rhetoric of Assent and the Believing Game Together – and into the Classroom', *College English*, 67: 388–99.

Elias, S. (2008) 'Eulogy for the Lord Cooke of Thorndon', *Victoria University of Wellington*, 39: 1–8.

Ellmann, S. (2001) 'To Live Outside the Law You Must be Honest: Bram Fischer and the Meaning of Integrity', *South African Journal on Human Rights*, 17: 451–76.

Finkelman, P. (1993) 'Sorting Out *Prigg v. Pennsylvania*', *Rutgers Law Journal*, 24: 605–66.

Fishbane, M. (2008) *Sacred Attunement: A Jewish Theology*, Chicago: Chicago University Press.

Fleckenstein, K.S. (1999) 'Writing Bodies: Somatic Mind in Composition Studies', *College English*, 61: 281–306.

Frame, A. (2000) 'Beware the Architectural Metaphor', in C. James (ed.), *Building the Constitution*, 426–33, Wellington: Institute of Policy Studies.

Fried, B.H. (1998) *The Progressive Assault on Laissez Faire: Robert Hale and the First Law and Economics Movement*, Cambridge, Massachusetts, and London: Harvard University Press.

Frost, R. (1931) 'Education by Poetry', *Amherst Graduates' Quarterly*; reprinted in H. Cox and E.C. Lathem (eds) (1966) *Selected Prose of Robert Frost*, 33–48, New York: Holt.

—— (1939) 'The Figure a Poem Makes', in R. Frost (1951) *Complete Poems of Robert Frost*, 17–20, London: Jonathan Cape.

—— (1946) 'Directive', *Virginia Quarterly Review*, 22: 1–3; reprinted in R. Frost (1947) *Steeple Bush*, New York: Henry Holt.

Fuller, L.L. (1949) 'The Case of the Speluncean Explorers', *Harvard Law Review*, 62: 616–45.

—— (1964/1969) *The Morality of Law*, New Haven and London: Yale University Press.
—— (1966/1999) *The Law in Quest of Itself*, Union, NJ: Lawbook Exchange.
Gaakeer, J. (1998) *Hope Springs Eternal: An Introduction to the Work of James Boyd White*, Amsterdam: Amsterdam University Press.
—— (2007) 'Interview with James Boyd White', *Michigan Law Review*, 105: 1403–20.
Gadamer, H.-G. (1975) *Truth and Method*, New York: Seabury Press.
—— (1981) *Reason in the Age of Science*, Cambridge, Mass.: MIT Press.
Gallop, D. (1999) 'Jane Austen and the Aristotelian Ethic', *Philosophy and Literature*, 23: 96–109.
Geyer, F. and Heinz, W.R. (eds) (1992) *Alienation, Society, and the Individual: Continuity and Change in Theory and Research*, New Brunswick: Transaction.
Gibson, W. (1959) *Seeing and Writing: Fifteen Exercises in Composing Experience*, New York: McKay.
Gibson, W. (1961) 'Literary Minds and Judicial Style', *New York University Law Review*, 35: 915–30.
Gibson, W. (1985) 'Theodore Baird', in J. Brereton (ed.), *Traditions of Inquiry*, 136-151, New York: Oxford University Press.
Glendon, M.A. (1994) 'Knowledge Makes a Noisy Entrance: The Struggle for Self-Appropriation in Law', *Lonergan Workshop*, 10: 119–44.
Guinier, L. (2008) 'The Supreme Court, 2007 Term – Foreword: Demosprudence Through Dissent', *Harvard Law Review*, 122: 4–138.
Hall, S. (1997) *Representation: Cultural Representations and Signifying Practices*, London: Sage Publications.
Hendrix, H. (1988) *Getting the Love You Want: A Guide for Couples*, Melbourne, Victoria: Schwartz & Wilkinson.
Hinton, A.L. (2002) *Genocide: An Anthropological Reader*, Massachusetts and Oxford: Blackwell.
Hodges, E.P. (1988) 'Writing in a Different Voice', *Texas Law Review*, 66: 629–40.
Huizinga, J. (1949) *Homo Ludens: A Study of the Play-Element in Culture*, London: Routledge and Kegan Paul.
James, C. (ed.) (2000) *Building the Constitution*, Wellington: Institute of Policy Studies.
James, W. (1890/1981) *Principles of Psychology*, Cambridge, Mass.: Harvard University Press.
Kahn, P.W. (1997) *The Reign of Law:* Marbury v. Madison *and the Construction of America*, New Haven and London: Yale University Press.
Kalscheur, G.A. (1996) 'Law School as a Culture of Conversion: Re-imagining Legal Education as a Process of Conversion to the Demands of Authentic Conversation', *Loyola University Chicago Law Journal*, 28: 333–71.
Karis T. and Carter, G.M (eds) (1977) *From Protest to Challenge: A Documentary History of African Politics in South Africa 1882–1964 – Volume 3: Challenge and Violence 1953–1964*, Stanford, California: Hoover Institute Press.
Kastley, J.L. (1997) *Rethinking the Rhetorical Tradition: From Plato to Postmodernism*, New Haven, Conn.: Yale University Press.
Klamer, A. (1984) *The New Classical Macroeconomics: Conversations with the New Classical Economists and their Opponents*, Brighton: Harvester Wheatsheaf.

—— (1987) 'As If Economists and Their Subject Were Rational', in J.J. Nelson, A. Megill and D.N. McCloskey (eds), *The Rhetoric of the Human Sciences: Language and Argument in Scholarship and Public Affairs*, 163–83, Wisconsin: University of Wisconsin Press.

—— (2007) *Speaking of Economics: How to get in the conversation*, Abingdon: Routledge.

Klare, K.E. (1998) 'Legal Culture and Transformative Constitutionalism', *South African Journal on Human Rights*, 14: 146–88.

Kofman, S. (1988) 'Beyond Aporia', in A. Benjamin (ed.), *Post-structuralist classics*, 7–45, London and New York: Routledge.

Kronman, A.T. (1993) *The Lost Lawyer: Failing Ideals of the Legal Profession*, Cambridge, Mass.: Harvard University Press.

Lakoff, G. and Johnson, M. (1980) *Metaphors We Live By*, Chicago and London: University of Chicago Press.

Lawn, C. (2006) *Gadamer: A Guide for the Perplexed*, London: Continuum.

Lawrence, F. (1972) 'Self-knowledge in history in Gadamer and Lonergan', in P. McShane (ed.), *Language Truth and Meaning*, 167–217, Gill and Macmillan.

Levin, D. (1989) *The Listening Self: Personal Growth, Social Change and the Closure of Metaphysics*, London and New York: Routledge.

Levinson, S. (1991) 'Conversing About Justice', *Yale Law Journal*, 100: 1855–78.

Lewis, C.S. (1961) *An Experiment in Criticism*, Cambridge: Cambridge University Press.

Litowitz, D. (2000) 'Reification in Law and Legal Theory', *Southern California Interdisciplinary Law Journal*', 9: 401–26.

Little, J.P. (1993) 'Simone Weil's Concept of Decreation', in R.H. Bell (ed.), *Simone Weil's Philosophy of Culture: Readings toward a divine humanity*, 25–51, Cambridge, England: Cambridge University Press.

Lonergan, B.J.F. (1957/1973) *Insight: A Study of Human Understanding*, New York: Philosophical Library.

—— (1972) *Method in Theology*, London: Darton, Longman & Todd.

—— (1985) 'Unity and Plurality: The Coherence of Christian Truth', in F.E. Crowe (ed.), *A Third Collection: Papers by Bernard J.F. Lonergan*, 239–50, New York: Paulist Press.

McCloskey, D.N. (1985) *The Rhetoric of Economics*, Wisconsin: University of Wisconsin Press.

—— (1993) 'Some Consequences of a Conjective Economics', in M.A. Ferber and J.A. Nelson (eds), *Beyond Economic Man: Feminist Theory and Economics*, 69–93, Chicago and London: The University of Chicago Press.

McDowell, M. and Webb, D. (2006) *The New Zealand Legal System: Structures and Processes*, 4th edn, Wellington: LexisNexis.

Mackenzie, N.H. (1981) *A Reader's Guide to Gerard Manley Hopkins*, London: Thames and Hudson.

—— (ed.) (1990) *The Poetical Works of Gerard Manley Hopkins*, Oxford, England: Clarendon Press.

Mahomed, I. (1997) 'Address by the Honourable Mr Justice Ismail Mahomed at a Dinner given by the Johannesburg Bar on 25 June 1997 to celebrate his Appointment as Chief Justice of the Supreme Court of Appeal', *South African Law Journal*, 114: 604–8.

—— (1998) 'The Bram Fischer Memorial Lecture', *South African Journal on Human Rights*, 14: 209–17.

Mandela, N. (1994) *Long Walk to Freedom: The Autobiography of Nelson Mandela*, Boston: Little, Brown & Co.

—— (1995/2003) 'Bram Fischer', in K. Asmal, D. Chidester and W. James (eds), *Nelson Mandela: In His Own Words*, 458–68, New York: Little, Brown.

Metge, J. (1976) *The Maoris of New Zealand: Rautahi*, London: Routledge & Kegan Paul.

—— (2001) *Korero Tahi: Talking Together*, Auckland: Auckland University Press with Te Matahauariki Institute.

Metge, J. and Kinloch, P. (1978) *Talking Past Each Other!?: Problems of Cross Cultural Communication*, Wellington: Victoria University Press.

Meyer, L.R. (2010) *The Justice of Mercy*, Ann Arbor: University of Michigan Press.

Miller, J.H. (1967) 'Literature and Religion', in J. Thorpe (ed.), *The Relations of Literary Study: Essays on Interdisciplinary Contributions*, New York: Modern Language Association; reprinted in J.H. Miller (1991) *Theory Now and Then*, 63–78, Durham: Duke University Press.

—— (1985) *The Linguistic Moment: From Wordsworth to Stevens*, Princeton, New Jersey: Princeton University Press.

—— (1987) 'The Ethics of Reading', *Style*, 21: 181–91; reprinted in J.H. Miller (1991) *Theory Now and Then*, 329–40, Durham: Duke University Press.

Mooney, E.F. (1996) *Selves in Discord and Resolve: Kierkegaard's Moral-Religious Psychology*, New York: Routledge.

Mootz, F.J. (1999) 'Natural Law and the Cultivation of Legal Rhetoric', in W.J. Witteveen and W. van der Burg, *Rediscovering Fuller: Essays on Implicit Law and Institutional Design*, 425–52, Amsterdam: Amsterdam University Press.

Morelli, M.D. and Morelli, E.A. (2002) *The Lonergan Reader*, Toronto and London: University of Toronto Press.

Mureinik, E. (1994) 'A Bridge to Where? Introducing the Interim Bill of Rights', *South African Journal on Human Rights*, 10: 31–48.

Myrdal, G. (1944/1996) *An American Dilemma: The Negro Problem and Modern Democracy*, New Brunswick: Transaction.

Nardin, J. (1973) *Those Elegant Decorums: The Concept of Propriety in Jane Austen's Novels*, Albany, NY: State University of New York.

Norris, K. (1998) *Amazing Grace: A Vocabulary of Faith*, New York: Riverhead Books.

Oakeshott, M. (1962) *Rationalism in Politics and Other Essays*, London: Methuen.

Ong, W.J. (1958) *Ramus, Method, and the Decay of Dialogue: From the Art of Discourse to the Art of Reason*, Cambridge, Mass.: Harvard University Press.

Ortega y Gasset, J. (1959) 'The Difficulty of Reading', *Diogenes*, 28: 1–17.

Paine, T. (1791/1998) *Rights of Man; Common Sense; and other writings*, ed. M. Philp, Oxford: Oxford University Press.

Phelps, T.G. (1994) 'The Power of *Persuasion*', *University of Cincinnati Law Review*, 63: 377–86.

Plant, S. (1996) *Simone Weil*, London: Fount.

Plato (*c*.360 BCE/1993) 'Crito', in *The Last Days of Socrates*, trans. H. Tredennick and H. Tarrant, London: Penguin.

Pocock, J.G.A. (1957) *The Ancient Constitution and the Federal Law: A Study of English Historical Thought in the Seventeenth Century*, Cambridge, England: Cambridge University Press.

Poirier, R. (1971) *The Performing Self: Compositions and Decompositions in the Languages of Contemporary Life*, New Brunswick, NJ: Rutgers University Press.

—— (1992) *Poetry and Pragmatism*, Cambridge, Mass.: Harvard University Press.

Posner, R.A. (1988) *Law and Literature: A Misunderstood Relation*, Cambridge, Mass.: Harvard University Press.

Pritchard, W.H. (1984) *Frost: A Literary Life Reconsidered*, New York: Oxford University Press.

—— (1991) 'Ear Training', in Amherst College Faculty, *Teaching What We Do*, 126–46, Amherst: Amherst College Press.

—— (2003) *Shelf Life: Literary Essays and Reviews*, Amherst: University of Massachusetts Press.

Ramstad, Y. (1986) 'A Pragmatist's Quest for Holistic Knowledge: The Scientific Methodology of John R. Commons', *Journal of Economic Issues*, 20: 1067–1105.

Robertson, L.G. (2005) *Conquest by Law: How the Discovery of America Dispossessed Indigenous Peoples of Their Lands*, New York: Oxford University Press.

Sammons, J.L. (2010) 'Justice as Play', *Mercer Law Review*, 61: 517–50.

Samuels, W.J. (1989) 'The Legal-Economic Nexus', *George Washington Law Review*, 57: 1556–78.

—— (1992) 'Warren J. Samuels', in P. Arestis and M. Sawyer (eds), *A Biographical Dictionary of Dissenting Economists*, 478–83, Cheltenham, UK: Edward Elgar.

Scragg, R. (2005) *New Zealand's Legal System: The Principles of Legal Method*, Auckland: Oxford University Press.

Sen, A.K. (1977) 'Rational Fools: A Critique of the Behavioral Foundations of Economic Theory', *Philosophy and Public Affairs*, 6: 317–44.

Shakespeare, W. (*c*.1595/1990) *King Richard II*, ed. A. Gurr, Cambridge, UK: Cambridge University Press.

Sheets-Johnstone, M. (1999) *The Primacy of Movement*, Amsterdam, Philadelphia: John Benjamin Publishing Company.

Smith, A. (1759/1974) *The Theory of Moral Sentiments*, Indianapolis: Liberty Fund.

—— (1776/1937) *An Inquiry into the Nature and Causes of the Wealth of Nations*, London: Routledge.

Swanson, J.B. (1981) 'Toward a Rhetoric of the Self: the Art of *Persuasion*', *Nineteenth-Century Fiction*, 36: 1–21.

Tave, S.M. (1973) *Some Words of Jane Austen*, Chicago: University of Chicago Press.

Teachout, P.R. (1986) 'The Soul of the Fugue: An Essay on Reading Fuller', *Minnesota Law Review*, 70: 1073–1148.

Terry, J. (1996) 'The Slow Process of *Persuasion*', in J. McMaster and B. Stovel (eds), *Jane Austen's Business: Her World and Her Profession*, 124–35, New York: St Martin's Press.

Tracy, D. (1970) *The Achievement of Bernard Lonergan*, New York: Herder and Herder.

—— (1975/1996) *Blessed Rage for Order: The New Pluralism in Theology*, New York: Seabury Press.

—— (1979) 'The Catholic Model of *Caritas*: Self-Transcendence and Transformation', reprinted in D. Tracy (1994) *On Naming the Present: God, Hermeneutics, and Church*, 94–106, New York: Orbis Books.

—— (1981) *The Analogical Imagination: Christian Theology and the Culture of Pluralism*, New York: Crossroad.

—— (1987) *Plurality and Ambiguity: Hermeneutics, Religion, Hope*, San Francisco: Harper and Row.

Trix, F. (1993) *Spiritual Discourses: Learning with an Islamic Master*, Philadelphia: University of Pennsylvania Press.

Tully, J. (1995) *Strange Multiplicity: Constitutionalism in an Age of Diversity*, Cambridge, England: Cambridge University Press.

Twain, M. (1884/1985) *The Adventures of Huckleberry Finn*, London: Penguin.

Van der Walt, A.J. (2001) 'Dancing with Codes – Protecting, Developing and Deconstructing Property Rights in a Constitutional State', *South African Law Journal*, 118: 258–311.

Vanhoozer, K.J. (2005) 'Discourse on Matter: Hermeneutics and the "Miracle" of Understanding', *International Journal of Systematic Theology*, 7: 5–37.

Varnum, R. (1996) *Fencing with Words: A History of Writing Instruction at Amherst College during the Era of Theodore Baird, 1938–1966*, Urbana: National Council of Teachers.

Vilhauer, M. (2010) *Gadamer's Ethics of Play: Hermeneutics and the Other*, Lanham: Rowman & Littlefield.

Waitangi Tribunal (2004) *Report on the Crown's Foreshore and Seabed Policy*, Wellington: Legislation Direct.

Warnke, G. (1999) *Legitimate Differences: Interpretation in the Abortion Controversy and Other Public Debates*, Berkeley and Los Angeles: University of California Press.

Weil, S. (1940–41/2003) *The Iliad or the Poem of Force: A Critical Edition*, ed. and trans. J.P. Holoka, New York: Peter Lang.

—— (1943/1977) 'Human Personality', in G.A. Panichas (ed.), *The Simone Weil Reader*, 313–39, New York: David McKay Company.

—— (1951/1973) *Waiting for God*, New York: Harper & Row.

Weisberg, M. (1999) 'Discerning the Gift', *Change*, 31: 29–37.

Weisberg, M. and Peters, J.K. (2007) 'Experiments in Listening', *Journal of Legal Education*, 57: 427–47.

White, J.B. (1973) *The Legal Imagination: Studies in the Nature of Legal Thought and Expression*, Boston: Little, Brown and Company.

—— (1984) *When Words Lose Their Meaning: Constitutions and Reconstitutions of Language, Character, and Community,* Chicago: University of Chicago.

—— (1985a) *Heracles' Bow: Essays on the Rhetoric and Poetics of the Law*, Madison: University of Wisconsin.

—— (1985b) *The Legal Imagination*, Abridged Edition, Chicago: University of Chicago.

—— (1986) 'Economics and Law: Two Cultures in Tension', *Tennessee Law Review*, 54: 161–202.

—— (1987a) 'Thinking About Our Language', *Yale Law Journal*, 96: 1960–83.

—— (1987b) 'Rhetoric and Law: The Arts of Cultural and Communal Life', in J.S. Nelson, A. Megill and D.N. McCloskey (eds), *The Rhetoric of the Human Sciences: Language and Argument in Scholarship and Public Affairs*, 298–318, Madison: University of Wisconsin Press.

—— (1989) 'What Can a Lawyer Learn from Literature?', *Harvard Law Review*, 102: 2014–47.

—— (1990) *Justice as Translation: An Essay in Cultural and Legal Criticism*, Chicago: University of Chicago Press.

—— (1994a) *Acts of Hope: Creating Authority in Literature, Law, and Politics*, Chicago: University of Chicago Press.

—— (1994b) *'This Book of Starres': Learning to Read George Herbert*, Ann Arbor: University of Michigan.

—— (1994c) 'Imagining the Law', in A. Sarat and T. R. Kearns (eds), *The Rhetoric of Law*, 29–56, Ann Arbor: University of Michigan Press.

—— (1996) 'Meaning in the Life of the Lawyer', *Cumberland Law Review*, 26: 763–71.

—— (1999) *From Expectation to Experience: Essays on Law & Legal Education*, Ann Arbor: University of Michigan.

—— (2001) *The Edge of Meaning*, Chicago: University of Chicago Press.

—— (2002) 'Legal Knowledge', *Harvard Law Review*, 115: 1396–1431.

—— (2006) *Living Speech: Resisting the Empire of Force*, Princeton: Princeton University Press.

—— (ed.) (2006b) *How Should We Talk about Religion?*, Notre Dame, Indiana: University of Notre Dame Press.

Wilkins, D.E. (1997) *American Indian Sovereignty and the U.S. Supreme Court: The Masking of Justice*, Austin: University of Texas Press.

Williams, J.H. (2005) 'Hillis's Charity', in B Cohen and D. Kujundzic (eds), *Provocations to Reading: J. Hillis Miller and the Democracy to Come*, 64–79, New York: Fordham University Press.

Wittgenstein, L. (1953) *Philosophical Investigations*, trans. G.E.M. Anscombe, Oxford: Blackwell.

Wollstonecraft, M. (1790) *A Vindication of the Rights of Men, In a Letter to the Right Honourable Edmund Burke; Occasioned by his Reflections on the Revolution in France*; reprinted in D.L. Macdonald and K. Scherf (eds) (1997) *The Vindications: The Rights of Men; The Rights of Woman*, Peterborough, Ontario: Broadview.

Index